Tom Pisso

THE MEDIEVAL CROWN OF ARAGON

The Medieval Crown of Aragon

A Short History

T. N. BISSON

CLARENDON PRESS · OXFORD
1986

Oxford University Press, Walton Street, Oxford OX2 6DP

Oxford New York Toronto
Delhi Bombay Calcutta Madras Karachi
Kuala Lumpur Singapore Hong Kong Tokyo
Nairobi Dar es Salaam Cape Town
Melbourne Auckland
and associated companies in
Beirut Berlin Ibadan Nicosia

Oxford is a trade mark of Oxford University Press

Published in the United States
by Oxford University Press, New York

British Library Cataloguing in Publication Data
Bisson, T.N.
The medieval crown of Aragon: a short history.
1. Aragon (Spain)—History
I. Title
946'.5502 DP125
ISBN 0-19-821987-3

Library of Congress Cataloging in Publication Data
Bisson, Thomas N.
Medieval crown of Aragon.
Bibliography: p.
Includes index.
1. Aragon (Spain)—History. 2. Catalonia (Spain)—History.
I. Title.
DP128.B57 1985 946'.5 85-21812
ISBN 0-19-821987-3

Set by Hope Services, Abingdon
Printed in Great Britain
at the University Printing House, Oxford
by David Stanford
Printer to the University

TO NOËL AND SUSAN

Preface

I HAVE tried here to sketch a historical theme on which it has become difficult to find discussions in English suitable for pupils and general readers. H. J. Chaytor's admirable *History of Aragon and Catalonia* (1933), although it remains useful, has been overtaken by new research on many points of fact and interpretation. For the later Middle ages the fullest up-to-date treatment of the Crown of Aragon in English may now be found in appropriate chapters of J. N. Hillgarth, *The Spanish kingdoms, 1250–1516* (Oxford, 1976–8), a work of sound learning to which I am glad to record my debt. While much of my Chapter II and some of Chapter III rest on my own researches, I have relied throughout on the recent publications of Spanish—and, above all, of Catalan—historians. These are cited in the Bibliographical Notes together with certain other works in foreign languages. Some important researches of Catalan scholars are still too little known outside Spain. But I have tried not to neglect the valuable new work being done by English and American specialists. Several of them contributed suggestions for improving the manuscript which I gratefully acknowledge. Philip Grierson kindly supplied the photographs and descriptions of the coins that appear on Plate VII.

Like all historians writing in English of Hispanic matters, I have had to wrestle with the problem of rendering proper names. Instead of burdening the preface, I have thought it best to explain my system in a Note on the Translation of Proper Names. The essential point of this system is to encourage readers to see in the distinct forms of certain names an agreeable clue to the multi-cultural reality of the Middle Ages. My preference for speaking of the dynastic rulers of Aragon and Catalonia as 'count-kings' is justified on p. 31

I wish to thank the Warden and Fellows of All Souls College, Oxford, where two chapters of this book were written during Michaelmas Term 1983. Other support came from generous grants by the Fulbright Commission and the Institute of International Studies at the University of California at Berkeley.

I also acknowledge previous fellowships from the National Endowment for the Humanities and the American Council of Learned Societies, for my sense of the wider and longer experience of medieval Catalonia goes back at least to 1975–6, when I spent a year in Barcelona with my family. At that time two small daughters were wont to exclaim wearily, at threatening moments: 'Not *another* cloister, Daddy!' Of course, there always *was* another cloister. They have grown to understand—and I to be thankful.

T. N. B.

Contents

List of Illustrations

THE illustrations, with one exception, are taken from photographs supplied by the Arxiu Mas of Barcelona, and are reproduced by permission. The coins illustrated in Plate VII are from the collection of Professor Philip Grierson, who has supplied the descriptions and captions.

List of Maps

Prologue

THE tourists who climb a dusty path of worn stones to the ruins of Monzón castle in Aragon might well be on their way eastward. Let us imagine them stopping off next at Poblet to admire the royal tombs in the monks' choir before arriving in Barcelona where, in the Plaça del Rei, they will be charmed by the old royal palace, the new (1547!) lieutenant's house, and Santa Agatha's chapel. They may not easily imagine what connects these monuments among so many others: has not the journey been filled with castles and churches, sights and sites, of every epoch? France lies ahead (or behind?), the Costa Brava tempts, Italy and Germany beckon. Yet if they can pause to visit—or at least to imagine—the graciously arched spaces of Santa Maria del Mar in the old marine suburb of Barcelona, or of Girona cathedral, or of the great merchants' *llotjes* at Barcelona, Valencia, and Perpignan, or, still at Perpignan, of the imposing palace of the kings of Majorca with its sun-drenched brick exteriors, then a more assured and coherent impression may result. For the castles, churches, tombs, and trading-houses that have been mentioned have not only their place in a European archaeology of diverse cultures and styles, they are, more precisely, the vestiges of a proud and expansive Mediterranean civilization. They evoke the ambitions of counts of Barcelona who were kings of Aragon by dynastic descent; the energies of knights and merchants who followed the count-kings* in overseas conquest and settlement, spreading Catalan speech throughout the Mediterranean; and the taste of artists aware of European fashion who devised a characteristic Gothic style of their own. These are the monuments of the medieval Crown of Aragon.

In this case the monuments may be more eloquent than the history. Among dynastic federations of the Middle Ages, the Crown of Aragon is not perhaps the most memorable. Upstaged from the start by the marriages uniting Anjou, Normandy,

---

* For this term see p. 31

Aquitaine, and England, it lacked the power and wealth of the combined Plantagenet domains, the grandeur of the Hohenstaufen empire, or the glamorous impudence of Charles of Anjou's. Set back by catastrophic defeat in the Albigensian wars and stripped of Provence in the thirteenth century, the union of Aragon and· Catalonia might then have seemed destined to vegetate in provincial squalor. Historians have lately stressed its political and economic failings in the later Middle Ages. Yet the Crown of Aragon long survived all the federations mentioned above, falling heir, indeed, to the Mediterranean spoils of two of them. Even as it lost most of its trans-Pyrenean annexes, it turned aggressively against the Moors and forged ties of marriage with the Hohenstaufen. Majorca, Valencia, Minorca; Sicily and Sardinia; Naples; the duchies of Athens and Neopatria —the list of conquests or settlements is long and glittering; and while not all its colonies were assimilated or suffered Catalan domination for long, the original dynastic union together with its Hispanic conquests outlasted the dynasty itself to become Ferdinand the Catholic's gift to the patrimony of modern Spain.

There was nothing chimerical about the Crown of Aragon. The marriage from which it stemmed, for all the problems to which it later gave rise, was an act of political logic that made sense in the twelfth century. It was neither the first nor the last dynastic union of peninsular lands that never knew a Philip Augustus in the Middle Ages. The Aragonese union early found positive expression in the collaborative activity of a bi-regnal court. Even when national jealousies arose to weaken the solidarity, Catalans and Aragonese who fought or traded abroad or benefited from subsidies or royal protection must have regarded their ruler as a multi-regnal dynast. The count-kings, for their part, did what they could to administer their lands *en bloc*. James II founded his new university at Lérida because of its centrality and convenience in his peninsular realms, and in 1319 he decreed that his realms should remain undivided. His successors continued to think of Mediterranean hegemony in federative terms. When the dynasty died out in 1410 the succession was resolved in counsels representing the notables of Catalonia, Aragon, and Valencia. And when Ferdinand and Isabella later created an enlarged Crown of Castile, Leon, Aragon, and Sicily, they not only replicated (and subordinated) the old Pyrenean union, they also drew on federative institutions pioneered by their Mediterranean forerunners.

So it may be said that the Crown of Aragon, considered precisely as a dynastic federation, had a history of its own. This history is the subject of this book—or, more exactly, its titular subject. The qualification is necessary, for to understand this subject it is not enough to examine a union that was often threatened and always artificial; not enough to adopt the inspiring perspective of rulers who were an untypical minority, to say the least. More fundamentally our subject must be the history of the lands they ruled, of societies in Aragon and the Catalan-speaking counties that were on the threshold of national identity when their ruling dynasties merged and that continued to evolve in distinctive ways. In one sense the histories of Aragon and Catalonia begin with the marriage of Ramon Berenguer IV and Petronilla in 1150 and what happened thereafter was much affected by the contacts and reactions of the two peoples with and to each other. But these histories were influenced by antecedent factors—geography, substructures of ancient and Visigothic culture, struggles against the Moors—which go far toward explaining the most salient peculiarity of the medieval Crown of Aragon: the rise of Catalonia to pre-eminence in the federation. This peculiarity creates a serious difficulty for any historian who seeks to be impartial. To this day some Catalans find it hard to understand why Ramon Berenguer IV or his son failed to assume the style of king in Catalonia, while some Aragonese resent the blatant partiality of James the Conqueror toward Catalonia. The political passions of the present are so bound up with the medieval past in the case of these lands that one is tempted to pass over such incidents in silence. Yet the historical explanations for them are often as illuminating as they are troubling; one cannot avoid them even at the cost of taking sides. If these chapters were merely to sketch the parallel histories of Aragon and Catalonia, they would surely fail to convey one larger lesson of our story. Neither land evolved freely of the other; still less do the post-conquest histories of the Balearic Islands and Valencia make sense in isolation. To write of one land is necessarily to write of all, and so, perhaps, to do less than justice to any. It is possible to interpret the medieval federation from an Aragonese point of view: José Maria Lacarra did so brilliantly. It is easier—and perhaps not more misleading—to lay stress on the centrality of Catalonia. That is what is attempted here. Catalonia was the Normandy of the late medieval Mediterranean. She did not give her name to the confederation, she was content to leave the crown to others. What she gave, above all, were the gifts of people and their language, of enterprise and culture. How did these things come about? What did they mean?

I
Before the Union

THE regions commonly spoken of as Aragon and Catalonia occupy some 89,000 square kilometres of the most diverse and accidented terrain in the eastern Hispanic peninsula. They have their northern sectors in the high Pyrenees, with valleys extending generally southward into plateaux and secondary ranges before dropping to coastal lowlands in Catalonia and to the Ebro valley in Aragon. But the eastern lowlands are both more spacious and more fertile than the Aragonese Ebro; moreover, the uplands extending north-east and south-west of the Ebro are so much more arid and extensive than anything found in the east as to define an unfavourable climate for agriculture in much of greater Aragon. Grains, vines, garden crops, fruits, nuts, and oil were widely cultivated in both lands, especially in the lowlands and the Segre and Ebro valleys. For all its aridity Aragon was well drained in its north-eastern sectors, its rivers creating communications with the Segre and the lower Ebro that helped compensate for Catalonia's better access to the Ebro delta and the sea.

Considered together, these lands were a crossroads and a homeland to prehistoric and ancient peoples. Traces of hunting-gathering cultures have been found which, in the eastern Pyrenees, may now be dated back some 300,000 years. No later than the fifth millennium BC came the fundamental shifts towards agriculture and the domestication of animals, followed around 2000 BC by metal-working. But it was only in the first millennium that there came the Indo-European and Mediterranean intrusions which left permanent marks on the language and topography of the eastern peninsula. Roman authors mentioned the 'Iacetans' and the 'Ilergetes' in localities corresponding to Jaca in old Aragon and Lérida (*Ilerda*) in the Segre valley, but many other Celto-Iberian groups have been identified. Osona, Berga, and Cerdanya take their names from such peoples. Greeks and Rhodians settled at Rhode and

Emporion from the sixth century BC (or before), profoundly influencing the indigenous cultures of the eastern littoral and touching those even of the Ebro valley. The use of coined money and the alphabet spread through such contacts from coastal settlements as far as the Ilergetes.

The Romans moved into the acculturated coastal lands during the Second Punic War (218–201). Easily imposing on a long zone extending south-west to the Ebro delta, they founded Tarragona (*Tarraco*) and penetrated Spain through the Ebro valley. They met resistance from the Ilergetes and later from other tribes in an interior belt extending from the eastern to the central Pyrenees. Romanization proceeded over many generations, resulting in the displacement of indigenous settlements and the establishment of colonies (*coloniae*) and *municipia* whose continuous history thus dates from Roman republican times. Barcino and Tarraco were *coloniae*, although Tarragona later became an imperial capital, dominating a *Provincia Tarraconensis* that encompassed all (and more) of what later formed Catalonia and Aragon. Countless towns and cities of these lands still bear the names the Romans gave them: Llívia (*Iulia Libica*), Girona (*Gerunda*), Caldes de Montbui (*Aquae Calidae*), Huesca (*Osca*), Zaragoza (*Caesaraugusta*), to name but a few; and the Latin forms were in use throughout the Middle Ages. Roman landlords organized farms or estates (*villae*), sometimes (as at Can Sent-romà near Barcelona) on indigenous or prehistoric sites), in the fertile zones running from the easternmost Pyrenees to the upper Ebro valley.

Two aspects of romanization had extraordinary importance for the future: linguistic transformation and the spread of Christianity. Almost everywhere the native tongues gave way to Latin, a sure sign of assimilation and submission if not always of the Iberians' numerical inferiority to Romans. Only in some remote uplands, such as Pallars and Ribagorza where a Basque-like dialect was spoken until the tenth century, can we discern the limits of Latin expansion. Of the Latin spoken in the Tarraconensis we know sadly little, but there can be no doubt that the romance vernaculars of the Middle Ages and after are descended from this speech. Why, then, do we find marked differences between modern Catalan and Aragonese (or Castilian)? Do these differences go back to the early confront-

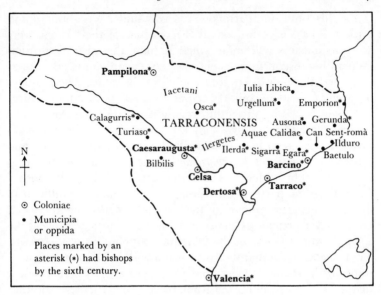

Pampilona*⊙

Iacetani

Iulia Libica•

Urgellum*•

Emporion*•

Osca*

Calagurris*•

TARRACONENSIS

Ausona*• Gerunda*

Turiaso*

Aquae Calidae Can Sent-romà

Caesaraugusta* Ilergetes Ilerda* Sigarra• Egara* Ilduro

N

Bilbilis

Celsa

Barcino*⊙

Baetulo

Dertosa*⊙

Tarraco*

⊙ Coloniae

• Municipia
  or oppida

Places marked by an
asterisk (*) had bishops
by the sixth century.

Valencia*

1. The Tarraconensis

ations of indigenous languages with Latin? If so, one might postulate a precocious ethnic differentiation antedating the Visigothic and Moorish invasions. But some philologists would place the determining changes later, as we shall see.

Of the transmission of Christianity to Spain next to nothing is securely known. It is no better than conjecture that ports of the Tarraconensis would have been the first communities to receive apostles or missionaries (possibly Saint Paul around AD 60?). The persecutions of Gallienus and Diocletian took their toll of martyrs, of whom Felix at Girona, Cugat at Barcelona, Fructuosus at Tarragona, and Vincent and Engracia at Zaragoza were among the most illustrious; their names with many others were perpetuated in countless altars and monasteries of later centuries. Tarragona and Barcelona were represented in the Council of Arles (314), but few bishops of Hispanic cities are known by name before the sixth century. Christian congregations evidently multiplied in the fifth and sixth centuries, when the councils of Tarragona (516) and Girona (517) testify to the administrative and liturgical organizing of affiliated bishops.

By this time the Tarraconensis was under Visigothic domination. The Visigoths, for all the violence of their kings, were tolerant masters who maintained Roman administrative order. Generally absent from their east Pyrenean lands, the kings governed through dukes and counts in the cities, where judges and *saigs* (agents of court) executed the law; most of these offices long survived the Visigothic regime in Catalonia. Alaric II's breviary of Roman law (506) served to preserve the Roman order. Reissued with accumulated additions by Recceswinth and later known as the *Liber iudiciorum*, this code remained the legal basis of public order in Catalonia until the eleventh century (and, on some particulars, still later). What is more difficult to grasp is the social impact of the Visigoths. Once the kings had converted to orthodox Christianity, there was little to prevent the assimilation of Goths in the Christian populations of the towns. Yet it seems likely that the Goths were seldom more than a small minority in the old towns, that they were absorbed themselves instead of transforming the Romanized populations. Little that was peculiarly Gothic survived in the art and liturgy of the early known monasteries, such as San Pedro de Séptimo in Aragon, although it was in the councils of the sixth and seventh centuries that ecclesiastical law was forged.

Visigothic administration collapsed before the onslaught of Muslim armies from Africa in the eighth century. Valencia was overrun in the years 711–13; the Ebro was breached in 714, when Tariq and Musa carried out devastating raids along the settled belt running from Huesca and Lérida to Tarragona, Barcelona, and Girona. Other expeditions crossed the Pyrenees, capturing Narbonne (720) and besieging Toulouse (721), but the strength of these advance positions was sapped by revolts and the defeat of a Moorish army near Poitiers by Charles Martel in 732. South of the Pyrenees the early Moorish incursions resulted in the replacement (or conversion to Islam) of urban administrators and the imposition of tribute on inhabitants. But there was no systematic expropriation for those—the vast majority— who accepted the new regime. Christians, called Mozarabs, maintained their clergy and churches in most cities, although monastic life seems to have been disrupted, and Jewish communities survived. Conversions to Islam were doubtless more general among the peasants, in the Ebro valley, for example, and the regions between Tortosa, Tarragona, and Lérida. In the course of time, many of the Roman-Visigothic estates changed hands, and were parcelled into smaller tenements.

From their earliest years the Moorish invasions created one fundamentally new condition: they divided the Tarraconensis into a southern zone of Muslim domination and an upland zone, generally north and east of the Ebro and in the Pyrenees, where the old Christian order persisted with little change. The resulting borderlands were ill-defined so long as they were not the scene of conflict. But the situation changed when, in 777, Moorish chieftains disloyal to the new emir 'Abd al-Rahmān I (755–88) negotiated for Charlemagne's support. The Frankish expeditions of 778, reaching Zaragoza by way of Barcelona and through the pass of Roncesvalles were unsuccessful, but they created the prospect of a Frankish protectorate that could only seem alarming to the emir. In 780–2 he recaptured Zaragoza and sent a punitive expedition through the upper Ebro lands, destroying strongholds and reimposing personal tribute in token of submission. From that point onward the Pyrenean valleys became a refuge for nonconformists, Muslims in some cases, but chiefly Christians for whom independence now took on new meaning. Most of the Moorish commands east of Tarragona were lost to the Franks by the end of the eighth century, but the Moors retained and confirmed their domination of Tortosa, Lérida, Huesca, Zaragoza, and Valencia, among other cities of the north-east. With a well-disciplined army of Berbers, 'Abd-al-Rahmān I laid the foundation of a Muslim dynastic state that lasted until 1031. Its greatest days came in the tenth century, when 'Abd-al-Rahmān III (912–61) governed a highly civilized court at Córdoba, then a prosperous city of some half a million inhabitants, and assumed the title of caliph in 929. In this period the provinces and major cities, such as Zaragoza and Valencia, were delegated to the *wālis*, under whom the *qādis* exercised justice, and the *muh-tasib* supervised markets, weights, and measures. The Moors developed irrigation for garden farming, notably in the Ebro valley and Valencia as well as in Andalusia, and cultivated oranges, sugar cane, rice, olives, and vines. They built baths and mosques, some of which are still visible (in Majorca city and Valencia); and city castles (*sudes*), such as may be seen at Tortosa, Siurana, and Lérida.

The great age of Islam in Spain passed with the tenth century, and the caliphate collapsed in 1031. From its ruins emerged a cluster of petty states, the *taifa* kingdoms, of which those at Valencia, Tortosa, and Zaragoza, were to be the principal adversaries of the Christian kings of Aragon and counts of Barcelona. The *taifas* in turn were mostly overcome by the Moroccan Berber Murābits (Almoravids), whose intense religiosity helped stir the crusading fervour that marked a new and decisive stage in the Christian Reconquista; and the Murābits were succeeded, in turn, by the Muwaḥḥids (Almohads), whose defeats at the hands of the count-kings in the thirteenth century were to be milestones in the early history of the Crown of Aragon.

Aragon (AD 800–1137)

From the efforts of Hispano-Visigothic chieftains to organize a rural population against the Muslims of the Ebro valley arose the kingdom of Aragon. Confined to tiny valleys above the river Aragón (barely 600 square kilometres), the Aragonese were dominated in the early ninth century by one Oriol (d. 809), doubtless in consequence of previous Frankish thrusts, and then by Aznar Galíndez (c.809–39), who was probably of native descent and was certainly recognized by Charlemagne. Culturally as well as politically the early county was oriented toward Frankland, easy of access through Hecho and Canfranc passes. The Benedictine house of San Pedro de Siresa, founded in the early ninth century, was nourished by the Frankish monastic reforms. When Saint Eulogius visited the monastery in 848 he found manuscripts of Virgil, Horace, and Juvenal; of Porphyry, and Aldhelm; and of Saint Augustine's *City of God*, none of which (he said) were then available at Córdoba.

The Frankish orientation did not last, for the Aragonese ceased to be threatened by the Muslims in the ninth century. In the Ebro valley survived a considerable Mozarab population, whose Arabic-speaking masters had long since quarrelled among themselves. The Christians in Zaragoza retained their bishop. Although the mountaineers were nominally subject to tribute, the effective Moorish domination reached no further north-east than Huesca, Barbastro, and Monzón. A daughter of Count Aznar II (867–93) married the *wāli* of Huesca. But the most influential political factor was Aragon's dynastic involvement with Navarre (or Pamplona) to the west. Her leaders were still no more than counts of uncertain title. Galindo Aznar (*c*.844–67) could only secure his father's claim to Aragon at the price of dependence on the king of the Pamplonese; his son Aznar II Galíndez (867–93) married the daughter of King García Iñiguez. In the tenth century a new line of Navarrese kings threatened to swallow up Aragon entirely. The Navarrese fortified devastated lands south of the river Aragón, thus encroaching severely on Aragon's zone of natural expansion. Aragon was to be virtually incorporated in the kingdom of Pamplona until the death of Sancho the Great (1004–35).

Nevertheless, the county of the Aragonese retained its social and administrative identity. One spoke of it in charters as the land of the 'Aragonese lords'. In the tenth century San Juan de la Peña, in the rugged frontier south of Jaca, replaced Siresa as the religious centre of Aragon. Traditionally associated with the arrival of Christian refugees from Zaragoza, the foundation of San Juan encouraged not only a restoration of Visigothic culture but also a patriotic militancy soon to be turned against the Muslims. Also symptomatic was the establishment of an Aragonese bishop in 922. The location of his see in the valley of Borau points to a growth of population in the upper valleys increasingly protected by military resettlement south of the Aragón river. Life in the latter zone, Aragon's first frontier, already contrasted starkly with that of farmers and shepherds in the unwalled hamlets of the mountains. Similar frontiers were being defined in Sobrarbe and Ribagorza to the east, where the early allegiance was to the counts of Toulouse, but where ties with the Aragonese become visible in the tenth century. There, too, monasteries were founded: at Alaón and Obarra (Ribagorza) in the early ninth century and later at San Juan de Matidero and San Victorián in Sobrarbe; and a bishopric was established at Roda in the tenth century.

Aragon became a kingdom in the eleventh century. Ramiro I (1035–69), who had ruled the county as deputy 'kinglet' for his father (Sancho the Great) since 1015, conceded his brother's supremacy in Navarre. He was permitted for his part to extend Aragonese authority deeply into the frontier formerly fortified by Navarre, a policy that resulted in a permanent enlargement of

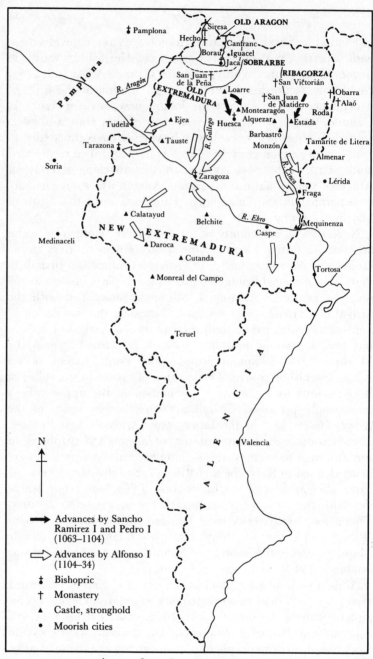

11. Aragon from the tenth century to 1134

Aragon. The incipient realm grew to more than six times the territorial extent of the original county; nor was this all, for in 1044 Ramiro annexed Sobrarbe and Ribagorza, where his father had campaigned to protect the Christian settlements. If Ramiro did not quite claim to be king himself (using the expression 'as if king'), he had manifestly assumed leadership in the struggle against the Moors, whose strongholds now faced his own across a long frontier. Ramiro's precedence in the dynastic patrimonies was confirmed when his nephew became king of Pamplona in 1054; his son Sancho Ramírez (1062–94) submitted Aragon to papal protection, a dependence converted into vassalage in 1089; and when Sancho himself succeeded his cousin in Navarre in 1076, the supremacy of Navarre was ended. Sancho styled himself 'king by God's grace of the Pamplonese and Aragonese'.

This political success was enhanced by singularly favourable circumstances. The Muslim cities, while continuing to prosper economically and culturally, lost the military initiative to strengthened contingents of mounted knights on the Christian side. With the pressure thus reversed, so also was the flow of gold. Sancho Ramírez was able to impose tribute on the Moors of Huesca, Tudela, and Zaragoza, and derived great wealth from it. Meanwhile Christian Aragon became a crossroads. The Gascon passes carried a swelling throng of merchants and pilgrims: the former trading cloths, weapons, and hardware for Muslim spices, fruits, and manufactures; the latter finding Jaca a convenient stage on the route to Santiago de Compostela. The tolls of Canfranc and Jaca produced spectacular profits for the Aragonese monarchy and church. In an upland hitherto without urban life, Jaca became an 'instant city'. It attracted settlers not only from its environs but especially from Gascony and Toulouse. Sancho Ramírez encouraged this movement, granting to Jaca a charter of liberties (1077) and instituting a silver coinage that would spread with the realm itself to become a national institution.

So transformed, the first city of Christian Aragon naturally became its ecclesiastical capital. What was conceived to be a restoration of the territorial church was inaugurated in a synod at Jaca (1063) attended by the archbishop of Auch and other prelates from both sides of the Pyrenees. The episcopal see traditionally belonging to Huesca was relocated at Jaca and grandly endowed. Its canons received the Augustinian Rule, which was also instituted in royal chapels at Siresa, Loarre, Montearagón, and Alquézar; the monastic customs at San Juan de la Peña and San Victorián were reformed; while churches throughout the realm gave up the Visigothic observance for the Roman liturgy. The bishopric of Roda, having been destroyed by the Moors in 1006, was restored under royal and papal protection in the 1070s. Together with economic prosperity the religious revival worked to revolutionize ecclesiastical architecture. The splendid cathedral at Jaca was built in monumental if eclectic styles drawing inspiration from Italy and France. There were similar innovations in the renovated churches at Iguácel (1063–72), San Juan (1094), and elsewhere; of the traditional, undecorated style little survived save, here and there, the Hispanic arch. Artists from southern France introduced new meaning and elegance to the sculpture of interiors and cloisters.

By the later eleventh century Aragon seemed to have come of age. Yet the young kingdom, so precociously expansive and receptive, was only then on the eve of conquests that would enlarge its territories nearly tenfold during the next two generations. There was nothing fortuitous about this renewed expansion. Jaca's designation as a bishop's see seems to have been provisional, pending the conquest of Huesca. Ramiro I died in conflict with the Muslims near Barbastro (probably in 1069), an event which, following on notorious struggles over Barbastro (1064–5), must have contributed to a hardening perception of the Moors as enemies of the Christian faith. French and Catalan-speaking knights were already fighting alongside the Aragonese in this zone of the frontier, and expeditions of this kind were to be promoted as pious works and, finally, as crusades. Progress, however, remained slow. The Muslims retained a string of fortified places well upland from the Ebro, extending from lower Ribagorza to Tudela. Moreover, the kings of Pamplona and Castile for a time supported the *taifa* of Zaragoza against the Aragonese. Then in the last quarter of the eleventh century the tide turned. The death of Sancho IV in 1076 ended the debilitating competition of Navarre, while Muslim leadership, threatened from the south by Almoravids, faltered with the death of al-Muqtadir of Zaragoza in 1081.

So a new wave of Aragonese conquests began in the later years of Sancho Ramírez. Acting as viceroy in Sobrarbe and Ribagorza, his son Pedro captured Estada in 1087 and Monzón in 1089, opening the way to rapid advances southward in the Cinca valley and as far east as Almenar (taken in 1093). Progress toward Barbastro and Huesca proved more difficult. Although Montearagón, within view of the city, fell in 1088, it was not until November 1096 that Huesca surrendered to Pedro I (1094–1104), now king of Aragon. Barbastro capitulated in 1100, leaving only Lérida unconquered among cities of the eastern frontier. To the west progress along the sparsely settled Gallego river had been no less spectacular. By 1101 Pedro's forces were in control of strong points virtually under the walls of Zaragoza and Tudela.

At this stage the campaign was slowed. Alfonso VI, who had previously resisted Aragonese expansion as a threat to Castilian destinies, was moved by the conquest of Huesca to renew his aid to the Moors. The Aragonese, for their part, while breaking the enemy frontier, had failed to secure the lands behind their advanced positions. Nor could the kings of Aragon yet safely commit all their resources to this enterprise. They had felt obliged to collaborate in Castilian expeditions to the lower Ebro and to Valencia so as not to jeopardize their own claims to rich coastal domains; Pedro I had allied with the Castilian mercenary Rodrigo Díaz de' Vivar (el Cid Campeador) against the Almoravids in 1097. The preoccupation with Castile continued during the reign of Pedro's brother Alfonso I (1104–34), whose stormy marriage to Alfonso VI's widow Urraca ultimately failed to effect a dynastic union. In his early years Alfonso I conquered Ejea and Tauste on the western frontier, thus gaining control of the Cinco Villas, and Tamarite de Litera in the east (1105–7), but another decade passed before the campaign against the *taifas* now dominated by the Banū Hūd dynasty at Zaragoza, Lérida, and Tortosa was seriously renewed.

Inspired by the crusading ideal then in its flower, Alfonso I welcomed papal support in the form of indulgences and military aid from foreign knights, notably Count Centulle II of Bigorre and Viscount Gaston IV of Béarn. Zaragoza fell in 1118 after a long siege, followed in 1119 by Tudela and Tarazona. In 1120 Soria was resettled and Calatayud besieged. News of a counter-attack on Zaragoza diverted the king to the Valencian borderland where at Cutanda his forces routed an Almoravid force in June 1120. Soon afterwards Alfonso captured Daroca and Calatayud. The destruction of the Moorish realm of Zaragoza was almost complete. Alfonso secured his southern positions against Valencia, and established knights under religious vow at Monreal del Campo and Belchite. To the east he established a new frontier extending virtually from Morella to Mequinenza, seriously threatening the Moors of the Cinca and lower Ebro. For all this success Alfonso was frustrated in his ambition to conquer Lérida and Tortosa, which lay in zones claimed for annexation by the count of Barcelona, who had made a treaty with the kinglet of Lérida in 1120. In 1134 the king of Aragon lost a battle at Fraga and died a few weeks later.

Alfonso I ('the Battler') ranks among the greatest kings of the Hispanic 'Reconquest'. His victories substantially defined the medieval realm of Aragon, establishing borders with Catalonia, Valencia, and Castile. Under him Aragon lost the defensiveness of her upland origins and assumed an expanded role as liberator of oppressed Christians. 'No king of Aragon was inflamed with a spirit so authentically religious and crusading as the Battler king', wrote Lacarra. It is in light of these circumstances that most historians have explained the strange testament by which Alfonso, childless and probably sterile, bequeathed his kingdom to the military orders of the Holy Land: an exalted but unrealistic act of piety. But it seems at least possible that this testament, which was composed in 1131 and confirmed shortly before the king's death in 1134, was a shrewd contrivance intended to have almost precisely the consequences that, in the event, ensued. The defeat at Fraga touched off Moorish uprisings in which the south-eastern frontier collapsed. Zaragoza was saved from recapture by forces of Alfonso VII of Castile (December 1134), who had a good dynastic claim to Aragon and Navarre. The purpose of the will may therefore have been to neutralize papal influence in support of this claim. The Aragonese magnates set aside the testament in favour of the Battler's younger brother, the monk Ramiro, who was married to Agnes of Aquitaine in order to beget the needed heir. In the end the Navarrese rejected this arrangement, choosing a king of their own, García Ramírez, descended from the old house of

Pamplona. Ramiro II (1134–7), for his part, retired to the monastic life after fathering a daughter, Petronilla, who was promptly betrothed to Count Ramon Berenguer IV of Barcelona. Aragon had escaped Castilian domination, at what cost remained to be seen.

Enormous problems of organization faced Alfonso I and his successors. Their domains, a compounding of frontiers, had multiplied too fast to be assimilated. South of the Pyrenean valleys in which Aragon had originated lay the 'old frontier' (*Vieja Extremadura*) dating from the tenth century. Next came the 'new land' conquered at the end of the eleventh century, the key points of which were Huesca and Barbastro. Relatively densely inhabited, this frontier was organized in military tenancies awarded to barons who had contributed service and fighting men in the campaigns, while its extension west of the Gallego remained an incompletely subjugated no man's land. Imported from the old frontier, the tenancies of the new land were devised to support fighting men on the produce of peasants progressively less free. That the king was obliged to create baronies in lands over which he claimed sole dominion points to a characteristic weakness in his position. The military obligations of (old) Aragon, having become customary at a level suited for defensive service, were too light to sustain the prolonged campaigns and sieges of the twelfth century. The king had to persuade and to pay. Less a popular than a royal idea, the expansion of Aragon obliged the king to raise up powerful tenants-in-chief in the new land.

The Ebro valley, with its old cities, gardens, and orchards, posed a different problem. This zone had to be secured and exploited without destroying its prosperity. The solution was to clear the cities for Christian resettlement, while allowing the Muslims to retain their movables and rural property. Every effort was made to preserve the traditional structure of obligations and irrigation in the countrysides. The king compensated his knights with properties confiscated in Zaragoza and Tudela and enticed settlers from the old Aragonese lands, the east Pyrenean counties, Gascony, and Castile, even Christians from Granada, to share in the spoils. Although many Muslims abandoned these homelands—particularly administrative officers and expropriated landlords—the mass of peasants and artisans

remained, so that the Mudejars, as they were called, long
outnumbered the Christians.

Finally, there was the 'new *Extremadura*' established by Alfonso
I on the borders of Castile and Valencia. Rugged and arid, this
sector was organized in military zones projecting from towns
such as Soria, Medinaceli, Calatayud, and Daroca. These places,
generally commended to the king's barons-in-arms, were settled
on unusually liberal terms which included freedom from prosecution for felonies. Castilians, Navarrese, and Gascons joined the
immigrants to this frontier. These were communities of peasant
warriors: foot-soldiers and mounted men shared a common
status. Governed by customary statutes (*fueros*) and by councils,
the early settlers here were resistant to seigneurial exploitation.

Aragon was, therefore, far from being a homogeneous state at
the death of Alfonso the Battler. Although the 'Aragonese'
(*aragoneses*) were fighting and settling on all the frontiers, the
term 'Aragon' (*Aragonia*) continued to be reserved for the old
mountain homeland, while the king's authority remained a
cluster of lordships: over Aragon, Sobrarbe, Huesca, Zaragoza,
etc. The process of assimilation was beginning, to be sure.
Settlers in Barbastro received the same privileges as the knights
(*infanzones*) of Sobrarbe. Alfonso I encouraged his followers to
serve him regardless of local custom. That is why in 1134 the
'*infançones* and barons of Aragon' insisted, in one of the earliest of
Europe's 'great charters', on having their customs confirmed as
they were in the time of Pedro I. Moreover, the Christian clergy
supported the royalist view that the war was a reconquest.
Bishop's churches were to be 'restored' where they once
existed—in Tarazona as well as in Huesca and Zaragoza, for
example—and they were endowed in similar ways, often by
expropriation of mosques. Upland churches lost their early
centrality and influence, becoming annexes of restored sees: Jaca
of Huesca, Roda of Lérida.

Yet the monarchy as an institution had evolved very little.
Alfonso I, like his ancestors, was a war-lord. He dominated and
rewarded followers who derived status and privilege from
association with him; acting through men of his court, their
functions unspecialized, he exploited his estates in the old
Aragonese lands and his rents, justice, and tolls everywhere.
While the common military obligation was derived from an

ancient conception of public order upheld by the king, the prevailing forms of service, obligation, and right were essentially personal and patrimonial. The situation was such that the king retained the initiative while the expansion continued; few military tenancies were yet hereditary in the early twelfth century. But the stability of this royal-baronial condominium remained to be tested.

East Pyrenean Counties and the Rise of Barcelona (800–1137)

Like Aragon the eastern Pyrenean regions later to be known as Catalonia were first organized as a Christian frontier against the Muslims. But the Frankish initiatives here were more important, and their impress more lasting, than in Aragon. Charlemagne himself ordered the campaigns in which Girona (785) and Barcelona (801) were reconquered. Moreover, the earliest counts of these districts seem to have been appointed by the Frankish king, as their successors certainly were. Whether the native peoples would necessarily prefer Frankish to Moorish masters was another matter. In Barcelona, as in Narbonne a generation before, the Muslim governor had found support among Christians who had prospered in the eighth century, and local coalitions of Goths and Moors would plague Frankish leaders for decades to come. On the other hand, Charlemagne's welcome to Hispano-Gothic refugees north of the Pyrenees together with his acceptance of Visigothic law as the basis of social order had fostered sentiment favourable to Frankish rule in the diverse lands (over 40,000 square kilometres) stretching from the Conflent to the Ebro. The Franks spoke of this region as the 'March of Spain' in the ninth century.

The Frankish protectorate extended naturally from positions north of the Pyrenees. The key figure was Count Guilhem of Toulouse (d. 812), a cousin of Charlemagne, whose first wife was probably a Visigoth, and who retired to the monastic life in 806 (he was later canonized) after valiant campaigns against the Moors. From his time date monastic foundations at Arles, Sant Andreu de Sureda, and Sant Genís de Fontanes in the Vallespir and the restoration of Gerri in upper Pallars; in most of these may be discerned the influence of the reformed Frankish observance of Benedict of Aniane. Saint Guilhem and his sons, in shifting and turbulent combinations, administered nine of the

III. East Pyrenean Counties (tenth century to 1137)

Legend:
- ‡ Archbishopric
- ‡ Bishopric
- † Monastery
- ▲ Castle
- Regions aggregated with Barcelona from the tenth century

Map labels:

ROUSSILLON (1172)
Elne
Sant Miquel de Cuixà
Sant Genís
Arles
VALLESPIR
CONFLENT (1117)
Vilafranca
CAPCIR (1117)
CERDANYA (1117)
Peralada
EMPÚRIES
Besalú
BESALÚ (1111)
R. Fluvià
Sant Joan
Ripoll
OSONA
†Vic
▲Malla
GIRONA
Girona
▲Fornells
BERGA (Berguedà 1117)
Cardona
MARCH OF BERGA
MARCH OF OSONA
Sallent
SEGARRA
Copons
▲Pierola
BARCELONA
R. Llobregat
†Barcelona
PENEDÈS
▲Olèrdola
MARCH OF BARCELONA
ANDORRA
La Seu d'Urgell
Lord Valley
URGELL (1314)
Tàrrega
MARCH OF URGELL
MARCH OF CAMARASA
VALL D'ARAN
UPPER PALLARS (1488)
†Gerri
LOWER PALLARS (1192)
RIBAGORÇA
Tàrrega
Tarragona
TAIFA REALMS OF LÉRIDA AND TORTOSA
▲Siurana
R. Segre
Lérida

N

fourteen counties that later constituted Catalonia. But the opportunism of Bernard of Septimania (826–44) alienated his indigenous subjects as well as King Charles the Bald, who found legitimist support in Sunifred of Carcassone (844–8), who was of Visigothic descent. Conquering Cerdanya (835) and Urgell (838), Sunifred seems also to have checked a Moorish invasion before it reached Septimania. These exploits, by a native equally loyal to his homeland and the king, were not forgotten. But Sunifred fell victim, before his sons were grown, to a revolt by Guilhem, son of Bernard of Septimania; and the king, having restored order (849), found it increasingly difficult to secure loyal and competent service from the Frankish counts he appointed to the Spanish March. As the kingdom itself reeled, it fell to the loyal house of Carcassonne to fulfill its destiny. Guifré (or Wifred) the Hairy, Sunifred's eldest son, seems to have been invested with Urgell, Cerdanya, and Conflent as early as 870; to these were added Barcelona and Girona in 878. Guifré associated his younger brothers Miró and Radulf in the administration respectively of Conflent and Besalú.

The Catalans of later times viewed the reign of Guifré the Hairy (870–97) as a heroic age of national formation. He was, in fact, the last count of the Spanish March to receive his commission from a king, and he supported popular initiatives in resettlement that helped to create a sense of political and cultural identity in his lands. Guifré and his descendants were to rule Catalonia for more than 500 years.

Already in the 870s Guifré had encouraged colonization of the wastelands in the Lord valley in the frontier of Cerdanya and Urgell. After 878 settlers spread into the plain of Vic and the upper Llobregat valley (the later Berguedà). Coming mostly from the Pyrenees, these people received lands on the liberal tenure of *aprisio*, which created a quasi-proprietary right under comital protection; the new county of Osona was organized. New parish churches were consecrated and endowed, old ones restored. The bishopric of Vic was restored by 887. The most notable of the new monastic foundations were Sant Miquel de Cuixà in the Conflent (878) and, in the newly resettled domains, Ripoll (879) and Sant Joan de les Abadesses (887). Nevertheless, the situation throughout this pre-Pyrenean frontier remained insecure. Guifré lost a battle against the Moors near Lérida in

884; and he was killed in 897 resisting a Moorish incursion that reached Barcelona. There had been no provision for the succession, still legally at the disposition of the Frankish king.

The crisis was resolved through the resolute efforts of Guifré's sons and grandsons, in whose time the Spanish March attained a new degree of political stability. The brothers of the first generation divided the counties among themselves, while reserving nominal superiority to the eldest, Guifré II (897–911), who administered Barcelona, Girona, and Osona. Miró II (897–927) succeeded to Cerdanya, Conflent, and Berguedà; Sunifred II (897–950) to Urgell. Upon Guifré II's early death, Barcelona passed to his younger brother Sunyer (911–47), an irregular devolution for which Miró II was apparently compensated by the succession to Besalú in 913. This remarkable condominium persisted in the second generation (and, in some respects, much longer), although the counties soon became heritable in themselves. The counties of Pallars and Ribagorza remained in an equivocal position, linked to Urgell and the eastern counties by their Frankish origin and Catalan speech, yet pressed from the ninth century onward to consolidate with the Aragonese.*

Juridically, nothing had changed. The embattled count Guifré II thought it prudent to do homage to King Charles the Simple (899), whose protection still seemed useful to March-land monasteries as well. As late as 986–7, following a devastating Moorish attack, appeals were directed to the king. In reality the counts had progressively assumed the Carolingian cause for their own, continuing the work of resettlement, notably in the lower Llobregat region and the Vallès, sponsoring ecclesiastical councils and inspiring a more aggressive resistance to the Moors. The accession of a new generation of counts was marked by political reorientation. From Cerdanya and Conflent were initiated contacts with Rome (950–1) which resulted in the first papal privileges of exemption for peninsular monasteries. At the same time an embassy to Córdoba from Borrell II of Barcelona and Urgell (947–92) concluded a treaty with the caliph that virtually nullified the historic dependence of the March on Frankland. Improved security and confidence encouraged a

---

* Pallars would later be incorporated in Catalonia (see below, p. 48), while Ribagorza remained, uneasily, a Catalan-speaking enclave of Aragon.

flowering of ecclesiastical culture. Bishops and abbots, typically scions of the comital lineages, splendidly promoted and endowed their congregations. Cuixà, Vic, and Ripoll became renowned centres of letters and learning. Vic must already have had cultural contacts with Córdoba when Gerbert of Aurillac sojourned there around 967–70. In the time of Oliba (b. 971), son of Oliba Cabreta (count of Cerdanya-Besalú, d. 990), abbot of Ripoll and Cuixà (1008–46) and bishop of Vic (1017–46), Benedictine observance came into touch with newly reformed religious currents in Frankland and Italy. Classical Latin, patristics, and Visigothic legal studies were revived at Ripoll, where, moreover, the recording of Frankish king-lists began to give way to commemoration of comital deeds. Lombard styling predominated in the churches dedicated at Ripoll (1032), Vic (1035), and Cuixà (1038).

Yet if the new culture was nurtured in the uplands, political and economic circumstances were raising Barcelona to pre-dominance in the condominium. Borrell II bore the brunt of al-Manṣūr's invasion which unexpectedly broke the peace in 985. His courageous defence of Barcelona nearly coincided with the demise of the western Carolingian dynasty, which explains why in 988 he styled himself 'duke and marquis by God's grace'. Under Ramon Borrell, count of Barcelona and Girona (992–1017), new thrusts by al-Manṣūr and 'Abd-al-Malik (1001–3) were not merely parried but reversed in damaging counter-attacks which culminated in a daring raid on Córdoba itself (1010). This exploit proved a turning-point. Henceforth the frontier west of the Llobregat (the Penedès) would be relatively secure, while the booty distributed among Christian warriors and the payments of tribute by *taifa* chieftains gave impetus to the economy.

For the renewed raids had done little more than deflect a movement of sustained economic growth in the east Pyrenean lands. Contacts with Moorish Spain friendly or otherwise resulted in exchanges of slaves, weapons, horses, and cloth. Muslim gold coins circulated around Barcelona in the 970s, and were minted there by 1018. Metallurgy developed together with new markets for rural exchange, such as at Sallent and Besalú; a fair was instituted at Urgell in 1048. Even more remarkable was agrarian expansion: continued resettlement, reaching to the coasts of Girona; the improvement of older peasant cultivations, as in the Vallès and the Gironès owing to better tools for labour; the exploitation of new and marginal lands, as in the lower Penedès and the Segarra, by terracing and ditching. Centred in the coastal plains and their hinterlands, the revitalized economy continued to draw people from the mountains. The primacy of the mountains came to its end earlier in this sector than in Aragon.

Traditional legal and institutional structures persisted intact into the eleventh century. Ancient settlements and public (fiscal) domains adjoined new peasant settlements in the coastal and sub-Pyrenean valleys. Small properties, parcels, and allodial farms were common everywhere. The law remained Visigothic, public and territorial; the administration Carolingian. Counts, viscounts, and vicars dominated their lands from well-spaced castles and relied on the military and economic services of a mostly free population. They held public courts assisted by judges and clerks learned in the Gothic law.

But this social and institutional cohesion collapsed in the second quarter of the eleventh century. Berenguer Ramon I (1017–35) was unable to sustain his father's momentum against the Moors, thereby depriving an upwardly mobile military class of its most cherished outlet. The castles of the aggressive lineages, manned by mounted warriors more numerous and less disciplined than their Aragonese counterparts, proliferated beyond comital control. Castellans fought among themselves, ravaged peasant lands, and requisitioned crops, and imposed upon helpless peasants an array of obligations that soon hardened into a custom of banal lordship. The old procedure of courts gave way to private settlements. Wishing to restore public order and perhaps encouraged by associated peasants, the bishops of Elne and Vic inaugurated the Truce of God (1027, 1033) so as to curb the excesses of the new militarism. Specific protections for the clergy, the monks, and the unarmed were defined under episcopal sanctions in a territorial statute that would later be appropriated by the counts. For the time being, however, the assault on comital prerogatives continued. The revolt of Mir Geribert, who styled himself 'prince of Olèrdola', took two decades (1040–59) to overcome.

It was Count Ramon Berenguer I (1035–76) who finally

prevailed and established a new political order. Regaining control of the principal castles, often by purchase (Pierola, Cardona, Fornells, Malla, Copons, etc.), he progressively secured the alliance or fealty of the other counts and viscounts as well as of other lords of castles. He insisted on the sworn fidelity even of subordinate castellans and knights together with the right of entry to castles. In using such methods, however, he was not reactionary: little of the old order survived. Ties of personal fidelity proliferated throughout society, replacing the weakened sanctions of the law. The fief, having originated in the Spanish March as a form of remuneration from fiscal land, became the normal reward, and eventually the pre-condition, for service and fidelity. Castellans and their enfeoffed knights formed a new aristocracy whose social superiority was progressively defined in rites of initiation. Most portentously, the old free peasantry disappeared wherever castles arose—that is, almost everywhere. Because the counts and viscounts as well as the new aristocracy had violated tenant liberties for economic gain, there could be no redress for the masses north and east of the Moorish frontier. They were becoming a subservient class. The new order was thus a feudal order dominated by the count of Barcelona. His domains came to be perceived by foreigners as a land of castellans (*castlàns*), whence the new appellation *Catalonia* that came into familiar use in the twelfth century.

About 1060 dawned the great age of independent Catalonia. Acting firmly as 'princes of the land' to secure the new internal order, Ramon Berenguer I and the countess Almodis imposed the Peace and Truce as a territorial statute in 1064. They legislated so as to bring the procedures and tariffs of the Visigothic law up to date, although it is not clear whether they sought to have these measures recognized in counties nominally independent, such as Empúries, Besalú, and Roussillon. Externally, Ramon Berenguer I renewed the pressure on *taifa* chieftains of Lérida, Tortosa, and Zaragoza, who were obliged to pay tribute.

Thenceforth the counts entered vigorously into affairs of the wider Mediterranean world. Ramon Berenguer II (1076–82) married a daughter of the Norman prince Robert Guiscard, and their son was to marry first the Cid's daughter and later the heiress of Provence. The Gregorian reform of the church was introduced to Catalonia in legatine councils held at Besalú (1077) and Girona (1078). Not even domestic violence, which for the first time jolted the peace of Guifré's dynasty, seriously disrupted political affairs: the matricide Pere Ramon was packed off to Castile, while Berenguer Ramon II (1082–96), charged with the murder of Ramon Berenguer II, was permitted to retain the comital title on condition of its passing ultimately to his nephew Ramon Berenguer III. Berenguer Ramon II fought to extend Catalonian claims far to the south-west of secure frontier positions. His attempts to capture Valencia (1085, 1089) were frustrated by the Cid, and settlers were still too few to justify attacking Tortosa. But the coincidence of Catalan advances in this zone with the Castilian reconquest of Toledo (1085), the primacy of which seemed to threaten Barcelona's ecclesiastical autonomy, led Pope Urban II to proclaim the restoration of the archbishopric of Tarragona (1089, 1091). This was premature. Political complications together with new invasions by the Almoravids, who devastated the Penedès in 1107 and threatened Barcelona in 1115, ended hopes of swiftly securing Tarragona and conquering Tortosa.

Ramon Berenguer III (1096–1131) devoted himself to the possibilities of his dynastic position in the old counties. In 1107 he married his child-daughter to the dotard Bernat III of Besalú on condition of succeeding to that county should Bernat die without leaving children. This condition was fulfilled, surely not unexpectedly, in 1111. Then at the death of Count Bernat Guillem (1109–17) without heirs, Ramon Berenguer annexed Cerdanya, the dynastic homeland. These devolutions, deliberately planned, went far toward reconstituting the Guifredian patrimony. But, as in the ninth, so in the twelfth century the Pyrenees were no barrier. Having inherited the suzerainty of Carcassonne and Razès, counties acquired by his grandparents in 1067, Ramon Berenguer III secured sworn fidelities from the men of Carcassonne in 1107 and the homage of their viscount in 1112. In that year, too, Ramon married Dolça of Provence, yet another diplomatic triumph. Entitled count of Provence from 1113 and possessed of trans-Pyrenean domains stretching from Nice to the Ariège, Ramon Berenguer III henceforth threatened the Occitanian hegemony of the count of Toulouse, with whom a treaty of partition was passed in 1125.

Since establishing ties with Norman Sicily, the lords and merchants of the coastal counties had taken to the sea. Toward 1100 Barcelona was a thriving place, rebuilding within its old walls, expanding in its suburbs, prospering in its trades and industries. Its mariners probably joined the Pisans and Genoese in complaining of piracy by Moors in the Balearic Islands. In 1114–15 Ramon Berenguer III, called 'duke of the Catalans' by admiring Pisans, led a coalition of crusaders to seize Majorca. Although the islands were promptly recaptured by the Almoravids, the exploit was symptomatic of enlarged Catalonian designs in the Mediterranean. In 1118 began new efforts to restore Tarragona. The count commended the city and its hinterland to Bishop Oleguer of Barcelona, who was designated archbishop of Tarragona by the pope. Another decade would pass, however, before resettlement began in earnest under the Norman knight Robert Bordet, to whom Oleguer ceded his jurisdictional rights in 1129. These were trying years on the Christian frontier, for the Almoravids had cut off tributory payments from *taifa* chieftains and otherwise discouraged campaigning. The Aragonese now seemed as threatening to Catalonian prospects as the Moors themselves. In his last years Ramon Berenguer III worked to secure his rights—to develop mercantile tolls, to correct violators of the peace—and he planned an overseas crusade.

In 1131 Ramon Berenguer IV succeeded to his father's peninsular lands and the suzerainties of Carcassonne and Razès, while Provence passed to his younger brother Berenguer Ramon (1131–44). He was faced at once with Aragonese advances on Lérida and Tortosa that were cut short by Alfonso the Battler's defeat and death in 1134. Three years later Ramon Berenguer IV was betrothed to the heiress of Aragon.

Catalonia was affected less than Aragon by events of the early twelfth century. The major social and institutional changes had occurred earlier, her greatest peninsular conquests still lay ahead. While the division separating what were later called Old and New Catalonia was well established by 1137, the latter remained a deep and insecure frontier of mingled Moorish and Christian settlements running from the hinterlands of Tarragona north and west through the massif of Siurana to Lérida. In the old counties the conditions of people remained diverse. The castellans and knights were not yet fully assimilated in the old aristocracy, which continued to command the greater fortunes. Lay estates and castles were becoming hereditary, while peasant tenants were progressively bound to their masters and the land. Towns of the old counties possessed a rising mercantile class, unlike the Aragonese, but only a few places in Catalonia—such as Vilafranca del Conflent and Tàrrega—could yet boast charters.

The exercise of power was hardly less rudimentary than in Aragon. The counts exploited their domains through castellans and bailiffs. They relied on favoured barons and clerics for counsel, and they rewarded a bellicose aristocracy in their campaigns. But the equilibrium between comital and baronial interests was balanced precariously on the prospect of continued conquests.

On the eve of dynastic union, the historic realities of the Tarraconensis must have faded from common memory. Where centuries of invasions and reconstructions had failed to obliterate an ancient if superficial unity defined by the Roman imperial province, the Christian baronial conquests from the ninth century created new cellules of power and society with astonishing rapidity and unprecedented solidity. Aragon and Catalonia are thus, strictly speaking, products of the Middle Ages; products of the confrontation between Islam and Christianity in the eastern peninsula. Neither had any basis in tribal culture, both were inherently geopolitical constructions. Yet the characteristic novelty in both stemmed from the Moorish conquest, which, prolonged over several centuries and experienced typically as disconcerting thrusts, forced those who resisted to consolidate in the Pyrenees and work their ways southwards. So for the first time in Iberian history the mountain resisted the plain, and prevailed. Yet, as elsewhere in the northern peninsula, it did so in the eastern and central Pyrenees in different ways, with different results.

In Aragon the Moorish imprint went much deeper. Most of the enlarged realm of the twelfth century lay in rugged lands lately conquered and incompletely assimilated. The cultural gulf between the Ebro and the Aragón corresponded more nearly to a geographical contrast than was true in the eastern counties.

Aragonese cultural identity was among the most precocious in all western Europe, defined from the early ninth century in relation to an upland system of natural drainage; the kingdom of Aragon proclaimed in the eleventh century was confined to this upland and its first tentative frontier, which lent it a precarious coherence that was weakened with the conquests of the twelfth century. In 1137 Aragon was a royal-baronial confederation for the exploitation of multi-cultured lands united by little more than name.

The situation in Catalonia was quite different. There, too, the Moors had struck in the eighth century, but in contrast to what happened in Aragon, the early Frankish retaliation had been decisive. Only in the south-west borderlands had Moorish settlements and protectorates lasted in the ninth century, so that while the occasional raids that long persisted helped to kindle a defensive militancy, they did not prevent the early demographic expansion from the mountains that resulted in a more culturally homogeneous society extending over most of historical Catalonia. The frontiers of Catalonia, save for that defined in the twelfth century when the days of Moorish domination were visibly numbered (and when all Christian fighting men were eager for the spoils), tended to be agrarian rather than military. On the other hand, while the Aragonese early found identity in their name and their king, the people of the eastern counties still lacked such marks of cohesion as late as the mid-twelfth century. As in the past, their rulers were counts and their law was Gothic and none but foreigners yet saw the need to name them according to a pancomital idea that seems to have had more to do with a new custom of the multiplied castles than with fears of the Moors. Something, after all, survived here from the old Tarraconensis.

It remains to mention language, perhaps the most mysterious and certainly the most influential survival in the two lands. The transformation of spoken Latin into Aragonese and Catalan must have been virtually complete by the middle of the twelfth century. Here we have the single clearest sign of ethnic individuation in our two realms and we may be sure that the differentiation had occurred no later than the time of the first Moorish invasions, when it was doubtless accelerated. There is reason to believe that, whatever influence may be attributed to the various tribal substrata of language, the contrast between Moorish occupation in much of Aragon and its early eradication in Old Catalonia largely accounts for the phonetic and dialectical differences between East Catalan and Aragonese. According to Badia i Margarit, moreover, it was Moorish settlement in the Ebro–Segre frontier that produced a deromanizing resurgence of a native substratum that brought about marked differences between the multifarious West Catalan forms of these border-lands and East Catalan. If this theory perhaps underestimates the strength, pervasiveness, and variability of the Latin sub-stratum, it none the less helps to explain how the processes of acculturation worked in the forming of Aragon and Catalonia quite independently of the reconquest politics of Christian kings and counts. The forging of divergent linguistic identities long antedated the new processes of national formation in Aragon and Catalonia in the early years of the union.

II

The Age of the Early Count-Kings
(1137–1213)

THE betrothal of the heiress of Aragon to the count of Barcelona inaugurated a dynastic union that would last for centuries. It is customary to speak of this union as the 'Crown of Aragon', although the term itself dates from much later times when the original federation had expanded; and of its rulers, who never ceased to style themselves 'count of Barcelona', as 'count-kings'.* Under the early count-kings the union worked well. Neither land was neglected, both societies prospered and matured, while joint lordship promoted the expansive ambitions that fired a later age of conquest.

The Principate of Ramon Berenguer IV (1137–1162)

The greatest of the early rulers was Ramon Berenguer IV (1131–62). Not the least of his achievements was simply to secure Aragon according to the terms of 1137. The betrothal to Petronilla had been a diplomatic triumph: it ended the threat of Castilian (or Aragonese) domination of the Moorish borderlands from Lérida to the lower Ebro, and it opened the prospect of a Catalan–Aragonese conquest of Valencia. Yet it was not an easy triumph. Many years were to pass before the infant Petronilla could marry Ramon Berenguer IV (1150). Meanwhile, the dispossessed military orders had to be compensated and the

* This usage, preferred by Catalan historians, may seem awkward to non-peninsular readers. Yet it is arguably the least misleading of appropriate alternative expressions. One may speak of the dynastic rulers of Aragon and Catalonia as 'kings', as I often do in this book; but to do so exclusively is to perpetuate an exaggeration of Aragon's place in the federation that pervades the older literature and common parlance in northern lands. The expression 'king-count' is similarly tendentious and even more obtrusive for being a neologism; it may further mislead in implying that the king was everywhere count (otherwise why not simply say 'king'?). The more familiar compound 'count-king', whatever *its* fault, has the advantage of expressing the characteristic precedence of Catalonia in most initiatives of the dynasty after 1162.

pressures of Alfonso VII resisted; nor could the papal attitude in
such circumstances safely be ignored. Ramon dealt resourcefully
with all these problems. He won renunciations from the orders of
the Hospital and the Holy Sepulchre in September 1140 on
condition of their retaining certain rights in Aragon. Although
the Templars did not join in these capitulations, they accepted
compensation that not only nullified their claim to Aragon but
sufficed to secure for the count-prince some reasonable expec-
tation of their military support against the Moors. By a charter
of November 1143 the Templars secured six Aragonese castles, a
tenth of royal revenues, plus 1000 sous per year from those of
Zaragoza, a fifth of all lands conquered from the Moors, and
exemption from tolls. The pope confirmed this agreement, and
thereby the count-prince's authority in Aragon; Ramon Berenguer IV, for his part, acknowledged papal suzerainty over
his lands. Towards Castile he was likewise conciliatory. To
prevent Navarre from falling dependent on Alfonso VII, Ramon
conceded Alfonso's lordship over Zaragoza and married his sister
to him. The count-prince seems to have collaborated with
Alfonso in an expedition against the Moors of Murcia in 1144;
and it was certainly in the service of Castile that he carried out
the dazzling exploit that first won him fame: the conquest of
Almería in 1147.

Having thus demonstrated his fidelity to his suzerains and his
capacity to lead and to reward, Ramon Berenguer IV had little
trouble securing support for campaigns against Tortosa and
Lérida. The Genoese were promised a third part of Tortosa, as
was Guillem Ramon Seneschal of Montcada; other contingents
from Catalonia, Occitania, and Aragon joined the army, which
received the pope's crusading privilege. After a long siege
Tortosa fell in December 1148. The Moors were allowed to retain
their customs and officials, commercial rights in the city, and
title to real property, although houses within the walls were to be
surrendered in a year's time. Christian settlers were guaranteed
personal and civil liberties in charters of 1148 and 1149. The
count-prince exploited the momentum of this success to attack
Lérida, which he captured, together with Fraga, on 24 October
1149. The leading coadjutor in this campaign was Count
Ermengol VI of Urgell, who—like Guillem Ramon Seneschal at
Tortosa—was to be co-seigneur for one-third of the city.

Christian resettlement was regulated in a charter patterned on that of 1149 for Tortosa (January 1150).

These conquests, largely the work of Catalans, were to become in time their reward. They came to define New Catalonia and its boundary with Aragon, while securing a vast frontier for Catalonian expansion. But for the time being Ramon Berenguer IV styled himself marquis of Tortosa and Lérida, making no overt gesture to reveal which one of his lands (if either) he considered to govern these marches. Of the great tenancies at Tortosa and Lérida, one may say that they were Aragonese in form and Catalan in substance, being ceded like Aragonese *honores* to Catalan barons according to the custom of Barcelona. The bishoprics of Tortosa and Lérida were restored and endowed, the latter at the expense of Roda-Barbastro. The reorganization of Christian Tarragona was accelerated, and in 1154 Pope Anastasius IV virtually revived the Tarraconensis as an ecclesiastical province, alluding expressly to the ancient order destroyed by the Moors, and prescribing the primacy of Tarragona over the sees of Girona, Barcelona, Urgell, Osona, Lérida, Tortosa, Zaragoza, Huesca, Pamplona, Tarazona, and Calahorra. The hinterlands were opened to immigration and settlement. Moorish strongholds at Miravet and Siurana fell in 1152–3. Rural churches were built, mosques were converted: monks of Ripoll later credited the count-prince with having 'extended the church of Christ by more than 300 altars'. The Cistercians of Occitania took a major part in this work. Guillem Ramon Seneschal endowed monks from Grandselve with lands on which arose the new abbey of Santes Creus, while Ramon Berenguer IV drew upon Fontfroide to establish the monastery later known as Poblet (1150–3). Lords of the frontier—the archbishop, barons such as the Cervera brothers, Templars, Hospitallers, and Cistercians, as well as the count—encouraged immigration by granting liberal terms of settlement.

His victories over the Moors strengthened Ramon Berenguer IV abroad. He regained the tribute from Valencia that had been lost in the early twelfth century. By the treaty of Tudillén (1151) he obtained Alfonso VII's recognition of a sphere of prospective Catalan-Aragonese conquest comprising Valencia and Murcia. In 1154 the magnates and free men of Béarn elected him their lord and tutor to the minor Gaston V, an event that prepared the way for a Catalan succession there in the next generation. And he enjoyed almost equal success in Occitania. Retaining the fealty of Guilhem VII of Montpellier and the viscountess Ermengarde of Narbonne, who had fought for him at Tortosa, Ramon Berenguer IV acquired that of Viscount Trencavel of Béziers-Carcassonne in 1150. Only in Provence did he have trouble. Acting there as protector of his nephew Ramon Berenguer (1144–66), whose father had been killed by pirates, the count-prince had to fight repeatedly against the counts of Saint-Gilles and their allies and against the castellan lineage of Les Baux. In 1162 he successfully negotiated his nephew's title to Provence with Frederick Barbarossa.

These military and political achievements together with the collapse of the Castilian hegemony at the death of Alfonso VII in 1157 left Ramon Berenguer IV the most powerful ruler in Spain. That he took his eminence seriously is evident from his policy in his ancestral counties, where he strove to rebuild the public order that had been weakened in the eleventh century. His legal experts produced the *Usatges of Barcelona*, a code (cunningly attributed to Ramon Berenguer I) that stressed the regalian authority of the count-prince: his ultimate judicial power, including jurisdiction over fortifications, the peace, and the coinage; and his right to the military service of all men in time of general war or invasion. Even the law of fiefs was integrated into this regalian structure. The old Catalonian counties were not mentioned as subordinate to the 'prince' because the count-prince envisaged a near future when he or his successors would have regained possession of them all. It was a sweeping programme, and not a purely theoretical one, for the *Usatges* were evidently designed for use by a reactivated comital court which, in fact, convened with some frequency after about 1150 to hear suits over land, administration, and jurisdiction. The barons and prelates who attended these sessions included specialists in law, notably *comtors** and judges; sometimes the magnates served as 'elected judges'. What is more, Ramon Berenguer IV was the first Catalan ruler to conceive of a uniform fiscal administration for his aggregated counties. A remarkable survey of peasant tenures and obligations in the regions of Barcelona, Girona,

* Barons of the old aristocracy of the counties.

Besalú, Vallespir, Conflent, Cerdanya, and the Ripollès was carried out in 1151 under the direction of the knight Bertran de Castellet. It seems to have been intended not only to improve the service and accountability of comital bailiffs but also to evaluate the old domain as collateral for credit in the post-conquest years when the old counties ceased to be the count's main material resource.

Of such policies in Aragon we have no record. But the negotiations with Castile, the conquests of Huesca (1154) and Alcañiz (1157) as well as of Lérida and Fraga, and other acts of lordship suggest no lack of concern for the kingdom Ramon had acquired for his offspring. It is possible that his caution with respect to the *Usatges* was dictated by a new interest in the count-prince's dynastic credentials, an interest complicated as well as enhanced by the recent triumphs at Moorish expense. To monks at Alaó Ramon's conquests had undercut the ambitions of the old counts and bishops of Ribagorza and Pallars, yet they could only represent the conqueror as successor to the kings of Aragon. Such a view could hardly be shared at Ripoll, where counts of Besalú and Barcelona lay buried. There the monks evidently had France in mind (as well as Aragon?) when in the early version of the *Deeds of the Counts of Barcelona*, composed towards 1162, they celebrated Ramon Berenguer IV as the restorer of Guifré the Hairy's patrimony while suggesting in a plausible fable that the count-prince was descended from Charlemagne. Such effusions had to be expressed, and received, with care, and they seem to have had limited currency. But since they were intended to commemorate a newly achieved principate, it is significant that they do so not in overtly Catalanist (or Aragonese) terms but simply by stressing legitimate dynastic descent from the heroic founders of the anti-Moorish cause.

Dynastic Policy (1162–1213)

When Ramon Berenguer IV died unexpectedly in Piedmont in August 1162, his eldest son was a child of five named Ramon. His succession to the 'honours' of Aragon and Barcelona was regulated according to his father's will in an assembly of Aragonese and Catalonian magnates at Huesca in October 1162; and there or soon thereafter, in significantly related acts, his name was changed to Alfonso (II in Aragon; Alfons I in

Catalonia)* and he received the royal title to Aragon that his father had never borne. Nominally the protégé of Henry Plantagenet, the boy-king was supervised for many years by advisers of his two realms. Their vigilance in external affairs, confirming Alphonse in his birthright impartiality toward his peoples, did much to secure the monarchical union during its first half century.

Indeed, it is difficult to distinguish Catalonian from Aragonese interests in the dynastic affairs of this reign. At first the regents were concerned to secure the territorial integrity of Aragon by resisting Castilian claims to suzerainty over the 'kingdom of Zaragoza'. In January 1174 Alphonse II was knighted, married Sancha of Castile, and issued a new coinage of Aragon in a festive court at Zaragoza attended chiefly by Aragonese magnates. He had already encouraged continued expansion towards Valencia. With the founding of Teruel (1169–71) and the death of King 'Lobo' (1172), the time seemed ripe for attacking Valencia, an opportunity that was lost when Sancho VI of Navarre invaded Aragon. In the treaties of Cazola (March 1179) the militant young kings of Aragon and Castile not only proposed to partition Navarre but also delimited anew their zones of prospective Moorish conquest: the kings of Aragon were to have Valencia, leaving Murcia to Castile. Catalan historians have sometimes denounced this treaty as a gratuitous concession to a potentially dangerous rival. But at a time when he lacked the means to resettle Valencia (let alone Murcia!) it was arguably better for Alphonse II to secure his Aragonese frontiers so as to devote himself to more pressing problems elsewhere.

In fact, the realism of Alphonse II's Castilian policy affords a clue to the meaning of his trans-Pyrenean programme. It was not a conscious imperialism, still less a cultural protectorate. Alphonse patronized the troubadours with their arcane forms of Limousin discourse, in which he was no mean dabbler himself, and so did his son. He found a champion in Peire Vidal of Toulouse—and a sometime enemy in Guillem de Berguedà. Yet one may search this literature in vain for a consistent ideology. If the Provençal politics had an underlying motive, it was to defend the Catalonian counties against the perceived threat

---

* To be spoken of hereafter as Alphonse; see p. 191.

of an expansionist Capetian monarchy allied with the count of Toulouse. The first version of the *Deeds of the Counts of Barcelona* betrays anti-Frankish chauvinism, and Alphonse and his courtiers were aware of Louis VII's expanding influence in Occitania. In October 1180 a provincial council at Tarragona decreed that scribes should henceforth date charters by the year of the Incarnation instead of regnal year of France.

Accordingly, the Castilian alliance, which entailed solidarity with the Angevins, was deployed in defence of Catalan-Aragonese interests in southern France. There was nothing foreordained about these interests. Provence might have remained in the hands of a cadet branch of the dynasty of Barcelona if Ramon Berenguer III had not been killed in 1166 without leaving a male heir. At this juncture Alphonse's advisers, goaded by Guilhem VII of Montpellier, seized Provence, thereby flouting the claim of the late count's daughter who had been betrothed to the count of Toulouse. This led to the renewal of conflict between Barcelona and Toulouse. The fighting, protracted and desultory, and marked by Genoese support of Raimond V, ended first in a truce influenced by Henry II in 1173, and then in the peace of Tarascon (1176), which reaffirmed the rights of Alphonse with compensation to the count of Toulouse. When the king's brother, called Ramon Berenguer IV in Provence (1166–81), met a violent death in his turn, another brother, Sanç, was appointed, only to be dismissed, for reasons not altogether clear, in 1185. The count-king now intended to rule Provence more directly, appointing the count of Foix as his procurator, and adding to his own titles that of 'marquis of Provence'. He found support in the rise of a legitimist sentiment in Provence based on the rights of his paternal grandmother Dolça; and he was able, for the same reason, to vindicate his dynastic claim to Millau, Gévaudan, and the Carladès.

But his success in Provence cost Alphonse II support elsewhere in the Midi. By 1176 most of the magnates of lower Occitania, including the viscount of Béziers, had aligned themselves with Toulouse. To counter these defections the king cultivated the Pyrenean borderlands, securing the vassalage of Maria of Béarn in 1170, that of Centulle of Bigorre by granting him the Val d'Aran in 1175, and the fidelity of Roger-Bernard of Foix. Such was the situation when churchmen at the Third

Lateran Council resolved in 1179 to combat heresy actively, a decision that rendered the lands of Béziers-Carcassonne particularly vulnerable in the existing political circumstances. In November 1179 Viscount Roger II dramatically upset the Toulousan hegemony by commending himself and his lands to Alphonse II, thus renewing an old tie that had been repeatedly undone. This windfall brought Catalonian dynastic influence in Occitania to a new peak.

Strengthened on his northern frontiers, Alphonse II returned to Hispanic affairs in his later years. He abandoned (1189–90) the alliance with Alfonso VIII of Castile, who had continued to be tempted by Aragonese borderlands and who had allied with Frederick Barbarossa, nominally lord of Provence. Alphonse II undertook agreements with Navarre which culminated in 1191 in a more general pact, extended to include Leon and Portugal, against Castile. But the defeat of Alfonso VIII by the Almohads at Alarcos in 1195 lent urgency to an effort by Pope Celestine III, who had spent many years as a legate in Spain, to unite the peninsular realms against Islam. Late in 1195 Alphonse II made a pilgrimage to Compostela in the course of which he encouraged such a crusade, but the enterprise was frustrated by his own death—he was not yet forty—in April 1196.

Pedro II (Pere I in Catalonia)* succeeded his father in Catalonia and Aragon as well as in most of the Occitanian suzerainties, while his brother Alfons inherited Provence, Millau, and Razès. Thus the original idea of a uniquely peninsular monarchy survived intact. Peter was bolder than his father but less prudent. Influenced by his mother, he revived the alliance with Alfonso VIII, who promptly exploited it at the expense of Navarre. In 1212 Peter achieved a spectacular success when he led a wing of the federated crusading army that crushed the Almohads at Las Navas de Tolosa. Serving Castile well—this had become the fashion of his dynasty—he was less fortunate in Occitania.

There Peter broke abruptly with tradition when he allied with Count Raimond VI of Toulouse, who married the king's sister. In 1204 Peter himself married Maria, the heiress of Montpellier; and a few months later he had himself crowned at Rome by Pope

---

* To be spoken of hereafter as Peter; see p. 191.

Innocent III, to whom he agreed to pay a tribute of 250 mazmudins each year. Despite this engagement there can be little doubt that the event was shrewdly staged by the king, possibly to counteract an incipient rivalry for the coronation between the Aragonese and the Catalans, certainly to enhance his prestige among Christian monarchs. For a king to submit himself in fealty to the pope could have no practical consequence save that of setting a good example to his own vassals; moreover, the fealty in this case (there is no mention of homage or vassalage) was of just that sort by which members of Mediterranean élites customarily entered into conventions of mutual trust. Yet the alliance worked badly during the Albigensian crisis. Like the Occitanian barons with whom he was allied, the king failed to foresee (or preferred to ignore) the consequences of not prosecuting heretics; he was slow to act on his suzerain rights and obligations; while Pope Innocent III, once the French crusade was launched, proved insensitive to Peter's efforts to mediate. In 1209 a formidable host led by northern magnates and prelates conquered Béziers (where the populace was massacred) and Carcassone; and when this army disbanded the French baron Simon de Montfort was left to implement a colonial settlement in the vice-comital lands. Of Peter's good will there can be no question: he not only served the Church valiantly at Las Navas de Tolosa, but also, following the defeat of Viscount Raimond Roger, accepted Simon de Montfort's fealty for Carcassonne. He gave to Simon the custody of his infant son and to the young Raimond VII his sister in marriage. But conciliation foundered as the increase of Simon's ambitions was matched by that of Peter's prestige. By January 1213, when Peter obtained the commendation of the counts of Toulouse, Comminges, and Foix, and of the people of Toulouse, he attained a pinnacle of political success in Occitania. It was not to last. On 12 September 1213 the hero of Las Navas lay dead on the battlefield of Muret, his newly enlarged cause in southern France shattered by his own tactical folly and by Simon de Montfort's well-drilled knights. The Catalonian-Aragonese suzerainty of Béziers-Carcassonne collapsed with the rest.

It is easy to exaggerate the import of this disaster. The Occitanian suzerainties had never been regarded as territorial extensions of Catalonia, and if Peter II entertained visions of the

dynastic conquest of Occitania (which is not impossible), he was
the first of his line to do so. The idea that the count-kings were
the natural protectors of Occitan culture owed much to the
literary interests of Alphonse II and his son, but it only became a
political idea in the next generation. Provence remained subject
to descendants of Alphonse II. Yet it was an undoubted
misfortune for the Crown of Aragon to lose two promising rulers
by untimely deaths at so critical a time in its early history.

Social and Economic Change (1150–1213)

It was a time of fundamental social evolution. The continuing
growth of population was linked to sustained agrarian expansion
and commercial prosperity, especially in Catalonia. In Aragon
the frontiers had been defined a generation before and the pace of
change was gradual. The great barons of the New Extremadura
and the military orders relied more on their Mudejars than did
lords of New Catalonia, although the reconquered Ebro and its
hinterlands also drew immigrants from old Christian lands. With
clearing of the lower Ebro, Christian Zaragoza recovered a
centrality at once commercial and political, connecting Navarre
with the Mediterranean, trading in spices, textiles, metalwork,
and wood, and sprouting a new suburb at the Puerta del Toledo.
By 1200 Zaragoza had eclipsed Jaca as the hub of the realm. Her
notables had formed a privileged *concilium* (council, *concejo*) from
the 1130s, but there, as also in the older *fuero* of Jaca and the
newer ones of Daroca (1142) and Teruel (1171), the liberties
were more civil than administrative.

In Catalonia we have some indication of a major demographic
expansion in the frequency of grants of rural charters. These
were very numerous: some fifty resettlement charters for New
Catalonia alone date from the years 1148 to 1162, and eighty
more were granted in the reigns of Alphonse II and Peter II,
many by these kings themselves. These charters represent more
than 80 per cent of all such grants in Catalan-speaking lands
during the period 1137–1213, a fact that points to a profound
demographic-social contrast between the old counties and the
frontier. Settlers streamed into the hinterlands of Tarragona as
well as to Tortosa and Lérida and their environs. They came
from near and far: people from Old Catalonia were especially
numerous at Tortosa, while Lérida drew chiefly upon Pallars,

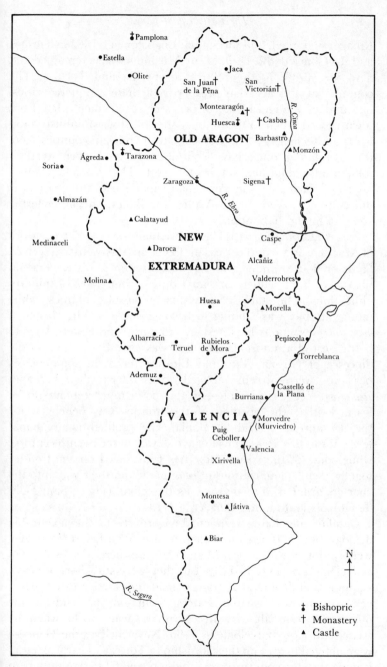

IV. Aragon and Valencia (1137–1479)

Ribagorza, Urgell, and Occitania; Englishmen settled in Tortosa
and the Conca de Barberà. Many Muslim hamlets remained and
new ones arose in the suburbs of Lérida and Tortosa. The
commercial and agrarian prosperity of these conquered cities,
like that of Zaragoza and, on a lesser scale, some other Ebro
towns, owed much to the maintenance of Moorish industry and
agrarian technology. In the old sub-Pyrenean counties, too,
the population must have continued to grow even as their
inhabitants emigrated south and west. The urban agglomer-
ations of Barcelona and Perpignan expanded in this period, as
did cultivated lands in the Vallès, the Bages, and other fertile
zones of inland habitation.

New Catalonia perhaps even more than the new Extremadura
of Aragon was a world of peasant freedom. Most settlers received
lands or houses under a lord's protection on terms of personal
liberty, of light renders or banal duties, sometimes of military
obligations. The status of peasants in the old counties, while
more variable, was tending to become onerous. The cluster of
mals usos—exactions for intestacy, adultery, and arson—later to
be the test of a notorious servitude was already common in the
dioceses of Girona, Vic, and Elne by 1150; in some places
peasants were already obliged to purchase their freedom
(*remença*). Yet it is possible—on this point much remains to be
learned—that the opening of the frontier was beneficial for
the peasantries of Old Catalonia. The proliferation of banal
lordships in this area seems to have slowed in the twelfth century,
while some of the specific liberties guaranteed on the frontier
together with renunciations of *mals usos* found their way into the
charters granted to towns such as Barcelona (1163), Sant Feliu
de Guíxols (1181), and Puigcerdà (1182).

Catalan merchants responded vigorously to the favourable
demographic and economic conjuncture. Well before 1200 they
were sailing in the eastern Mediterranean; there was a colony of
Barcelonans at Tyre in 1187. But they were still short of heavy
shipping and the lucrative trade in gold and slaves created strong
competition in Hispanic waters. Benjamin of Tudela saw
merchants from all over the Mediterranean world when he
passed through Barcelona in 1160. Nevertheless, the Genoese
were obliged to give up their lordship in Tortosa as early as 1153,
leaving it to the count-prince's creditors and Christian settlers to

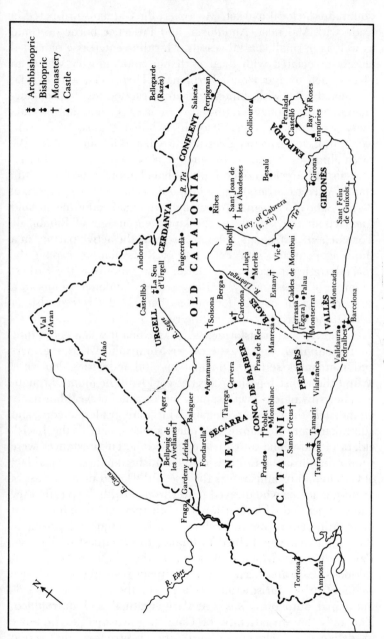

v. Catalonia (1137–1479)

R. Ebre

N

R. Cinca

Val
d'Aran

† Alaó

Fraga

Gardeny ▲
Lérida †
Fondarella

Bellpuig de †
les Avellanes

Balaguer

Ager ▲

Agramunt

Castelbó ▲

Andorra

† La Seu
d'Urgell

URGELL

R. Segre

Puigcerdà •

CERDANYA

R. Tet

CONFLENT

Bellegarde
(Razès) ▲

Salses ▲

Perpignan •

OLD CATALONIA

Ribes •

Sant Joan de
† les Abadesses

Vcty. of Cabrera
(s. xiv)

Collioure ▲

EMPORDÀ

Peralada ▲
Castelló •

Bay of Roses

Empúries ▲

Besalú •

Ripoll †

R. Ter

† Solsona

Berga •

Cardona ▲

BAGES

Manresa •

Lluçà ▲
Merlès •

Estany †

Vic †

Caldes de Montbui †
Palau •
Terrassa
(Egara) •
Montserrat †

Girona ‡

GIRONÈS

Sant Feliu
de Guíxols †

Cervera •
Tàrrega •

Prats de Rei •

SEGARRA

NEW

CONCA DE BARBERÀ

† Poblet
• Montblanc

Prades •

CATALONIA

Santes Creus †

PENEDÈS

Vilafranca •

Tamarit †

Tarragona ‡

Montcada ▲

VALLÈS

Valldaura •
Pedralbes †

Barcelona †

Tortosa †

Amposta ▲

dominate the local market. Moreover, the Catalans prospered in trade with Valencia, Andalusia, and Provence borne overland as well as in small coastal vessels. Maritime enterprise remained closely associated with local exchange and industry which, in places such as Barcelona, Perpignan, Tarragona, and Lérida, connected city with hinterland: real estate, textiles, money-changing and money-lending, provisioning. Catalonian productivity was already diversified: it included grains, wine, salt, wood, iron, implements, dyestuffs, wool, and finished cloths. We catch glimpses of some of the successful entrepreneurs: of Bernat Marcús of Barcelona, who built a chapel about 1166–70 (it still stands, carrer Carders) and a hospital in the *vilanova de la mar*; of Bernat Sanç of Perpignan (d. *c.*1186), who made a fortune in land transactions and supply to the king's entourage; of Ramon de Torredela of Tarragona, who in 1194 was the active partner in a shipping contract with Pere Poc of Roussillon to exploit the coastal trade in slaves. The latter case, affording the earliest example of a *commenda* yet discovered in Catalonia, points to a new interest in capital formation that can be traced also at Lérida and Barcelona during the reign of Peter II.

Urban life was transformed. At Barcelona it was a boom time for the suburbs, such as the carrer Montcada, where mariners and merchants settled. Older shops and industries flourished within the walls; Jewish properties could still be found throughout the growing city, with some concentration of wealth already in the *call*, their owners engaged in small trades, credit, and administration. Benjamin of Tudela spoke highly of the Jewish elders of Barcelona and their culture. The circumstances were similar in Girona and other towns. But the dominant social fact of Catalonian urbanism was the rise of the 'good men', a class of proto-patricians who derived power from wealth. Typically they had co-operated with their lords: at Vic they had won important mercantile rights from the bishop as early as 1139, and a group of Barcelona's citizens helped to finance the conquest of Tortosa. Lay lords—the Montcadas at Vic, the count of Urgell at Lérida—taxed and licensed trade without insisting on exclusive rights of urban jurisdiction. As a result, the evolution towards municipal autonomy was singularly gradual and untroubled. The only known attempt of Catalan townsmen to organize in defiance of seigneurial authority occurred in the period

1180–84 at Vic, where the scheme 'to institute a consulate' was quashed by an episcopal tribunal. In 1182 Alphonse II authorized his knights at Cervera to form a *confratria* with elected consuls, a concession enlarged by Peter II in a charter of more comprehensively municipal character (1202). By that time the inconvenience of a purely seigneurial mode of urban authority was being felt in other Catalonian towns, and it was in charters granted to Lérida, Perpignan, and probably Barcelona (the text, in this case, is lost) soon after Peter's accession that the men of these towns received the right to appoint consuls and counsellors.

For the military and clerical élites that dominated the peasants and townspeople it was a time of legal and administrative consolidation. In Aragon the diversity of social status was simplified by the diffusion of local customs, such as of Zaragoza and Teruel. By the early thirteenth century one could cite the 'custom of Aragon' for treachery. The charter of 1134 (above, p. 28) came too early to represent definitively the military obligations of the greater barons, but it pointed clearly to the characteristic strength of the king's position *vis-à-vis* the *tenencias*: namely, that the king shared their revenues and recovered them on their holder's death. Under such an arrangement the aristocracy remained an open class of king's retainers, envious of the Catalonian custom of fiefs, covetous of the spoils of war. Such men could hardly think of themselves as vassals in a land where every free man was expected to do homage and fealty to the king; where vassalage, if little more than a reinforcement of fidelity, implied a systematic structure of royal power untroubled by the anomalies of private or fragmented right.

In Catalonia the *Usatges of Barcelona* depict a lay aristocracy becoming conscious of its own stratification, yet by no means closed. The old ruling group—counts, viscounts, and *comtors*—still counted as the 'most noble' in the contemporary sense of those best fitted to rule; but their prestige declined as the old counties disappeared, their numbers were reduced—to perhaps less than twenty families by 1200—and they took little part in exploiting the frontier. Something of their frustration may be glimpsed in the cruel gossip of Guillem de Berguedà and the insubordination of the viscounts of Cabrera and Castellbò, although the old families were far from uniformly dissident. The castellan lineages were numerous and vigorous. Some, like the

Montcada, had won the patronage of the counts of Barcelona by their eminence or ability; for others, like the Castellet, loyalty led to prosperity in the princely service; still others, like the Gurb and the Odena, contented themselves with a local pre-eminence and independence. Many such families fought in the campaigns of Ramon Berenguer IV and shared the rewards of his victories: most notably, the Montcadas, with their lordship in Tortosa and other domains scattered in New Catalonia. The knights— typically men who held knights' fiefs (*cavalleriae*) carved from domains dependent on castles—were the most numerous element of the lay aristocracy, very much an open class but economically precarious in status. Men of all these groups were hungry for land and castles, yet reluctant to be regarded as vassals. They were knit together in a bewildering skein of pacts and conventions having to do more often with fidelity and property (castles) than with fiefs; there was no hierarchy of fiefs but only of fidelities; and while much land in Catalonia, especially in Old Catalonia, was enfeoffed, the revival of regalian power and the spread of non-military tenures with the Hospitallers and Templars imposed limits on the feudalizing tendencies that had arisen so strongly in the eleventh century. Only toward 1200 do we find the concept of vassalage gaining general currency, a reflection, perhaps, of its cultivation as a moral ideal by the troubadours and of quickened contacts with France. By that time, too, the court poets were distinguishing among the élite a *nouveau riche* element alleged to lack the nobility of the old aristocracy.

The secular clergy became better organized under the arch-bishops of Tarragona. Ramon Berenguer IV gave up the seigneurial prerogative of despoiling widowed churches, and episcopal elections were relatively free thereafter. The disciplin-ary tenets of the reformed church were promoted through legatine councils held at Lérida in 1155 and 1173, councils that illustrate the pontifical view of the churches of Aragon and Catalonia as an indistinct provincial entity; this view doubtless influenced the organizers of the military orders. The restored episcopate of Aragon was defined in the metropolitan privilege of 1154 (see above, p. 33), including Huesca (translated from Jaca) and Lérida (translated from Roda-Barbastro). Among the regulars in Aragon the royal house of Montearagón eclipsed San Juan and

San Victorián in prestige, coming to dominate 104 churches in the time of Abbot Berenguer, half-brother of Alphonse II and pluralist bishop of Lérida (1176–91). The Cistercian nunnery at Casbas, founded in 1172 by a dowager countess of Pallars, became a retreat for the aristocracy of both realms. Knights-regular of the Hospital and Temple developed commanderies in all parts of both realms, but were especially active in the newly conquered borderlands. The castellany of Amposta, near Tortosa (founded 1154), served as an administrative centre for the Hospitallers of both realms; that of Gardeny, near Lérida (1156), for the Templars. In 1188 Queen Sancha founded the Hospitaller priory of nuns of Saint John at Sigena, which became a preserve of her family, a royal hostelry on a main route to Huesca, and the burial place of Peter II.

To the Catalonian sees listed in 1154 may be added Elne, which passed with Roussillon to the count-king in 1172, although it remained a suffragan of Narbonne. Bishops and canons in Catalonia regulated their endowments, the system of mensual administration through provosts being adopted by most of the chapters in the years 1160–75. But the episcopate, recruited as a rule from the scions of castellan families that dominated the cathedral chapters, remained deeply involved in temporal affairs. Saint Oleguer (d. 1137) helped to organize a secular seigneury over Tarragona and its hinterland (*camp*) that his successors turned into the most thoroughly vassalic principality in Catalonia, while the bishops of Vic, Urgell, and Girona struggled to retain their castles and urban jurisdictions. Arch-bishop Hug de Cervelló (1163–71) was assassinated in re-taliation for the murder (by another) of his co-lord of Tarragona Guillem Aguiló; and his successor Berenguer de Vilademuls (1174–94) met the same fate at the hands of Guillem Ramon I of Montcada in consequence of a personal dispute. One understands why the Catalans took enthusiastically to the cult of Saint Thomas Becket during these years—witness an altar dedication in the cathedral of Barcelona and the fresco still visible in Santa Maria of Terrassa—but there was no move to canonize their own. As in Aragon, prelates moved easily from one post to another or accumulated posts. Bishop Guillem de Torroja of Barcelona (1144–71), the most influential counsellor of the young Alphonse II, succeeded one murdered archbishop and preceded the other (1172–74). Ponç de Monells retained the abbacy of Sant Joan de les Abadesses (1140–93) when he was elected bishop of Tortosa in 1165.

The Benedictines of Old Catalonia retained a prosperity by this time more worldly than spiritual. Their old ties with communities north of the Pyrenees were progressively dissolved, Ripoll securing its independence of Saint Victor of Marseille in 1172. The monks of Ripoll could take pride in their historic affiliation with the dynasty of Ramon Berenguer IV, who was buried there. But the older abbeys no longer possessed the undeveloped lands, or for that matter the inspirational capacity, to duplicate the agrarian enterprise they had promoted in the past. Benefactors princely and humble henceforth preferred to give to canons-regular, Cistercians, Hospitallers, and Templars —and chiefly to their plantations in New Catalonia. The Augustinian rule for canons, often in the austere form emanating from Saint-Ruf of Avignon, became the basis of some thirty new foundations in the twelfth century, many of them on the frontier. The chapters of Tarragona, Tortosa, and Lérida likewise adopted the customs of Saint-Ruf, while in 1166 Count Ermengol VII of Urgell instituted the even stricter observance of Pré-montré at Bellpuig de les Avellanes. The Cistercians at Santes Creus and Poblet were enormously popular in the later twelfth century, attracting benefactions and converts, encouraging rural enterprise, and exerting a stabilizing influence over fast-growing regional populations. Alphonse II, having held a major court at Poblet in 1194, was the first of his dynasty to elect burial there.

Institutional Foundations (1150–1213)

The consolidation of Aragonese- and Catalan-speaking lands was virtually completed in the reigns of Alphonse II and Peter II, but in different ways. In Aragon the territorial conquest reached its natural term, notably in the borderlands of Valencia. Among the major settlements were Valderrobres (1169), Teruel (1169–71), Rubielos de Mora (1203), and Ademúz (1210); these lordships among others were commended to great barons, such as Pedro de Arazuri, or to the military orders. In Catalonia the process was political. Roussillon devolved to Alphonse II in 1172 when Count Guinard II died without heirs. In 1192 Dolça de So, the last survivor of another old comital lineage, ceded

Pallars Jussà to Alphonse. And when Ermengol VIII of Urgell died without male heirs in 1209, the dowager-countess gave possession of that county to Peter II in return for the protection of her daughter's right. It is clear that the king meant to annex the county, for he betrothed his infant son to the heiress. Although this marriage never took place, royal influence in Urgell was henceforth assured. By the end of Peter's reign only Upper Pallars and Empúries among the old Catalan counties remained independent of the king. Already around 1200 it had become customary for courtiers and scribes to speak of these aggregated counties together with the newly settled frontier as a political unit. In 1173 the peace statutes of Fondarella were instituted in all the king's lands 'from Salses as far as Tortosa and Lérida and their borders', a phrase that recurs in subsequent statutes until in those of Peter II it is made explicit that the territory so defined was *Cathalonia*. As the coinages of annexed counties were discontinued, that of Barcelona assumed expanded currency throughout the principality, coming into touch with the Aragonese coinage of Jaca in the Segre-Cinca frontier.

Neither Catalonia nor Aragon yet had territorial governments as the conquests wound down. The count-kings worked through curial officers, like the *mayordomo* in Aragon or the seneschal in Catalonia, who remained primarily domestic servants bound in personal fidelity; untitled barons and scribes supervised the farmers and auditors (*merini* in Aragon, bailiffs in Catalonia; peasants, merchants, Jews) who managed the royal or comital estates. Accordingly, the decision in 1173 to transform the old diocesan Peace into an instrument of regalian territorial administration was of fundamental importance for the future of Catalonia. The idea may have had a trial run in Aragon as early as 1164, when the boy-king, seeking to quell disorder, required oaths of magnates and urban notables assembled at Zaragoza to secure the realm until he reached the age of knighthood. In 1188 he apparently went much further, prescribing in a solemn court at Huesca a sweeping royal jurisdiction over the peace complete with judicial remedies. If this programme had been enforced, it might well have displeased the honorial barons, but we hear nothing of new sanctions—and, in general, still know sadly little about this critical moment of administrative innovation in Aragon.

In Catalonia the adaptation of the diocesan peace was first effected in Roussillon following the annexation of that land in 1172, and was then extended to the rest of the old comital domains, doubtless upon the recommendation of Archbishop Guillem de Torroja, in the statutes of Fondarella. The latter enactment confirmed the public-legal implications of the *Usatges* at precisely the moment when the law of the judges of Barcelona became the law of Catalonia. It imposed on the barons and castellans of the expanded county of Barcelona (and not only those commended to the king) a specifically custodial and deliberative function, for it was they who were obliged to confirm and observe the statutes; and it inaugurated a tradition of associative legislation that was to be institutionalized a century later in the Corts.

Yet the Peace enacted in 1173 was substantively archaic: injunctive and normative, it retained the bishop's share in the jurisdiction while lacking mechanisms of enforcement. What made it effective was the supplementary decision—this must have been reached toward 1173–8—to reform the old lay vicariate, and to entrust to vicars once again firmly subordinated to the (count-) king the administration of the Peace. The vicars and bishops were empowered to convoke householders of the diocese to combat recalcitrant malefactors. The remodelled vicars, chosen generally from among lesser knights without ties to the castellan lineages, became the first efficient agents of local administration in Catalonia. By the early thirteenth century their functions were becoming territorial as their powers expanded from police to fiscal and military supervision.

The reform of the vicariate coincided with a reorganization of the comital management of castles. Alphonse II reacted vigorously against the pretensions of third- and fourth-generation castellans to exploit their strongholds independently. For example, in 1180 he sued Pere de Lluçà for 'power' of access to the castles of Lluçà and Merlès, and when Pere claimed that these castles were his allodial property the king drew upon records 'from his archive' to prove that Pere's ancestor had held them in fealty from Ramon Berenguer I. Now the king could not have won this case if his archive, here mentioned as such for the first time, had not been classified according to lineages and castles. And there is strong reason to believe that this work of classification had been

undertaken within the preceding two years. Directed by Ramon
de Caldes, dean of Barcelona cathedral, the enterprise continued
thereafter and culminated in 1194 in the compilation of
the 'Great Book of Fiefs' (*Liber feudorum maior*), one of the
earliest—and finest—administrative registers of a medieval
monarchy.

Yet a third considerable reform in these years was that of the
fiscal service. By the time Alphonse II came of age, the survey of
comital domains executed in 1151 was out of date, while his
courtiers were losing control of bailiffs who were all too often
creditors to the king. Here again the responsibility fell to Ramon
de Caldes, often working in association with the scribe Guillem
de Bassa and, in later years, with Templars from Palau de
Plegamans. Updating the inventories, auditing the accounts
rendered periodically by the bailiffs, and preserving copies of the
statements of account in a new fiscal archive, these courtiers
effectively replaced the disorderly reliance on credit with a direct
management of domains. Their system all but collapsed,
however, under Peter II, whose inability to live within his means
was notorious. Credit was revived and the Templars replaced
the king's court as the primary agency of account.

One need not exaggerate the effectiveness of these reforms to
appreciate their significance. Royal finance remained dynastic
and itinerant, without treasury or budget. Of the omnicompetent
courtiers who supervised vicars and bailiffs, it may be said that
they were trying to organize a local administration without a
central one. The king's rule in Catalonia (as in Aragon)
remained very personal, even arbitrary. But we can see more
clearly than in Aragon how the political theory of the *Usatges* and
of the Peace together with the territorial consolidation of
Catalonia required the delegation and specialization of powers
that would progressively be institutionalized. So while the old
curial title of 'seneschal' became hereditary and honorific in the
Montcada family, ministerial functions in diplomacy, justice,
and finance evolved in the king's court among the more
enterprising knights, such as Bertran de Castellet in the time of
Ramon Berenguer IV or Guillem Durfort in that of Peter II, but
especially among the secular clerks and scribes through whose
labours professional literacy became indispensable to government. In this sense Ramon de Caldes and his associates were not

so much the reformers as the founders of public administration in Catalonia.

These institutional tendencies sat poorly with the military élite of Old Catalonia, the one social element of that realm that had ceased to prosper in the late twelfth century. Its anxiety may have been shared in Aragon, where there was more surely another cause of distress common to both realms. As time passed the great triumphs of Alfonso I and Ramon Berenguer IV assumed new meaning as regretted glories. Alphonse II did not lack energy but his campaigns in Occitania and Navarre were hardly productive of spoils. In Aragon dissatisfaction with the slackened pace of the Reconquest may perhaps be discerned in the appearance of a pseudo-Alfonso the Battler toward 1174. To discredit him the king felt it necessary to draw public attention to his great-uncle's tomb at Montearagón. There were repercussions in Catalonia, where the impostor was said to have been hanged in 1181; subsequently the troubadours Bertran de Born and Guiraut de Luc not only alleged that Alphonse II had hanged his predecessor but also charged the king with crypto-Moorish habits. The case of the false Alfonso probably helped to revive designs against Valencia and Majorca in 1178–9, but nothing came of these campaigns except the treaties at Cazola by which Castile and Aragon redefined their zones of future expansion. Although he persisted to the end in his dream of conquering Valencia, Alphonse II was less given to mobilizing his warriors than to perambulating his domains in leisurely tours.

It looks as if events of the 1170s had hastened a profound change in the structure of power in Catalonia. Influenced by his prelates, the king ceased to share the exploitative ethos of his barons as he came of age, substituting a political conception of territorial order for the traditional dynamic of expansionist aggression. While the count of Urgell might be persuaded to institute a Peace and Truce for his lands (1187) in conformity with the statutes of Fondarella, it was more difficult to win compliance from the lesser barons and knights organized for the very kinds of violence prohibited by the statutes. Nor were these men educated for such compliance. Prelates such as Guillem de Torroja, whose predecessor had been murdered in 1171, must have urged all the magnates to ratify the statutes under oath, but there is no reason to believe that these campaigns met with much success. The political effect of the statutes was therefore to drive a wedge between those magnates who felt an overriding loyalty to the king and those who felt threatened by the Peace.

This issue precipitated a constitutional conflict, the first in Catalonia's history. The struggle is poorly known, for it left no trace in the annals and the statutes were contrived to hide it, but it lasted for a quarter of a century and exerted a powerful influence on the rise of legislation and taxation in Catalonia.

The early phases of this conflict are especially obscure. It seems that some barons claimed exemption from the statutes of Fondarella on grounds that they had not consented or sworn to them, but that a more serious opposition arose from the allegation that the statutes were in conflict with the *Usatges*. At Girona in 1188 the magnates insisted (among other things) that the statutes should not derogate from the *Usatges* in respect to procedures over the possession of castles, a point that the king accepted in order to secure confirmation of the programme of Fondarella together with additions relative to enforcement. This must have been a stormy session that satisfied no one, and it was followed by a yet stormier assembly at Barcelona where Alphonse was forced to give up his Peace and Truce entirely. The king's next move was to prepare a revised text which he judged consistent with the traditional Peace as codified in the *Usatges* together with additions devised to maintain the executory force of the statutes of Girona while associating the barons in the work of enforcement. This text was published at Barbastro— was it impossible to meet in Catalonia?—in November 1192, apparently without general consultation, but with an address extended, for the first time, to the 'good men and people of the cities and towns' as well as the barons and knights of Catalonia.

But the struggle had already spread to other fronts. For the barons to contend that their lordships were exempt from the Peace was to encourage the king to expand his own claims of lordship and overlordship. The suits against rebellious castellans were part of this campaign, and so, too, we may conjecture, were Alphonse's interventions in the wars of Urgell (1186–94). Although these wars remain poorly understood, they cannot have been motivated solely by political grudges. They were in some measure the opposition of upland against lowland, for the king's domains and allies were concentrated in the old coastal counties. Guillem de Berguedà deplored royal expansion into the Bages and spoke (bitingly?) of the *rei de Barcelona*. Persistently the king sought—and won—recognition of his suzerainty, first from Ermengol VIII, later from the viscounts of Cabrera and Castellbò. But not even the count-king could hope to control the 'power' of all the castles, and the dangers of excessive insistence on his personal lordship became apparent during the reign of Peter II. At Barcelona in 1200, then more emphatically at Cervera in 1202, the barons set about once again to amend the statutes so as to exempt from the Peace the men and animals of lords not personally commended to the king. Although by this time the royal vicars had gained full control of enforcement of the Peace, their sphere of operation had been reduced in practice to the comital-royal domains. In 1202 the barons spoke of the 'Peace and Truce of the lord-king' as if the Peace had become a seigneurial institution.

The conflict was further complicated by fiscal issues. Like the barons the kings suffered from the constriction of military opportunity. Alphonse II retained a costly entourage and his son tended to extravagance. But their fiscal resources in both lands were limited to ordinary revenues from and occasional tallages upon people of their domains, to tolls, and to the proceeds of coinage; they lacked the right of northern lords to levy aids on fiefs. In 1173 Alphonse II made the Peace of Fondarella the occasion for imposing a general tax on Catalonia. This imposition, first called *bovaticum* (Catalan: *bovatge*) in an account of 1174–5, cannot have been successful. It was a novelty almost everywhere in Catalonia (justified only by remote and dubious precedent in Cerdanya), and in 1188 the king promised not to levy it again. But this promise, which in any case may have been jettisoned with the other statutes of Girona, did not bind Peter II, who imposed the *bovatge* anew at his accession. Meanwhile, Alphonse II had attempted to manipulate the silver coinages of Barcelona and Jaca for profit, and Peter II imposed a 'redemption of the money' in at least one Catalonian town to compensate for his confirmation of the coinage of Barcelona in 1197. These taxes together with other novel exactions deepened the existing unrest and led to a new confrontation between the king and his magnates.

The details of this encounter, too, are poorly recorded. All we know is that by an act attributed to him in March 1205 at Girona, Peter II solemnly renounced the new taxes, retaining only customary impositions on his own domains. He promised to reserve appointments of vicars for knights of Catalonia who were to be chosen 'with the counsel of great and wise men of the land'; the vicars must swear to govern lawfully. He also promised to maintain the coinage of Barcelona stable for his lifetime, and to refrain from exacting ransoms of the coinage or the peace. These engagements were incorporated in a charter—indeed, a *magna carta*, which, like other 'great charters' of its day, was secured by oaths of the king's barons—directed to the clergy, magnates, knights, and good men 'of all Catalonia'.

Had these concessions taken effect the struggle would have ended in a compromise not unlike that reached in the amended statutes of the Peace seventeen years before. In fact, the articles on vicars and *bovatge* in 1205 were probably patterned on baronial petitions first accepted at Girona in 1188. But there is no evidence that the charter of March 1205 was ever promulgated, let alone observed. Ever more urgently in need of money, Peter II not only imposed a new money-tax on both his lands in November 1205 but also debased the coinage of Barcelona without notice in 1209. He borrowed heavily. He taxed ecclesiastical lands, not always with prior consent, before giving way to a better organized opposition of prelates assembled at Lérida in March 1211, where he granted individual charters of non-prejudice.

So the initiative remained with the king. The instituted Peace, however truncated, survived baronial dissidence to become the basis of Catalonian public order in the later Middle Ages. Like his father, Peter II found natural allies in his townsmen, granting them specific protections in the statutes of 1198 and afterwards; and he may have been the first to summon representatives of towns to 'full' or 'solemn' courts. He legislated on heresy and marriage as well as the Peace. But his most audacious innovation was to devise a form of taxation adequate to the enlarged needs of the new principality. Territorial in basis, levied by paid collectors, his taxes became a major source of revenue. Peter capitalized on precedent by calling some of his impositions *bovatges* or *monedatges*, and it was a consequence of his reign that the *bovatge* came to be admitted as a customary accession-tax in Catalonia; but the king overcame the unpopularity of these levies by invoking the 'urgent necessity of the Saracen war' (1197) or the expenses of the crusade of 1212. In theory if not yet entirely in disposition, these were the first public subsidies in the history of the Crown of Aragon.

The troubles in Catalonia stemmed partly from baronial anxieties that must have been shared in the two lands and partly from royalist pressures that seem to have been confined to Catalonia. The appetite for spoiling the Moors, whetted now and then, was neither satisfied nor overcome, yet it coexisted in aristocracies that were parting ways. In Aragon the tenancies remained more the king's than the barons', in Catalonia the envied 'custom of Barcelona' was in process of creating a hereditary baronage heedless of the regalian principate defined by the *Usatges*. So the common pacification aroused hostility only (or chiefly) in Catalonia, where the terrifying licence of brutal cavalcades remained a viable substitute for rewards of the frontier at the cost of rural security. Aragonese barons may have found it easier to accept a role as royal agents, which would explain why in 1183 Alphonse II appointed Pedro Jimenez de Urrea to serve as his vicar in Cerdanya and Conflent, where some of the (Catalan-speaking) lords were then disaffected. It would also explain why in 1188, in the great court at Girona which approved revised statutes of the Peace, the count-king was obliged to promise to appoint none but Catalans as vicars from 'Salses to Tortosa and Lérida'.

This was a historic occasion. Here for the first time some barons of Catalonia were acting as virtually a national opposition. Moreover, here for the first time we catch a glimpse of something like political confrontation in a general assembly of Catalonia, for in securing concessions relative to the vicariate and *bovatge*,the magnates were imposing a quid pro quo. From this assembly (if not already from that of 1173) may be dated the origins of the Catalonian Corts as a solemn forum for reconciling the regalian peace with tenurial privilege. Similar things, to be sure, were happening in Aragon. The great courts of Zaragoza (1164, 1174) and Huesca (1188) showed that the king and his biregnal entourage were responsive to proto-national expressions of custom and right. The sixteenth-century historian Zurita tells of disorders following the proclamation of the *monedaje* in 1205 that anticipate those of the 1220s. But the affirmations of Catalonian identity were more characteristic of the reigns of the early count-kings, and they were bound up with administrative innovations such as would ultimately make of Catalonian domains the heartland of the Crown of Aragon. Royal scribes as well as barons and troubadours began to speak of the aggregated counties as 'Catalonia'.

Yet the early count-kings never lost their dynastic perspective. To appoint an Aragonese vicar of Cerdanya was for them, one suspects, like asking Catalonian scribes to register the records of Aragon together with the Catalonian oaths and conventions, as was done in the *Liber feudorum maior*. And if we can discern precedents of the national Cort(e)s in assemblies concerned with custom and the peace, so too we may trace the earliest Cortes of the Crown of Aragon in the dynastic celebrations of Huesca (1162) and Lérida (1214). The newly political ideas of Aragon and Catalonia coexisted with the dynastic idea of a joint monarchy—of a *Corona de Aragón*—so prudently nurtured in the king's court from the early days of the union.

III

James the Conqueror (1213–1276)

WITH the catastrophe of Muret the Crown of Aragon was plunged into its first major crisis. The new king was a child of five in the custody of his father's conqueror at Carcassonne. The fiscal resources were exhausted: James I later declared that his father had pledged all his revenues and given away most of his knights' fiefs. 'And one day when we came to Monzón, we didn't have anything to eat, so badly was the land destroyed and pawned!' The barons and townspeople felt exploited and deceived: 'troubles spread in [the late king's] lands, where unheard-of confederations and conspiracies of the towns arose.' It was a dangerous situation in need of the remedy of prompt and prudent leadership.

The Early Years (1213–1228)

A critical factor in the months after Muret was the willingness of the Catalans to negotiate with Pope Innocent III for the release of the child-king, thereby conceding the pontifical right of wardship. Few could blame the Church for a defeat attributed even by his subjects to the late ruler's folly. In the spring of 1214 the cardinal-legate Pierre de Douai arranged for the regency and secured the delivery of James to a deputation of Catalonian magnates and townsmen. The legate accompanied the child-king and his escort to Catalonia, where it was decided to entrust James's nurture to the Templars at Monzón (then considered a border-land castle), and the regency (*procuracio*) of his realms to Sanç of Provence, the king's great-uncle. In these events may be discerned two symptomatic influences: first, that of the queen-mother Maria, who had designated the Templars as custodians of her son by her first testament in 1209, and the pope by her last soon before she died in Rome in 1213; secondly, that of the newly elected provincial master of the Templars, Guillem de Montrodon, who shrewdly suspected that Count Sanç would make a worse tutor than regent. Not only Sanç, James later recalled, but also his uncle Ferrando 'had the hope of being king'.

It remained to pacify the disordered realms. In the summer of 1214 Pierre de Douai, acting in the king's name, summoned Aragonese and Catalonian prelates, barons, and towns through their deputies to a general *cort* which convened at Lérida, probably in August. There the legate imposed carefully revised statutes of the Peace on Catalonia ('as far as the Cinca') together with the significantly novel stipulation that these be ratified under oath by all lay men of Catalonia aged fourteen or over. Nor was this all. In a dramatic ceremony without precedent—James remembered it as the culminating moment of the assembly—all those present from the two realms were required to swear fealty to the king.

These were events of transcendent social solemnity, the liminal phase of a historic *rite de passage*. Some of the men convoked were in revolt, many were disgruntled, yet all were exalted through deliberately refashioned ritual to a new level of political solidarity. We know of no attempt to impose or confirm a statute for Aragon in this assembly. In that for Catalonia the legate and his advisers reacted firmly against baronial encroachments on the Peace while reaffirming the crown's regalian powers. They added the coinage of Barcelona to the list of protected persons and things. Most originally, they instituted a new mechanism for the maintenance of peace in the cities (see p. 76). But they did not merely impose. The revised statutes of 1214 also incorporated important concessions to dissidents, including some that the barons had formerly urged without visible success on Peter II and his father. Vicars should not only be Catalans, but should swear publicly 'to defend the peace' according to a prescribed form. The late king's abolition of new tolls (this is not otherwise recorded) was confirmed. And by 'special grace' of the legate and his charge the cities were exempted from all new taxes until James reached the age of puberty, with the limiting proviso that inhabitants of pledged lands might be tallaged 'moderately' for the redemption of those lands.

Such was the programme that the regent-procurator was charged to implement in Catalonia. But Sanç's was no easy commission: he was overshadowed by the cardinal-legate, who negotiated a truce with the Moors among other initiatives; and there was unrest in Aragon, where the abbot Ferrando resented being excluded from the regency. Worse still was the fiscal problem. Little progress toward the recovery of pledged domains seems to have been made in 1214–15, partly because the authority for this work had not been clearly defined, but chiefly because of the remission of taxation promised at Lérida. In 1215 Sanç appealed to the pope for a strengthened commission, which was granted by Innocent III in a remarkable series of orders dated 23 January 1216. The procurator was to be assisted by an administrative council representative of his two realms, leaving responsibility for the fiscal work to Guillem de Montrodon; moreover, a subsidy for the redemption of pledges was imposed on the cities of Catalonia and Aragon.

Thereafter, the regency worked better. But Count Sanç was increasingly drawn into the Occitan struggle against Simon de Montfort at the inevitable cost of papal benevolence. In December 1217 Honorius III threatened Catalonia with foreign invasion; about September 1218 Sanç resigned his *procuracio*; and by 1219 James and his counsellors, influenced by the Templars as well as by the Holy See, had virtually abandoned the alliance with the Raimonds of Toulouse. It was a fateful decision, reached by (or, more likely for) a king not yet twelve years old. James ratified it, in effect, by his passivity in face of the Capetian crusade in 1226.

Meanwhile, the first signs of fiscal recovery were evident. The king left Monzón in June 1217, after making a profitable settlement with Guerau de Cabrera, who was allowed to retain Urgell without prejudice to the rights of the heiress Aurembiaix. By 1221 important domains pledged by Peter II in both his lands had been recovered. It is clear that Sanç's successors were influential in these matters: Guillem de Montcada in peninsular Catalonia, Guillem de Cervera in Montpellier, and Nunyo Sanç in Roussillon. In 1220 the Templars secured an enlarged commission to serve as chief accountants in both realms, where they tried to restore the administrative methods of Ramon de Caldes. Nevertheless, major debts remained outstanding—and new ones were contracted, the baronial counsellors having fewer scruples about credit than the Tempars—and it was necessary to resort to taxation to discharge them. Such was probably the purpose of the *bovatge* granted by the Catalonian prelates and barons in a general Cort at Monzón in June 1217, as it was expressly the purpose of the Aragonese money-taxes (*monetatica*) imposed at Lérida in 1218, at Huesca in 1221, and at Daroca in 1223. The *bovatge* could no longer be resisted as an accession-tax in Catalonia. But it was otherwise with the (Catalonian) *monedatge*. Given the arbitrariness of Peter II's monetary policy, it is surprising to find no evidence of reaction after his death. There was no confirmation of the quaternal silver of Barcelona* in the great Cort of 1214 nor was the *monedatge* imposed or collected thereafter in Catalonia. This can only mean that the Catalonian magnates, persisting at this critical juncture in the position they had taken in 1205, insisted that their coinage 'be diligently conserved' (as the *usatge Moneta autem* put it) without cost to the people. It was a brave defiance that would not lack constitutional influence in the future. But for the moment it fairly invited the crown to manipulate the coinage of Barcelona for profit—which is precisely what happened when the *doblench* money,† which had been temporarily imposed by Peter II, was definitively instituted in 1222. At that time a royal ordinance overvalued the new money in relation to the old by 25 per cent, 'even though', the king admitted, 'it may seem . . . that . . . some people are unjustly troubled'.

As James came of age he was caught up in baronial politics—and frustrations. He was first influenced (after the Templars) by the Aragonese, who arranged his marriage to Leonor of Castile and his knighting (February 1221). But the magnates of Aragon were not subject to a territorial Peace as in Catalonia, the young king had already been drawn into their private wars in 1220 (he was then twelve), and he was obliged henceforth to create factions of his own. James learned how to fight and how to negotiate in Aragon—and men learned to respect him there. 'Take care not to go against our lordship,' he said to the rebel Pero Ahones in 1225. But there was more to be learned on both sides. The costly and unsuccessful siege of Peñíscola (September 1225) together with the king's harsh treatment of Ahones resulted in the organizing of a league of magnates and Aragonese towns over which James prevailed with difficulty only in 1227. This league was not a national uprising,

---

* A silver coinage of four-twelfths fine silver (hence quaternal) had long been minted at Barcelona.

† That is, pennies at two-twelfths fine.

nor was it ever, for all we know, very representative of Aragonese sentiment. Momentarily uniting the Cervera, the Montcada, and other Catalonian barons with Jaca, Huesca, and Zaragoza, and through them with the Infante Ferrando, Ato Orelia, Cornel, and other magnates of Aragon, it betrayed the desperation and jealousy of courtiers who felt their influence with the king slipping, as well as genuine doubts about royal monetary policy (in both realms) and new projects for conquest.

Catalonia was not spared. There was renewed conflict with Guerau de Cabrera over Urgell, a debilitating rivalry pitting Guillem de Montcada against Ramon Folc III of Cardona, and, most destructive, an inscrutable war between Guillem de Montcada and Nunyo Sanç (1223–5). Of the latter affair, which surely arose from some deeper cause than the dispute over a goshawk recorded in the *Libre dels feyts*, the king retained a bitter memory. He had been swept into a rivalry between two of his powerful administrators, who in the end took advantage of his troubles in Aragon to arrive at a settlement more favourable to themselves than to the king. Yet this settlement together with the premature campaigns against the Moors in 1225–6 marked a turning-point in James's fortunes. Aged seventeen and ex- perienced beyond his years, he was henceforth in firm command of public order and fiscal administration. In February 1228 he secured the allegiance of the Aragonese to his infant son Alfonso in a general court at Daroca. And his settlement of the war—let us call it the affair—of Urgell a few months later was to be an even more striking demonstration of his political maturity.

Guerau de Cabrera's possession of the county of Urgell, based on his descent from Ermengol VII, had not been permitted to supersede the right of Aurembiaix, daughter of Ermengol VIII, should she return from Spain to claim it. In the summer of 1228 she appeared before the king at Lérida and expressed her claim. Did she know that James had tired of his wife (that the oaths lately sworn to his son in the court of Daroca were preliminary to seeking a divorce on grounds of consanguinity)? In any case, Aurembiaix was young and attractive, she had once been betrothed to James, and if her claim could be vindicated, James could reasonably expect to annex the county through alliance with her. The law and fortune alike favoured the king. Aurembiaix was seconded by her distinguished stepfather

Guillem de Cervera and the jurist Guillem de Sassala of Lérida
in an impeccable judicial proceeding that left Guerau and his son
Ponç no alternative but a hopeless resistance. On 1 August
Aurembiaix performed homage and fealty to James for the
comital rights in Lérida and for the county of Urgell on condition
that the king recover the county for her; in October, acting on his
procedurally established protectorate of an orphan, James
captured Balaguer and other castles of lower Urgell in a brilliant
campaign incomparably described by the *Libre dels feyts*;—and
on 23 October 1228 Aurembiaix, proving her own sagacity,
contracted a secret protocol of concubinage with James confirming her tenure of Urgell and securing the succession to her
inheritance of any son born of their union. On that day—she let
it slip—James was already thinking of an expedition to Majorca.

Conquests and the Conqueror (1228–1276)

The Moorish regimes of Majorca and Valencia had existed for
generations on borrowed time. Both lands had come under
Roman rule in the second century BC. The Balearic Islands
(chiefly Majorca and Minorca) fell to the Vandals in the fifth
century AD, were conquered by the Byzantines in 534, and while
not untouched by early Muslim incursions passed definitively to
the emirate of Córdoba only in 903–4. Later part of the *taifa* of
Denia, Majorca was already threatened by the Almoravids when
the Catalans and their allies momentarily captured the island in
1115 (above, p. 27), only to be ejected by the Almoravids, who
ruled there for nearly half a century. When Al-Andalus fell to the
Almohads (1158), the islands achieved *taifa* status under the
Bānū Ġāniya, but with diminished and vulnerable authority.
Valencia's Roman-Visigothic history was uninterrupted until the
Muslim invasions, which culminated after troubled centuries in a
remarkable prosperity in the eleventh century. Menaced by the
Castilians from 1065 and later subject to the Cid and his allies,
Valencia submitted to the Almoravids in 1102. After the
conquests of Ramon Berenguer IV, she remained the lone
bastion of Moorish power in the eastern peninsula, weakened by
struggles of Muslim chieftains in which independence of the
Almohads required the purchase of protection from the count-
kings.

In his resolve to renew the time-hallowed conquests, King

James responded to the hopes of his peoples, the Templars, and the pope alike. In his decision to attack Majorca first, he satisfied chiefly the Catalans, among whom the merchants of Barcelona had complained of Moorish piracy. The Aragonese hoped that the king would revive his earlier initiatives against Valencia, but they had not supported those initiatives very well, and James saw no urgency in invading a land in manifest political decline from which he was collecting tribute. Accordingly, the Majorcan campaign, although it seems to have been declared a crusade and certainly drew contingents from Occitania and Provence as well as some of the king's honorial tenants in Aragon, was projected as a Catalonian enterprise. To justify and support it the king held a *Cort general* in December 1228 in his palace at Barcelona, where a new *bovatge* was ordained and the statutes of the Peace renewed. The prelates and barons agreed to furnish determined numbers of knights and foot-soldiers— Guillem de Montcada 400 knights, for example; the abbot of Sant Feliu de Guíxols five—on condition of receiving proportional shares of conquered properties. The men of Barcelona, Tarragona, and Tortosa promised ships. Ramon de Plegamans, a wealthy entrepreneur with long experience in the royal service, was charged with building and provisioning the fleet.

Sailing from Cape Salou on 5 September 1229 in some 150 ships—'all the sea seemed white with sails', the king remembered —a force of 800 knights and several thousand foot landed in Majorca two to four days later. They met no naval resistance, but had to fight the Moors on the heights of Portopí before they could move on to besiege the city of Majorca (the modern Palma), which fell after a prolonged siege on 31 December. The capture was violent and bloody, a lesson for the king as well as his adversaries, of whom a good many, nevertheless, were permitted to flee; most of the rest of the island was soon overrun. Among the Christian dead were Guillem and Ramon de Montcada, their famous lineage's emblem becoming henceforth symbolic of Catalonian valour. The preponderance of Catalans in the resettlement, notably of people from Empordà, can be seen in the register of partition. The men of Barcelona were rewarded with a charter of trading rights in the Balearic Islands; those of Marseille obtained 300 houses and the sixth part of the town of Inca, among other rights. The king remained in Majorca during most of the year 1230, then conferred its administration on Bernat de Montgri de Torroella. In 1231 Pedro of Portugal, whose marriage to Countess Aurembiaix had nullified her engagements to James, was granted Majorca as a fief for life in exchange for the conveyance to the king of his title to Urgell. The *Usatges of Barcelona* were imposed in Majorca as fundamental law, together with a privilege for the city patterned on the charters of Tortosa, Lérida, and Agramunt. Although the *wālī* Abū Yahya Hiquem had been captured, some pockets of Moorish resistance held out until the king's expeditions in 1231 and 1232. The isle of Minorca became tributary in 1231, that of Ibiza fell in 1235 to a force led by Guillem de Montgri, sacristan of Girona and (unwilling) archbishop-elect of Tarragona, and his brother Bernat.

Thus opening up another New Catalonia for agrarian and commercial expansion, the conquest of Majorca was an unmitigated triumph for James I and his people. The king had won independence of action as well as prestige. Having divorced Leonor of Castile in 1229, he was tempted by the prospect of a marriage to the heiress of Leon, then by that of a treaty through which he might reasonably hope to succeed the ageing king Sancho VII of Navarre. Nothing came of these negotiations, and James waited until 1235 to marry Yolanda of Hungary (called Violant in Catalonia), whose endowments in northern France and Flanders seemed to an approving pope to pose no threat to Capetian interests in the Midi. Meanwhile, impatient Aragonese barons had forced the king's hand in Valencia. In 1229 James had secured the collaboration of the deposed *wālī* Abū Zayd, who agreed to hand over six castles, including Peñíscola and Morella, in return for a share in the Christian conquest. When Morella fell to Blasco de Alagón in 1232, the king himself directed a campaign (1233) that led to the capture of Burriana and Peñíscola. A more urgent—and, in view of the rights of the first-born, more sinister—motive for the conquest of Valencia arose from James's engagement to cede the Balearic Islands and Valencia to the sons of his second marriage.

The campaign against Valencia city was projected in a general court celebrated at Monzón in October 1236. Monzón was still regarded as a borderland Aragonese town and the attendance on this occasion—prelates and barons of both realms, deputies from

Aragonese towns (including Lérida), plus Tortosa—reflects an intention of encouraging Catalan participation in the expedition while limiting the financial burden this time chiefly to Aragon. A statute of pacification was ordered and the standards of the Aragonese coinage (which circulated around Lérida and Tortosa) were confirmed, in compensation for which a tax of one morabetin per solvent hearth was established. This imposition, like the Catalonian *bovatge* in 1228, was manifestly a war subsidy (although, unlike the *bovatge*, it was to be levied repeatedly at intervals of seven years). Operations began with the capture of Puig de Cebolla (Onion Hill), where James installed a garrison (1237) which was severely tested in a Moorish counter-attack before the king could return with forces sufficient to lay siege to Valencia city. Meanwhile, the king had prevailed on the pope to have the campaign preached as a crusade. Reinforcements swarmed southward, from Occitania, some even from England, to join the Aragonese and Catalan knights in 1238. The siege lasted from April until 28 September, when Valencia surrendered on terms permitting the Moorish ruler Zayyān and his followers to depart in peace. King James was obliged to restrain his own men bent on pillage; but more serious problems arose when the Aragonese, who had marked out Valencia for their own, found themselves outnumbered by Catalans in the Christian resettlement. The custom of Aragon had prevailed in charters granted during the earlier phases of the conquest (1232–8), and Aragonese settlers in the northern borderlands continued to institute their own law thereafter. But in 1239 the king promulgated a new territorial custom for Valencia, an enactment that not only recognized that land to be a distinctive realm in itself (as, indeed, it had long been) but also ensured that Catalonian influence there would remain strong. The *Furs* of Valencia, eclectic, Romanist, and receptive to the customs of New Catalonia, were composed in Latin, then republished in Catalan in 1261. Settlers came chiefly from the plains of Lérida and Urgell, in considerable numbers. James I later estimated the Christians of Valencia at 30,000, but they certainly remained the minority in a predominantly Mudejar population. Expropriations were exceptional, the king confirming Muslim law and religious observance in many communities. The conquest was virtually completed with the capture of Játiva (1244) and Biar

(1245), although the Valencian Moors were in touch with their unconquered co-religionists in Granada and the Maghrib, and uprisings continued for many years.

With the annexations of Majorca and Valencia, James I fulfilled the ambitions of his forefathers. Pressing almost to the limit of the peninsular zone prescribed in 1179, he completed a dramatic enlargement of his ancestral realms. Beyond Valencia he would not go, not at least on his own account. When the Moors of Alicante offered to submit to him in 1240, James refused on grounds of his 'agreements with the king of Castile'. The Infante Alfonso of Castile was less scrupulous, not hesitating to move aggressively in Valencia, even against Játiva, in fear for his dynastic claim to Murcia. Exasperated, James seized border places in Murcia so as to teach Alfonso a new respect for the old treaties. But as a rule James continued to treat Castile with the Christian altruism traditional in the dynasty of Ramon Berenguer IV, not always to the satisfaction of his subjects. When the king of Granada incited revolts in Andalusia and Murcia toward 1264, Alfonso (now King Alfonso X) sought aid from James, who placed the matter with all good will before his *cort(e)s*. The Catalans reluctantly agreed to help, and even voted a new *bovatge* for the purpose; but in Aragon the magnates refused, advising the king to chastise Alfonso for past offences. Following preliminary thrusts by his son Pere, James himself directed the winter campaign in which Murcia was besieged and captured (January 1266). Granting the Moors the religious and legal concessions they had learned to expect of him, James settled his own men, mostly Catalans, there; and then—in a characteristic display of loyalty resented by some to this day—he turned over Murcia to Castile.

These relations with Castile were much influenced by domestic considerations. Queen Yolanda helped to settle the early dispute with Alfonso by promising to marry her daughter to him. She energetically pressed the interests of her sons against that of her stepson, encouraging the king to think of the royal inheritance as a proprietary dynastic condominium against all considerations of administrative integrity. In 1241 James's second son Pere was promised the succession to the Balearic Islands, Valencia, and Montpellier, plus Roussillon and Cerdanya (the latter two still in the hands of the king's uncle, Nunyo

Sanç, who died in the same year). But the birth of a third son, Jaume, necessitated a second partition (1244) in which the eldest son Alfonso's share was reduced to Aragon while Catalonia was destined for Pere. This unprecedented scheme to separate the heartland realms was symptomatic of the increasing estrangement of King James from Alfonso, whose Castilian sympathies grew stronger as his political ambitions were thwarted; moreover, the king favoured Catalonia (and Pere) by pronouncing its western limits extended so as to include Lérida with its environs, which had hitherto been regarded as Aragonese for political purposes, and even Monzón. Nor was this the end of partitions, as the birth of Ferran (1248), his death (1251), and the death of Alfonso (1260) occasioned new arrangements.

The Conqueror's success in Spain was offset by reverses in the Pyrenees and southern France. In Navarre, where he lacked native support, James was obliged to acknowledge the succession of the late king's nephew Thibaut of Champagne in 1234. In Béarn the heiress to Gaston VII was married to Alfonso of Aragon, but the union proved fruitless and the viscounty passed ultimately to Foix. More ominous was the failure of the counts of Toulouse and Provence to beget male heirs, for the sons of James I were too closely related to the heiresses to compete for their hands with Capetian princes. One may wonder why, at the death of Ramon Berenguer V (1245), James did not simply seize Provence by reversionary title, as his grandfather's men had done eighty years before. But the Provençal line was now one generation removed from Catalonian domination and southern traditions of partible inheritance remained strong. Despite protracted negotiations to prevent it, James saw Provence pass to Charles of Anjou (1246) and Toulouse to Charles's brother Alphonse of Poitiers (1249). Meanwhile, the dispossessed viscount Raimond Trencavel II found James a better protector than ally in his vain struggle to recover his lands.

Ferran Soldevila has movingly evoked the poignant paradox that ties of blood between their ruling houses should have prevented the maintenance of political solidarity between these peoples of common descent on either side of the Pyrenees. Yet while some lament was heard for the passing of native dynasties in the Midi, notably from the troubadours, there is no evidence that the Conqueror viewed the king of France as other than a fellow crusader. By the treaty of Corbeil (May 1258) James renounced all his rights and claims in Occitania, except those over Montpellier and the Carladès, while Louis IX gave up his ancient title to the counties of Barcelona, Urgell, Besalú, Roussillon, Empúries, Cerdanya, Conflent, Girona, and Osona; and in July 1258 James ceded his claim to domains in Provence to Queen Margaret of Provence and France. To complete this diplomatic reversal, which effectively legitimated Capetian expansion almost to the Pyrenees, James's daughter Isabel was betrothed to Philip, the heir to the kingdom of France.

From the Catalan-Aragonese point of view, the treaty of Corbeil was realistic as well as conciliatory. Even in his birthplace of Montpellier James had experienced increasing difficulty in exploiting his seigneurial rights. He was obliged to acknowledge the suzerainty of the bishop of Maguelone, and finally the overlordship of the king of France. These circumstances help to explain why King James designated Montpellier as the portion of his infant son Jaume (who was also born there) in 1243. To insist on his insubstantial suzerainties elsewhere in the Midi after the failure of his dynastic negotiations in the 1240s would have been to encourage Capetian jurists to define James's status—like Henry III's in Gascony—as that of a vassal of France. But it was one thing to treat with Saint Louis, quite another to allow the ambitious Charles of Anjou a free hand in the Mediterranean. In 1262 the Infant Pere married Constance of Hohenstaufen, the daughter of Charles's enemy Manfred and heiress to Sicily. The event caused consternation in papal-Angevin circles and stirred a pro-Catalan reaction in Provence. King James assured the Holy See and the king and magnates of France that no disloyalty to the pope or to Charles was thereby entailed; but Pere himself, the principal heir since his elder brother's death, made no such promise—and his day would come. By a new act of partition Pere was designated to inherit Aragon, Catalonia, and Valencia, while his younger brother Jaume was to have the Balearic Islands, Montpellier, Roussillon, and Cerdanya—the complex later spoken of as the Kingdom of Majorca.

The Sicilian marriage was by no means the only cause of papal uneasiness about the Conqueror. As early as 1237 Pope Gregory IX had excommunicated him for obstructing the consecration of the bishop-elect of Zaragoza, a sanction reimposed by Innocent IV in 1246 after James's intemperate punishment of a bishop of Girona—his tongue was cut out—charged with indiscreet revelation of the king's confession. Less damnable but more consequential was the ambivalence of James's attitude toward the infidel. His conquests, for all their crusading allure, remained chiefly cultural (if not yet quite national) undertakings. From Majorca and the ports James looked out upon the Maghrib somewhat as his forefathers had viewed Valencia: a zone inviting political as well as commercial exploitation. He entered into negotiations with the hafsid caliph of Tunis soon after the conquest of Majorca, authorized mercantile colonies and mercenary forces to operate in Tunis, and collected tribute. There were similar initiatives in Ceuta, Tlemcen, even in Egypt. James defended these pacts against his son-in-law's alarmist exhortations to unrestricted war against the Moors in 1260; and still later against Capetian–Angevin crusading activity. On the other hand, when this solidarity was broken in the Murcian uprisings of the 1260s, James could declare that all Saracens were his enemies. He proposed a crusade (by which he meant an expedition to the Holy Land) to Pope Clement IV, only to be told that he was morally unfit for such a cause. Even so, in 1267 James was inspired by an invitation from the Mongol Khan— and perhaps also by the urgings of his unendowed bastards Fernando Sánchez and Pedro Fernandez—to mobilize a major crusade that set sail for the East two years later. James seems to have hoped thereby to allay the pope's suspicions and to cap his own life's work. Once under way, however, he lost his nerve in a storm and put ashore, with most of his fleet, at Aigues-Mortes; only the ships of the Infants reached Acre, but with too few men to accomplish anything. Pope Gregory X tried to restore James's ardour for the crusade without success. Negotiations at the council of Lyon in 1274 foundered on mutual pretensions of honour unredeemed by understanding.

Within his ancestral realms the Conqueror's capacity to govern was affected diversely by his military settlements. In Aragon the hopes held out by the annexation of Valencia soon turned sour. The decision that Valencia should stand as a distinct realm with its own law countered the initiatives of Aragonese barons and led to a general reaction in Aragon which undermined the dynastic *entente* that had long prevailed in the king's court. In Catalonia James understandably fared better. Urgell continued turbulent, it is true. The king could not retain it in the teeth of local sentiment favourable to claimants of the old dynasty. In 1236 he recognized Ponç de Cabrera's title to the county, granting him the southern castles in fief except Lérida and Balaguer (although Ponç later acquired Balaguer). Two decades later the curious affair of Ponç's bigamous son Alvar split the baronage and obliged the king to side with the partisans of Constança de Montcada. In 1267 James regained control of Urgell by guaranteeing Alvar's debts, but at the inevitable cost of antagonizing both Alvar's heir Ermengol and his brother Guerau, who regarded Ermengol as illegitimate. These troubles were compounded by wider issues. The barons, especially those of Aragon but progressively the Catalans, too, became dissatisfied with a military programme apparently limited to fighting Castile's Moorish wars for the benefit of Castile, and when James treated their violence with leniency he ran foul of his own more demanding son Pere, who was appointed procurator in Catalonia in 1257 and later administered Aragon as well. Pere feuded with his half-brother Fernando Sánchez, who ultimately betrayed his father by siding with the dissident Aragonese. This event reconciled James with Pere, who led the force that crushed the revolt in 1275. But the revolt had originated in Catalonia, where Viscount Ramon Folc IV of Cardona took the lead in resisting the king's summons to military service in Granada (1273). When the viscount refused to render power of his castles for this alleged breach of obligation, James convoked a punitive militia from the towns of Catalonia—an unprecedented testimony to the gravity with which he viewed this defiance. Negotiations continued unsuccessfully in 1274 as the counts of Empúries and Pallars and the pretender (Ermengol) to Urgell joined Ramon Folc. But the king once again rose to the occasion, himself directing the campaign in the Empordà (summer 1275) which broke the Catalonian resistance. Meanwhile, clouds were gathering elsewhere. For those who, like the Infant Pere, questioned the wisdom of the capitulations in Occitania, the death of King Henry of Navarre in 1274 afforded a belated ray of hope; yet despite native sentiment favourable to Aragon, this succession, too, went to France. And in 1275 disorders in Valencia city escalated into a general rebellion of Moors which the king again, indefatigable to the last, acted firmly to subdue before falling ill. The Infant Pere was engaged in restoring order when his father died at Valencia on 27 June 1276.

Institutions, Societies, and Economies (1213–1276)

Throughout his domains, but especially in his old lands, government and society matured during the long reign of James I. One can hardly underestimate the contribution of the Conqueror himself to these processes. His exercise of power was characteristically personal, even impulsive. It found support in the regalian theory of the *Usatges of Barcelona* and the Romanist thinking of his own jurists, as may be seen from his commission to the Infant Pere as procurator-general of Catalonia in 1257. Pere was to do justice and enforce the Peace and Truce, acting himself or through judges-delegate; to appoint and dismiss vicars; and generally to do all that was necessary for the king's utility and for the defence and good government of all Catalonia. Feudal obligations were appointed to public purposes: it was to maintain the 'king's utility' that James convoked his Catalonian 'nobles and knights' in 1260 on account of the 'fiefs and honours which they hold of him'. The *Commemoracions* of Pere Albert confirmed the *Usatges* in reserving to the king of Aragon (with other kings) the power of 'ordering his vassals to follow him' in battle against the Saracens. But the evolution of Catalonian and Aragonese institutions in the thirteenth century was very much an associative process in which the king—whose office, we must remember, unlike that of his procurators, was neither Catalan nor Aragonese—responded to clerical or baronial or mercantile interests often coincident with his own and sometimes inconsistent with pan-regnal impartiality. In Catalonia the status of the *rey d'Aragó* was codified as co-ordinate, as that of a superior and directing but not absolute authority; there and even more so in Aragon the law was as much concerned with the rights of the other estates as with the king's.

It was the function of the higher clergy to uphold the king's status, something most of them did faithfully if not always efficiently during James's minority. In the 1220s not only Dominican and Franciscan houses but also the order of Mercy for the redemption of captives were founded at Barcelona; the friars were soon spreading throughout the province. James took personal interest in the order of Mercy, as did the great Dominican jurist Ramon de Penyafort (d. 1275), who served as the king's adviser and confessor and later promoted missions to the infidel. Both men supported the papal inquisition, which was introduced to Catalonia at the Council of Tarragona in 1234 and which led to prosecutions for heresy throughout the reign. The provincial episcopate had become excessively worldly. Archbishop Sparago (1215–33), who did not attend the Fourth Lateran Council, showed no interest in reform until pressed by the legate Jean d'Abbeville. The succession to Sparago proved a nightmare: not until 1238 could a candidate both competent and willing be elected. Pere d'Albalat (1238–51) worked tirelessly to impose the Lateran reforms, enjoining against clerical concubinage, pluralism, marriage within the prohibited degrees, and the relaxation of monastic discipline. He relied on the Cistercians and especially the Dominicans: five members of the latter order were promoted to suffragan sees. The metropolitan jurisdiction over Valencia was disputed with Toledo before passing to Tarragona in 1241; Majorca was placed in immediate dependence on the pope. The reform movement collapsed with the election of Pere d'Albalat's rival Bernat de Rocabertí (1252–68), whose sympathy for Bishop Ponç of Urgell, however, did not prevent the latter from being degraded for simony, incest, and adultery (1254). In 1257 a papal commission ordered the reform of Ripoll, which had fallen badly into debt.

The lay aristocracies were affected diversely by the conquests. In Aragon the barons (or *ricos hombres*) were frustrated by the limitations set on their exploitation of Valencia. The spirit of militant collaboration between king and magnates declined as the historic opportunity passed; in their own honours the barons worked to weaken the king's dominion. James resisted their pressure to make the honours hereditary, but to insist on this custom only lent force to the baronial claim of exemption from *bovatge* as a territorial privilege. Withholding their support for the Murcian campaign, many Aragonese lords were in virtual revolt during James's last years, some even declaring their allegiance to the royal bastard Fernando Sánchez against the Infant Pere.

In Catalonia none who fought had cause to regret the conquests. The counts and viscounts—such as the Empúries and the Cardona—struggled to maintain their dignity against royal officials and new baronage alike. Their horizons expanded apace with the king's: Ponç Hug III of Empúries (1230–69) married into the Castilian family of Lara, served James in war and negotiation, promoted urban enterprise, and even sought to restore the ancient colony of Empúries. His son Hug V (1269–77), less loyal but no less vigorous, took a leading part in the general rebellion of James's last years. The greater lords tried to limit the rights of superiors to take power of castles, which had become the king's chief procedural resort against refractory barons. Royal administrators sometimes referred to the higher aristocracy of Aragon as well as of Catalonia as 'nobles', implying that the knights (*cavallers*) were less than noble (above, p. 45); the *Libre dels feyts* used the Aragonese term (in Catalan form) *rics-hòmens* to describe the greater lords. At all levels tenants in homage were more freely spoken of as 'vassals', their tenures as 'fiefs', than in the twelfth century.

Among the masses of lesser estate the townsmen and, on the whole, the Jews continued to prosper. In Aragon peasant status remained variable, but with a tendency for the harsher tenures of the old uplands to become general. By the *fuero* of 1247 a lay lord could execute a peasant who had killed another. In Catalonia the customary law recognized distinct forms of peasant tenure toward 1250; and whereas in New Catalonia the sons of tenants were not bound to their fathers' lords, in lands east of the Llobregat peasants could escape an onerous domination only by purchase (*remença*) or by flight for a year and a day. Both in Aragon and Catalonia the hardening terms of agrarian lordship appear to be, in some part, the reaction of aristocracies to the royalist programmes of the Peace. Slavery persisted chiefly in Catalonian towns. The stratification of urban society created by the multiplication of artisans and wage-workers was recognized in administrative law: the electors at Lérida in 1214 comprised the 'greater men' and the 'people'; at Barcelona by 1226, the 'greater' and 'lesser hands'. Jewish communities flourished notably at Barcelona, Perpignan, Girona, Huesca, and Zaragoza. The *aljama* of Girona was distinguished for its learned defence of religious orthodoxy against Maimonides. Jews became heavily involved in credit for the campaigns of conquest, an unpopular enterprise that lent a spurious urgency to clerical efforts to stigmatize them as a people apart. Ramon de Penyafort and the king promoted disputations between Dominicans and rabbis, of which the best-known took place in the royal palace of Barcelona with a view to converting the Jews (1263). But James was less insistent than the friars on measures that for a time threatened the religious freedom of Saracens as well as Jews. Heavily taxed by the crown, both communities retained their social and judicial autonomy.

The relations of these classes with each other, their prosperity, and their utility to the king were increasingly regulated through legislation and administration. The statutes of the Peace, significantly amplified in 1214 so as to create a sworn solidarity amongst all Catalans, were reissued from time to time with additions relating to the exclusion of heretics and the security of Jews and Moors (1218 and after), the regulation of prices, and the prohibition of tournaments (1235). The disengagement of legislation from the traditional Peace was accelerated in the years between 1228 and 1235, when separate statutes were issued limiting interest payable to Jews to 20 per cent, prohibiting appointments of Jews as vicars or judges, and instituting the inquisition. As the royal jurisdiction expanded beyond the limits of the Peace in Catalonia, the barons sought to uphold custom against the influx of Romanist and canonist principles and procedures (statutes of Barcelona, 1251). The need of interpretation and reconciliation in the face of jurisdictional conflict explains the remarkable efflorescence of legal codifications in these years: the 'Customs of Lérida' by Guillem Botet (1228); the *Commemoracions* of Pere Albert, reinterpreting the *Usatges* with respect to homages, fiefs, procedures, and power of castles (and incidentally defining explicitly the customary zones of Old and New Catalonia); and the *Costumes de la Mar* (?c.1250), the precocious nucleus of the maritime law for which Barcelona was later to be famous; not to mention the great works—the *Decretals* and the *Summa de casibus*—which the Catalan Ramon de Penyafort contributed to the law of the Christian church as a whole. In Aragon, where the peace legislation had lapsed, various local customs persisted when it was decided after the conquests to codify the *fuero* of Jaca in a revised form suited to the courts and judges of the whole realm. Compiled by the jurist-bishop Vidal de Canyelles and promulgated in a general *Cort* at Huesca in 1247, the *fueros de Aragon* drew on Roman-canonical practice for principles of equity and written procedure. They were adopted rather widely save in the New Extremadura, where the laws of Albarracín and Teruel long held out. The *Furs* of Valencia (mentioned above, p. 66) were among the most important of these compilations, confirming in their definitive redaction (1261) the Catalan predominance in the post-conquest settlement of Valencia.

Everywhere, but especially in Catalonia, the regulation of urban and commercial affairs assumed great importance. The early impulse came from the legatine statutes of 1214 which introduced from Occitania a municipal administration of the Peaçe. Vicars were to be supplemented in the Catalonian cities by 'peace-men' (*paciarii, paers*) elected in pairs to represent the greater and lesser citizens. At Barcelona, and doubtless elsewhere, the *paers* became the first administrators of the urban community, comparable to the jurates in the Aragonese *concejos*. Following the early conquests, royal fiscal and jurisdictional pressures on the towns led to a renewal of the municipal initiatives that had first surfaced under Peter II, henceforth with more permanent results. In 1242 Tàrrega was authorized to elect four local men to govern in consultation with the good men and the bailiff. In 1243 James confirmed the customs of Perpignan; in 1246 he reorganized the consulate of Montpellier; and in 1256 he laid down the procedure by which the zalmedina (or justiciar) of Zaragoza was elected. At Barcelona the king experimented in a series of charters between 1249 and 1274 in order to arrive at a just balance between royal authority and local autonomy. The *paers* were replaced by counsellors (1258) who were progressively freed from the control of the vicar, and, in 1274, even from that of the bailiff; the general assembly was reduced to the *Consell de Cent* in 1265. These measures helped to secure a political autonomy commensurate with the maritime ascendancy sanctioned by a great charter of 1227, which effectively guaranteed Barcelona a monopoly of Mediterranean shipping so long as her merchants and seamen had ships available to load or to dispatch. This privilege was strengthened in 1268 when the king prohibited foreign merchants in Barcelona to charter or load merchandise other than their own. In the same year the counsellors and good men of Barcelona were authorized to appoint consuls in foreign

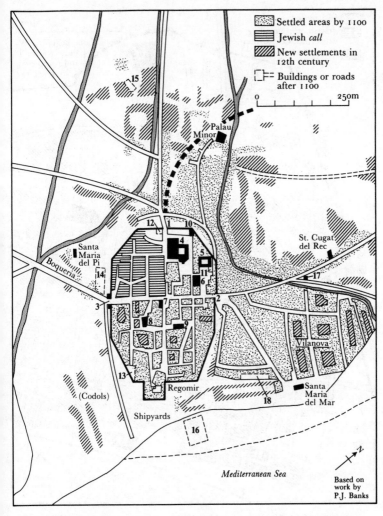

Note unsettled lands within the walls; these were filled in by 1200. The cathedral canons came to own most of the property between the Bishop's Gate and the Comital Palace in the eleventh century. The *vilanova* was established by the canons c.1080. Items 11 to 18 are structures of the 12th c. Not shown: to E: Sant Pere de les Puelles, Santa Eulàlia del Camp; to W: Sant Pau del Camp. In all the areas marked as settled by 1100 and in the 12th c. the street plan was more complex than shown here. Some of the streets marked in Map VI.B surely date back to 1200 or before.

1. Bishop's Gate (note the 'ancient arches', or *Arcs antics*, marked ■■■, that ran north from here.
2. Old Castle (*Castell Vell*) and ? market
3. New Castle (*Castell Nou*)
4. New Romanesque cathedral (1058); cemeteries to NW and SE.
5. Count's Palace.
6. Hospital of En Guitart (c.1045); fell into disuse c.1140.
7. Parish church of Sant Jaume.
8. Parish church of Sant Miquel (in the Roman baths)
9. Parish church of Sant Just and Pastor.
10. Cathedral hospital; canons' dormitory above.
11. Comital chapel of Santa Maria; later Santa Àgata.
12. New Bishop's Palace (c.1150)
13. Templar residence (by 1134); later a church.
14. New Baths (*Banys Nous*) 15. Santa Anna.
16. Old *Drassanes*, on extended shore-land.
17. Chapel of Bernat Marcuç. 18. Alfondecs.

VI. A Barcelona about 1100 (showing growth to 1200)

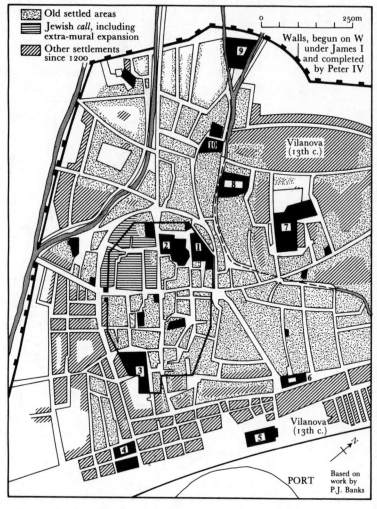

Old settled areas

Jewish *call*, including extra-mural expansion

Other settlements since 1200

Walls, begun on W under James I and completed by Peter IV

0   250m

Vilanova (13th c.)

Vilanova (13th c.)

PORT

Based on work by P.J. Banks

Structures identified on Map VI.A are not labelled here (with certain exceptions). Note the increased size of rebuilt structures (e.g., nos. 1,6). The street-plan, particularly in old extra-mural settlements, is here much simplified. Not shown: NW: to churches of Natzaret (1312), Montalegre (*c.*1360), Clarisses of Pedralbes (after 1327), Carmelites (1290s); to SW: Franciscans (1232; expanded late 13th c.); new *Drassanes*, (1370s); to E: Sant Agustí Vell (1309); Hospital of Pere Desvilar (*c.*1308).

1. Major Royal Palace.
2. Rebuilt cathedral and cloister.
3. Minor Royal Palace (1350s).
4. Mercedarian church and residence (1330s).
5. *Llotja* (begun 1382).
6. New church of Sant Maria del Mar (1320s).
7. Santa Caterina (1223–43).
8. Hospitallers' church (*c.*1207).
9. Santa Maria de Jonqueres (1293)
10. Magdalenes (1360s).

VI. B Barcelona about 1360 (showing growth since 1200)

ports to look after their commercial interests there. The tariffs of Barcelona, Tamarit, and Collioure not only prove a continued expansion of Catalonian productivity—we begin to hear now of millstones and saffron—but also suggest a Catalan role in the trade between the Mediterranean and the western peninsular realms. The Ebro valley towns shared in this trade. James's monetary policy likewise favoured commercial interests: his institution of the *doblench* coinage at an inflated rate in 1222 and his minting of imitation Muslim dirhems, notably at Montpellier, where in 1272 James also inaugurated a *gros* coinage in silver. The *doblench* proved a little too weak even for trade, so in 1258 the king was prevailed upon to establish the ternal coinage (three-twelfths fine) which was for long thereafter to be the standard petty silver in Catalonia.

The institution of the ternal money was of historic importance in two other respects. By specifying that the citizens of Barcelona received this privilege on behalf of his other subjects of Catalonia as well as for themselves, James acknowledged with singular emphasis Barcelona's economic and political ascendancy. Even more remarkable, by promising never to exact a *monedatge* in compensation for the confirmation, James capitulated publicly to the Catalans' traditional insistence on the gratuitous immutability of their coinage. This unprecedented concession does not mean that the king renounced a lucrative prerogative. There is no evidence that James I ever collected a money-tax in Catalonia, before or after 1258, save that collected in the borderlands where the coinage of Aragon circulated. This is why the *bovatge* was so important to him. It was his only customary subsidy of comprehensive incidence in Catalonia at a time when his extraordinary expenses continued to mount. Yet the *bovatge* was at first customary only as an accession-tax. When James wished to levy it a second time for the Balearic war and then again for a campaign in aid of Castile (1264) he was obliged to seek the consent of the Catalans, and this obligation proved in time to be the foundation of the powers of the Corts. In Aragon the situation was the reverse. There the magnates rejected the *bovatge* as a foreign custom, but they could not undo the traditional royal charge, dating from 1205 and repeated in 1218 and after, for the confirmation of their coinage's standards. The king consulted the Aragonese towns with the magnates when he wished to exploit the coinage, which thus played the role of the Catalonian *bovatge* in the genesis of the Cortes.

The Cort(e)s of both old realms may thus be said to date from the reign of James I. That was when the occasional summons of magnates to form plenary sessions of the king's court was transformed into institutions of the estates of Aragon and Catalonia. One must not exaggerate the personal influence of James in this process. He was only a child when some of the more important assemblies took place. But James was the first ruler of his lands to realize the potential of the Cort(e)s for mobilizing in defence of privilege and the first, accordingly, to convoke them as a matter of political discretion. In fact, he convoked them less often in his later than in his earlier years, complaining of their impertinent debates and remarking that 'in no country of the world has [counsel] the sense or value that it ought to have'. Fundamental innovations were apparent as early as 1228. First, it became customary to summon the towns together with the bishops, abbots, and barons. Cities and towns of both realms were represented at Lérida in 1214; of Catalonia at Vilafranca (1218), Tortosa (1225), Barcelona (1228), and on later occasions; of Aragon at Monzón (1217), Daroca (1223), Barbastro (probably, 1224), Daroca (1228), Monzón (1236), and afterwards. According to the *Libre dels feyts*, ten men from each city attended the *Cort* of 1214; some of the deputies from Aragonese towns in this assembly are known to have appeared in subsequent Cortes of Aragon and it is highly probable that Catalan townsmen gained similar experience in consultation during these years. Secondly, there evolved a formal procedure which, if not yet invariable, clearly anticipated the mature ceremonial of the late medieval Cort(e)s: the hortatory proposition by the king or by a prelate speaking for the king; the responses by *ad hoc* delegates of the clergy, barons, and towns, followed by discussion within the orders; and the public agreements and decisions: vote of *bovatge* or *monedaje*, determination of a date of muster, promulgation of statutes. In 1264 at Zaragoza there was a demand for redress of grievances prior to deliberation on the king's request. Occasions of this sort often required two or more ceremonial sessions, each of which was regarded as a *cort*, whence the familiar designation 'Cort(e)s'.

But the Cort(e)s were not yet constitutional organs of the

estates. The king retained the initiative, he sometimes convoked prelates and barons without towns or towns without magnates, he legislated with or without the assent of the estates. One factor inhibiting the constitutional evolution that was rapidly completed in the reign of Peter III was the persistent confusion of Catalonian interests with Aragonese. When it was a question of dynastic or military problems common to his realms, the king (or his advisers) found it expedient to summon general Cort(e)s in his borderland towns—Lérida (1214, 1275) or Monzón (1217, 1236)—as his predecessors had sometimes done. The procedures developed on these occasions doubtless influenced those in the Cort(e)s limited to Catalonia, Aragon, or Valencia, and may help to explain some structures common to the three institutions: the forms of summons and of urban representation, for example. What differentiated the assemblies was the tendency toward the middle of the thirteenth century for military and fiscal issues to become matters of territorial privilege. And one reason for the mounting insistence on privilege or custom was the king's increasing administrative power.

Curial officers became more numerous and more specialized. The procuratorships exercised by the king's sons and others were made necessary not only by the accumulation of realms but also by the multiplied demands on the king's attention to local affairs. Military and palatine supervision in Catalonia were co-ordinated in the hands of Pere de Montcada Seneschal (1228–67), who claimed them as of hereditary right; he supervised the *maior domus* whose office had originated in Aragon and persisted there distinctly. The chancellor is mentioned for the first time during James's minority, although his functions continued to be discharged routinely by notaries. Fiscal supervision, having been charged at first to the Templars, seems to have been relocated in the chancery after the conquests, for the first extant registers, in a series beginning around 1250, contain records of account as well as of military, economic, and judicial regulation for all the realms. As a fiscal delegation the *Procuració reial* dates from 1263 in Roussillon-Cerdanya. The enregistration of administrative correspondence, while not without precedents antedating 1200, was one of the major institutional innovations of James I. Although it surely owed something to the increased supply of paper made available by the conquest of Valencia, it also points to the progress of public-bureaucratic ideas. So too, even more emphatically, does the king's retention of Bolognese-trained jurists, such as Guillem de Sassala and Vidal de Canyelles, in his entourage; and James regularly appointed judges *ad hoc* to deal with matters beyond, or appealed from, the vicar's jurisdiction.

Royal authority was felt more and more pervasively in the localities of his realms. Alongside the older *merinus* in Aragon figures the *zalmedina*, once the *walī's* urban agent, and now chiefly a judge, notably at Zaragoza; in other towns and in Valencia appear judges so-called (*iusticia, iudex*). In Catalonia the vicariate remained the basic unit of justice, military muster, and police. Despite baronial complaints the jurisdiction of vicars expanded as the king's men delegated powers beyond the limits of the Peace. The Peace itself was strengthened in 1257, when the king charged the vicar of Barcelona to administer a militia of peasants on ecclesiastical and municipal lands in the Vallès: the so-called *sometent*, which later spread to other districts. The vicars, who were still normally knights but sometimes townsmen, employed retainers and in some places appointed sub-vicars. In towns and cities they worked with the *paers* or good men, not always harmoniously; from their conflicts of jurisdiction evolved the concessions to municipal autonomy that have been mentioned. The fiscal or patrimonial administration continued to be exercised by bailiffs, whose power often depended on their ability to extend credit to the king. With the recovery of pledged lands, and especially after the conquests, it became possible once again to hold bailiffs directly accountable for their domains. But James cannot have viewed this matter very differently from his father: in his later years he pledged major domains to his barons and Jews, especially the latter. The bailiffs were frequently Jews—at Barcelona, Tortosa, Lérida, Besalú, and elsewhere; there were Jewish bailiffs also in Zaragoza—although Baer has argued that Jewish participation in administration declined after 1250. The more lucrative bailiwicks, such as at Lérida, tended to be compounded with those of neighbouring domains in the hands of agents, far stronger than rural bailiffs, who exercised powers of police in addition to fiscal authority.

Like his father and grandfather James the Conqueror commonly thought of his realms in federative terms. His court continued to direct a unified administration of the two original lands even as it developed offices appropriate to each. We have noticed the ambiguous character of the general Cort(e)s in this respect. The conquest of Valencia, while more a Catalonian venture than the Aragonese wished, was by no means exclusively Catalan; the constitution of Valencia as a separate realm with its own *Furs* and Corts was, indeed, a curious compromise between Catalan and Aragonese pretensions. All this said, it remains true that James I was the first ruler of the Crown of Aragon who could be called Catalan by emotional preference: the first to show partiality for Catalan designs and interests, the first to adopt the Catalan language as a medium for commemorative prose. The Aragonese uprisings of his early years had left their scar. The exuberant vitality of his alliance with Catalonian knights and townspeople in the conquest of Majorca helped to nourish a Catalanist political mythology which, for a time, seemed to threaten Aragonese territorial integrity itself. Most revealing in this respect was the king's impulsive declaration before a stubborn Aragonese Cortes in 1264 that Catalonia 'is the best realm of Spain, the most honourable, and the most noble'; a land, he added, whose counts, barons, knights, clergy, and patrician citizens (*ciutadans honrats*) far outnumber those of Aragon.

Whether in dynastic policy (the redefinition of the Ilerdan borderlands) or in the discouragement of Aragonese baronial designs to appropriate Valencia, such partiality left its mark on Aragon. For the first time we hear of baronial protestations of national right, none the less interesting for being recorded by the king himself. 'Aragon and the clearly Aragonese', writes Sesma Muñoz, 'will rise by reaction to Catalonia and the Catalan.' Yet it was not so much the king or the Catalans that brought this about as the demographic, economic, and political realities of the post-conquest years. Valencia's role was critical. She was populous and prosperous, a land to be exploited rather than settled, and to accomplish this the king had the choice of leaving it to Aragonese barons or, in alliance with Catalans, dominating it himself, which in the event he proceeded to do. In time this policy would create a realm eclipsing the old homelands themselves. But that time had not yet come. Catalonia's population was far larger in the thirteenth century, and her

wealth at least the equal of Valencia's.* The real importance of
Valencia (and Majorca) in the thirteenth century was to provide
outlets for the expansion of Catalonian institutions and culture,
to ensure that Catalonia's geopolitical advantage in a mercantile
age was secure for the future. The king found it expedient to ally
with a process not of his own making.

He was not one to put sentimentality before reality. Seeking
first to govern all his peoples, James was an outstanding ruler in
an age of famous kings. A successful warrior (if not a great one),
he knew when and where to negotiate. No king in history ever
revealed himself better to posterity, and in writing (or inspiring)
the *Libre dels feyts*, James celebrated his peoples as well as himself
in the afterglow of their most durable triumphs. His crusading
piety was matched by his humanity: an impressive integrity in
dealing with fellow rulers and foes alike—and a notorious
weakness for women. He was a grand king, and was so perceived
(he noted with satisfaction) at the solemn Council of Lyon
(1274). Yet in the end he may be judged to have fallen short of
the highest attainment in medieval statecraft. He had not the
wisdom of Saint Louis nor the learning of Alfonso X—nor,
perhaps, the political astuteness of either. He found it harder
than Louis to discipline his barons, yet he was influenced by the
Capetian in his patience with Alfonso. James has been severely
criticized for failing to exploit his opportunity to annex Murcia,
although this criticism (whatever its merit) fails to do justice
to James's powerful defence of his policy as a matter of Christian
statesmanship. His grandeur may be felt to lie in the com-
manding energies of his early years and his conciliatory
sympathy with the constructive forces in the associative life of his
peoples.

The brilliance of James's reign has understandably obscured
the history of his predecessors. His grandfather had postponed
the conquests of Valencia and Majorca, his father had squandered all in a vainly personal politics. The Conqueror must have
appeared to his compatriots more truly the heir of Ramon
Berenguer IV, whose conquest of New Catalonia antedated that

* One must not be misled by contemporary estimates of Valencia's
surpassing revenues. In Catalonia James I merely shared in the wealth
according to an old patrimonial disposition; in Valencia he collected as a
dominating conqueror.

of Majorca by eighty years. Yet it was precisly during those eighty years—during a period beginning long before James's reign—that Catalonia and Aragon evolved from aggregates of archaic counties into administrative units and finally into political structures. This evolution was largely determined by underlying social forces—demographic, commercial, urban—yet it also owed much to Alphonse II and Peter II, who took the initiatives in resettlement, administration, and taxation as well as in dynastic and foreign policy, that James was to exploit and fulfil. James was an heir as well as a conqueror. He built as effectively on his institutional heritage as on his conquests to create that expanded confederation we call the Crown of Aragon.

IV

Mediterranean Expansion (1276–1336)

JAMES I was also a dynastic founder. The chronicler Muntaner represented his birth as miraculous, retaining no traditions about the earlier marriages of the house. From his perspective (Muntaner wrote in 1325) the dynastic patrimony included Montpellier and Majorca as well as the old peninsular lands and the former were, respectively, the maternal inheritance and the conquest of James I. In bequeathing them together with Roussillon and Cerdanya to his second (surviving) son, James created a dynastic federation that was, in the hands of James II of Majorca (1276–1311), to assume a political life of its own. The other conquest, Valencia, passed to the principal heir Peter III, thus confirming a union with Catalonia and Aragon that would henceforth persist intact.

Peter III is that rarity in history: the greater son of a great father. Faced with two dangerous challenges—rebellious aristocracies in Aragon and Catalonia and the collapse of Angevin rule in Sicily—Peter accepted both, and prevailed. In so doing he opened a new phase of dynastic and colonial expansion that threatened for a time to turn the Mediterranean into a Catalonian lake. The 'business of Sicily' remained to challenge Peter's sons Alphonse III (1285–91) and James II (1291–1327), and to plague the pope and his Angevin allies. It was the shoal on which foundered the older crusading idealism of 'good king James' and left the Crown of Aragon vulnerable to the consequences of its own success. 'And so the king of Aragon', wrote Desclot in reference to negotiations with France and Castile in 1282, 'is between two kings who are the most powerful in the world.'

Peter III (II in Catalonia, 1276–1285)

Peter succeeded his father, a grown and tried ruler. Born in 1240, procurator in Catalonia since 1257, he had resisted the Aragonese rebels more firmly than his father, and, despite falling

from favour for a time, was again fighting the king's wars when
James died. It took Peter more than another year to put down the
Moorish revolt in Valencia, during which time he left the war
zone only long enough to be crowned at Zaragoza (November
1276), taking care not to use the royal title until then. The
Valencian revolt ended with the capture of Montesa followed by
the surrender of other castles in 1277, leaving Peter free to
deal with constitutional problems in his other realms. When he
tried to collect a *bovatge* without first promising to uphold
the privileges of Catalonia, he met general resistance which,
momentarily appeased in 1278, was followed by risings in upper
Catalonia. Supported by the counts of Pallars and Foix and the
viscount of Cardona, Ermengol X fought for a claim to Urgell so
clouded that the king had virtually controlled the county since
1270. Peter III captured the rebels at Balaguer in 1280, won
their loyalty in generous negotiations, and soon released all
except Roger Bernard of Foix, who had induced the king's
brother James of Majorca to join the rebels. Of James Peter
demanded nothing less than homage and fealty for his inherited
lands, relenting only on condition that James's successors render
such submission. The demand was significant, for it showed that
Peter intended to restore the unitary administration of all the
dynastic lands.

Peter now took bold initiatives. He tried to neutralize Castile
and France at a stroke by seizing the Infantes de la Cerda, the
disinherited grandsons of Alfonso X and the sons of Blanche of
France. He projected a Portuguese marriage for his daughter and
an English marriage for his son. He arranged a truce with
Granada and renewed his protectorate over Tunis. And it is clear
that he was thinking of Sicily when he prepared fleets for service
on the Tunisian coasts in 1281 and 1282; his wife's claim to her
father's inheritance had not been forgotten and his court had
long harboured Hohenstaufen dissidents. When the Sicilians rose
against the Angevins and massacred the garrison soldiers on
30 March 1282, Peter readied himself for their call, and he
landed at Trapani to an enthusiastic welcome five months later.
Having received the Sicilians' fealty and confirmed their
customs—those of their 'good King William' (1166–89)—he
drove the Angevin fleet from Calabrian waters.

Never had a realm been so easily annexed to the Crown of

Aragon—nor so precariously. Pope Martin IV, a Frenchman, was furious and so was Charles of Anjou, whose harsh exploitation of Sicily had precipitated a crisis that wrecked his long-laid plans for east Mediterranean expansion. Their alliance in the months ahead posed the most dangerous threat the Crown of Aragon ever faced in the Middle Ages. Peter III had stoked their anger by negotiating cynically for papal support of his campaign against the infidel Tunisians even as he prepared to invade Sicily, an appeal that left the pope no acceptable response. After the uprising Martin lost no time condemning the rebels and their allies, he excommunicated Peter and placed Sicily under interdict in November 1282, and in the following year he relieved Peter's subjects of their fealty and offered the kingdom of Aragon to a son of Philip III of France. Meanwhile, Charles of Anjou challenged Peter to regulated combat at Bordeaux, an engagement that Peter accepted, then prudently evaded (1 June 1283) when it appeared that his adversary's guarantees could not be relied upon.

Peter had now to deal with his own peoples. In a stormy Cortes at Tarazona (September 1283) the Aragonese protested that they had not been consulted about the Sicilian project and that they were being taxed unlawfully; they demanded that the *Fueros* of Aragon be imposed in Valencia. When the king's reply was found inadequate, the nobles and towns united at Zaragoza to demand a general confirmation of their privileges, which the king was obliged to accept in October 1283. Thus originated the Aragonese 'Union', a coalition of élite forces that was to have constitutional influence for decades; from this time, too, dates the power of the *Justicia* to mediate between the king and the Aragonese *ricos hombres*. The Catalans were hardly less angry before Peter finally convoked them in December 1283 at Barcelona. It was there laid down that prelates, barons, knights, and towns should be assembled in Catalonia once a year, that legislation should have their consent, and that taxes (including *bovatge*) should be levied only as heretofore customary. The Catalans, too, had formed a representative union, but unlike the Aragonese had contrived to render their general Cort the instrument of its expression.

Not all discontent was allayed. When Juan Nuñez de Lara pretended to an independent (and hostile) lordship of Albarracín,

Peter reacted vigorously and captured Albarracín in September 1284. In the spring of 1285 an uprising of working men at Barcelona, led by the demagogue Berenguer Oller, was cruelly suppressed. It was no time to cross a ruler under ecclesiastical sanctions and threatened with foreign invasion. Meanwhile, naval war continued in Sicily and Calabria, in the course of which Charles the son of Charles of Anjou was captured for the Catalans by the admiral Ruggiero di Loria. In February 1284, overcome by papal pressure, the royal council of France persuaded Philip III to accept the kingdom of Aragon for his second son, Charles. War became inevitable—a crusade against Aragon by no means universally approved in France and financed by the church as well as through aids and loans levied by King Philip. On the other side, Peter III was unable to persuade the Aragonese to mobilize in Catalonia against the French. Moreover, James of Majorca, strategically placed in the royal palace at Perpignan, chose to support the French-papal crusade.

In late spring 1285 Philip III crossed the eastern Pyrenees with some 8,000 men, forcing Peter and his chiefly Catalan forces into defensive positions in the Empordà. Girona fell to the French on 7 September after a summer-long siege that enabled Peter to harass the enemy from backland positions and gave his admiral Ruggiero di Loria time to bring his fleet from Sicily. When Loria destroyed Philip's ships in the Bay of Roses on 3–4 September, the French position became untenable; the capture of Girona a few days later proved useless. Battered by the Catalans, the Capetian forces struggled back to Perpignan, where Philip III died on 5 October. Peter III, for his part, moved with characteristic vigour against those of his own realms who had failed him; he was planning an expedition to wrest Majorca from his insubordinate brother when he fell ill himself and died on 11 November 1285.

'Peter the Great', wrote Soldevila, 'had triumphed over all his enemies.' He had gained Sicily; he had pacified and defended his realms. He had instituted a new coinage, the silver croat—corresponding to the old Barcelona sou of account and well adapted to new commercial needs—that would be the monetary standard of his peoples for generations to come. But his achievements came at high cost. He had fundamentaly altered the constitution by conceding baronial and municipal autonomy only after such spirited resistance that he was forced to allow the power of the estates to be institutionalized. It remained to be seen whether the Aragonese could be reconciled to an expansionist regime so evidently responsive to Catalonian interests or whether Sicily could be defended against Angevins, Capetians, and militant popes. The peoples of the Crown of Aragon remained under ecclesiastical censures.

The 'Business of Sicily' (1285–1337)

These problems clouded the reigns of Alphonse III (II in Catalonia, 1285–91) and his brother James II (1291–1327). Their father, it is true, may have tried to renounce Sicily on his death-bed as the price of his peace with the church, but if so this was not divulged. Sicily passed to James (his younger son) while Alphonse inherited the other realms together with the hostility of his uncle James. It was Alphonse's achievement to complete his father's (and grandfather's) unfinished work. The expedition to Majorca resulted in the reconquest of Majorca city and the surrender of Ibiza. In the momentum of these victories the days of Moorish Minorca were numbered. The isle fell to a second campaign (January 1287) that resulted in a wholesale displacement of Moors, many of whom were sold in the slave-markets of Majorca, Valencia, and Barcelona, while their homeland was resettled by Catalans.

The conquest of the Balearic Islands can only have helped Alphonse in his relations with France and the papacy. But the negotiations with France were stalled as long as Charles of Salerno was imprisoned, and went badly once he was released. One difficulty was that the dispossessed James of Majorca continued to resist the status quo and to negotiate with France; a more serious difficulty was that the Aragonese remained disaffected. Their *Unión*, now including all the towns, insisted on controlling the king's fiscal administration and his foreign affairs; it even sent envoys to Alphonse's enemies in the matter of Sicily. When the Aragonese barons tried to impose their *fueros* on Valencia by force, Alphonse was obliged to resist them with Moorish mercenaries. In the end Alphonse capitulated to the *Unión*, believing like his father that the issues of Mediterranean pacification mattered more than the royal prerogative in Aragon.

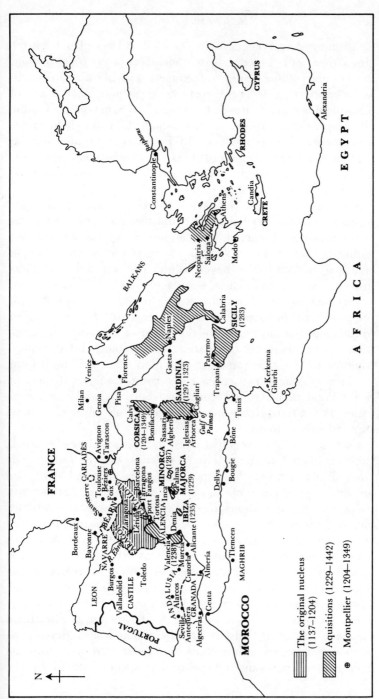

VII. The Mediterranean Crown of Aragon (1137–1479)

The original nucleus
(1137–1204)

Aquisitions (1229–1442)

Montpellier (1204–1349)

Confirming the privileges of the *Unión* on 28 December 1287, the king swore not to proceed against members of the *Unión* without the consent of the *Justicia* of Aragon and of the Cortes. In 1288, moreover, Alphonse lost the diplomatic advantage of championing the Infantes de la Cerda when Sancho IV of Castile allied with France. It became increasingly difficult to hold out for a comprehensive pacification. In February 1291 at Tarascon Alphonse reluctantly agreed to withdraw support from his brother in Sicily and to offer his obedience to the pope, who would lift the sanctions.

This agreement collapsed when the king died in June 1291. James of Sicily succeeded to the peninsular domains, leaving his younger brother Frederick as viceroy in Sicily. For a long tense moment (1291–3) James struggled to master a Crown of Aragon enlarged and united as never before. But when the Catalans proved unwilling to insist on sovereignty over Sicily at any cost, he revived his brother's initiative. In the treaty of Anagni (20 June 1295) he agreed to convey Sicily to the Holy See (and so to the Angevins) in return for the lifting of sanctions; to marry Blanche, the daughter of Charles II of Naples; and to restore Majorca to his uncle James on condition of his holding it from the king of Aragon in vassalage. To compensate for the loss of Sicily Pope Boniface VIII promised Sardinia and Corsica to James II, and in 1297 James received the solemn investiture of these islands at Rome.

Once again the powers had failed to reckon with the Sicilians. Refusing their fate they elected Frederick king in 1296, a *fait accompli* that neither the pope nor James II could undo. In an unlikely reversal of alliance James campaigned against Frederick; he and Ruggiero di Loria even won a sea-battle against him in July 1299. But the results were inconclusive and the Sicilians continued resolute. At Caltabellotta in August 1302 a new compromise was reached. It was settled that Frederick should reign in Sicily for life, after which time that realm should devolve to Charles of Naples (or to the heir of Frederick and Eleanor, Charles's daughter, whom Frederick would marry); Frederick gave up Calabria. So Sicily remained effectively Catalan, attracting settlers from Catalonia and developing commercial ties with the peninsula. Frederick proved to be an energetic, independent, and (politically) unconciliatory king. He baited the popes by allying with Henry VII of Germany and by favouring the extreme Spirituals of the Franciscan order. From 1313 there was renewed war with the Angevins of Naples. And in 1322 the Sicilians defiantly swore fealty to Frederick's son, Peter, who succeeded his father in 1337. Thanks to Frederick and their own political temper, the Catalanophile Sicilians were to live a troubled independence for much of the fourteenth century.

Frederick's most curious promotion was an expedition of Catalonian mercenaries that led in time to Sicilian-Catalan settlements in Greece. Finding himself unable to support these warriors when the Sicilian war ended in 1302, the king gladly fell in with the scheme of their leader Ritxard de Flor* to sell their services to the emperor Michael IX who was beleaguered by the Turks. Ramon Muntaner took part in the expedition (playing Villehardouin to another Fourth Crusade), and he told the story with endearing fervour but considerable inaccuracy as a feat of the Catalan-Aragonese dynasty. The *almogàvers* who chiefly composed the force were veterans of the Valencian border wars whom Peter III had employed in his Tunisian-Sicilian expeditions and the conflict that resulted. Desclot had described them as 'men who live only by war, who are not in cities and towns but only in mountains and woods, and they fight daily with Saracens . . . Very strong men and swift,' they go days without eating, wear short shirts, and bear knives, 'a good lance, two darts', and a bread bag.

The expedition, numbering some 8,000 people (half of them foot soldiers) including sailors, women, and children, sailed in Sicilian transports in the summer of 1303. Flor married the Byzantine princess Maria and took the title of Megaduc. After clashes with resident Genoese, the Catalans defeated the Turks in several battles before lapsing into conflict with the Greek authorities, whom they found bad paymasters. The treacherous assassination of Ritxard de Flor in 1305 seriously weakened the expedition, which persisted even so under Bernat de Rocafort and others. Frederick of Sicily became involved in 1307, but it was only in 1311 that he sent his son to Greece as deputy governor, thus founding a Sicilian duchy of Athens that lasted until 1387. For all this, the episode had little to do with the

* This is Muntaner's rendering of a German name, equivalent to Rutgar von Blum (or Ruggiero di Fiore).

political and economic expansion of the Crown of Aragon, merely leaving its mark in Byzantine lore and Catalanist imaginations inspired by Muntaner.

James II (1291–1327): Foreign Affairs

James II, for his part, acted with energy and caution on all his frontiers. He began by doing what his brother and his father had failed to do: he reconciled himself with his peninsular subjects. This was one of the most important events of the reign. Muntaner tells us how, having first settled with Castile on terms that restored harmony between the Infantes and Sancho IV, James visited 'all his realms and lands in peace and tranquillity, so that before long he had put all the land in peace and concord . . . he himself imposed peace and concord among all his barons, who had ever been used to fighting; and he even put down and prohibited factions in the city of Barcelona . . . [and] in all the towns.' Behind these redundant words we may discern something like the old programme of the regalian Peace, setting limits on and sanctions for private war, a programme made possible by the king's willingness to swear to uphold the privileges, first in Barcelona, then in Zaragoza, where he was crowned. In the Cortes at Zaragoza neither the king nor the estates mentioned the privileges of the *Unión*; the castles Alphonse III had been obliged to cede as securities in 1287 were restored; and the assembly granted the king a considerable subsidy. The pendulum swung back in favour of royal authority. A revival of the *Unión* in 1301 centred on the particularist demands of a minority in the nobility. As a rule James could count on Aragonese support in his Mediterranean campaigns as well as in those against Castile.

When Alfonso de la Cerda was excluded from the succession to Sancho IV in 1295, the time was ripe to reopen the question of Murcia. The delivery to Castile of this last conquest of James I rankled among those who had favoured the Infantes, and Catalans and Aragonese continued to settle in Murcia. James II therefore concerted with Alfonso to send an Aragonese army against Castile while the former himself overran Murcia. But the Castilians resisted, thanks in no small part to the selfless energies of the queen-mother María de Molina. Faced with complicated alternatives James thought it better to join with Castile against

Moorish Granada than face the prospect of eviction from Murcia by Castile in alliance with Granada. Giving up the Cerda cause he compromised on Murcia, retaining Alicante and other places north of the Segura in the peace of Agreda (1304). This considerable territory continued to be administered as an annex of Valencia.

These events cleared the way for an enterprise that became rather surprisingly the one major setback of James's reign. In 1308 the kings of Aragon and Castile agreed to take advantage of the failings of Muḥammad III by attacking Granada. The Moorish realm was to be partitioned, with the zone of Almería passing to Aragon in compensation for military support. The Catalan-Aragonese forces converged on Almería by land and sea while Fernando IV's army attacked Algeciras. Both campaigns failed, and the Aragonese were obliged to withdraw with appalling losses. For some time thereafter Valencia suffered raids from Granada as the balance of power seemed, at least morally, to shift. In 1323 James II negotiated peace with the emir Ismāʿīl of Granada.

In North Africa James promoted military and commercial interests, notably in Tunisia, but also, during the Castilian war, in Morocco, and even as far east as Egypt. In 1293 a treaty negotiated with the sultan Khalil rendered the count-king virtually the protector of Christians in the post-crusade Levant. James's third marriage, to Marie de Lusignan in 1315, was designed to enhance this east Mediterranean role, for Marie was a potential heiress to Cyprus and Jerusalem; but this prospect collapsed when she was disinherited in favour of a nephew.

As for Sardinia, where Genoese and Pisan resistance was inevitable, James II bided his time for a quarter century. He was canny enough to see that a campaign confirming his subordination to Boniface VIII would hardly justify the best possible outcome, optimistic enough to put his trust in negotiation. Only in 1322 did he plan an expedition, and then with characteristic care. The Infant Alfons was put in charge of a force of Catalans and Aragonese said to number 15,000 men, a force supported chiefly by Catalonia and Majorca, and welcomed by the Sardinian judge Hug II of Arborea, a descendant of the Catalonian family of Cervera. King James sent the fleet off from the port Fangós (near Tortosa) with a stirring speech (31 May

1323), then stood on the beach with his queen (wrote Muntaner), 'watching [the ships] until they were lost from view'. Arriving in the Gulf of Palmas on 14 June, Alfons received the fealties of many Sardinian lords, then divided his force so as to besiege the castles of Iglesias and Cagliari simultaneously. Iglesias fell in February 1324 but Cagliari resisted with the aid of Pisan reinforcements until 12 July 1324, when peace was made with the Pisans. Made easier by the Sards' contempt for the Pisans, the conquest had taken just a year. Its completion was a signal for the rival Genoese to stir the natives to rebellion. To describe Genoese perfidy, Muntaner asserted, not all the paper made in Játiva would suffice. When the Genoese allied once again with the Pisans, James II had to send another fleet to Sardinia. New uprisings in 1325 postponed a final settlement until June 1326, when Pisa renounced all her rights to Sardinia. James proceeded to organize a new administration of the island, with the main public offices passing to Catalans and Aragonese, who profited from commercial privileges and introduced settlers. Unrest continued, however, for in Sardinia the Catalans had to dominate as colonial masters, like the Angevins in Sicily, and their rule was seldom secure. The conquest of Corsica was put off indefinitely.

James II: Government and Culture

If his grandfather was the great conqueror and his father the great defender of the dynasty, James II was arguably the greatest of its governors. He was a man of piety, prudence, and perseverance. His family life was correct and intense. The love of his life was his second wife, Blanche of Naples (d. 1310), who bore (among many other children) his sons Jaume and Alfons. Her influence countered the Ghibellinism traditional in the Catalan-Aragonese court, opening it to a strong current of Franciscan piety, and Blanche accompanied the king on several of his expeditions. In her lifetime the accords with the Capetians and Angevins held firm; after her death the king used their children, in a manner curiously reminiscent of his grandfather's policy, to create influence in or even claims to Castile. In 1312 his daughter Maria was married to the Infante Pedro, brother of Fernando IV (1295–1312), while Leonor of Castile was entrusted to James II as the future bride of his son Jaume. Yet another son, Joan, was preferred to the archbishopric of Toledo, a post that ensured that Castile would keep no secrets from the count-king. But James could be overbearing with his own kin as with others. He lost touch with his son Jaume, whom he had appointed procurator-general and groomed for the succession. Increasingly eccentric, Jaume balked at the marriage long planned, then bowed to the pressure of his father and the pope, only to flee from his Castilian bride on their wedding-day (1319). He renounced his right to the succession and took vows as a Knight of Saint John. It was a cruel blow to a carefully nurtured Castilian policy. James II now put his hopes in Alfons, who proved his worth in the conquest of Sardinia.

The count-king's international court gave expression to a new conception of the Crown of Aragon as a Mediterranean power. Rejecting the policy of dynastic partition, James II prescribed in the Corts of Tarragona in 1319 that his realms be henceforth indivisible. He insisted on his suzerainty over Majorca, and refused at first to recognize the succession of his cousin's nephew in 1324. Sardinia would be the Crown's like Valencia (and unlike Majorca and Sicily), but if their statutes differed, the overseas lands would be comprehended none the less in a coherent politics. In his old lands James II was attentive to the Aragonese from the first years of his reign. In 1300 he established a university at Lérida, the most central of his cities.

James II loved administration. A contemporary said of him that he sent 'more solemn envoys to the papal court in one year than the kings of France and England in ten!' Through tireless diplomacy he recovered the Val d'Aran from France (1295–1312), dissolved the Templars without losing their property, and secured the homage of Sanç of Majorca in 1321. The pope was persuaded in 1317 to create a new military order of Montesa, to be endowed with the consolidated holdings of the Templars and Hospitallers in Valencia, and with those of the Templars in other lands. In Catalonia the old work of territorial unification was practically completed as the counties of Urgell (in 1314) and Empúries (in 1322) were annexed to the comital patrimony.

The comital-royal court became more professional, with increasingly specialized delegations for the several lands. The least bureaucratic of these charges, perhaps, was the general procuratorship, which the Infant Jaume held before his disgrace, and through which he or occasionally others of like standing had direction of military and judicial affairs of the highest order. Each realm had also its *procurador reial*. Administrative functions of the itinerant court were concentrated in a council (*Consell reial*) comprising the chancellor and his deputy, procurators, treasurer, and secretary. These offices and their scribes managed and registered an administrative correspondence vastly expanded since the early thirteenth century. For most of the reign of James II Ramon Despont, bishop of Valencia (1291–1312), served as chancellor, and Bernat d'Aversó as protonotary in charge of the seals. Each realm continued to have its *maior domus*. The royal household was regulated in ordinances issued first by Peter III and supplemented by his sons; the treasure remained normally itinerant with the count-king. Any of the courtiers might keep his own accounts in an unsimplified system of finance that culminated in the *Mestre Racional*, whose office was instituted for the federation after the conquest of Sicily. In each realm the 'general bailiff' had responsibility for the royal patrimony, which continued to be administered by bailiffs in Catalonia and Valencia and (usually) by *merini* in Aragon. From registers made in the time of James II we can see that the fiscal renders from Catalonia were much increased since the early thirteenth century, and that efforts were being made to total and compare the revenues of the peninsular realms in forms as nearly standard as practical. Administrative justice now culminated in the *Audiència*, presided by the chancellor or vice-chancellor. Local jurisdictions continued as in the past (see above, p. 82), but were subjected to improved curial control.

Nowhere perhaps did James II display his ability to better effect than with the Cort(e)s. By summoning them early, before the estates in the old realms were tempted to act on their own, and by working through them, the count-king defused political opposition. By precedent and statute (1283) the Cort(e)s were now institutions, subject, indeed, to annual summons. Yet they were not summoned, after James's inaugural celebrations, from 1292 to 1300. In 1301 the Catalans allowed their statute to be made triennial, a periodicity not too badly observed during the rest of the reign; in 1307 James arbitrarily altered the Aragonese privilege so as to require biennial assemblies, apparently without demur, and in this case clearly without observing the interval thereafter. But in both realms (the Corts of Valencia were hardly yet an institutional force) the count-king's careful agreement to regard the Cort(e)s as having custody of the privileges enabled him to preserve the assembly as a royalist celebration, and so to preserve the political initiative. A custom of the summons and of attendance took form in the later thirteenth century. In Catalonia and Valencia men of the clergy, the barons, and the towns were now regularly convoked; in Aragon, where the lesser baronage was summoned distinctly from the *ricos hombres*, the clergy were included only from 1301. In both Catalonia and Aragon the increasing solemnity of the notarial record, incorporating letters of summons together with summations of procedure, points to a new recognition of the Cort(e)s as a celebration of the associated powers of king and estates. The assemblies met in order to treat of the 'reformation and conservation of justice and peace', to approve statutes, and to vote taxes for justified reasons. A delegation of assembled men first appears in 1289 in the general Cort(e)s of Monzón, with the charge of collecting the subsidy there voted (see below, p. 118).

For all the king's solicitude for the federation and for the customs of each realm, there can be no doubt that Catalans dominated the expansion of the Crown of Aragon. West Mediterranean trade—grain from Sicily, salt and silver from Sardinia, cloth from Catalonia—fell increasingly into Catalan hands. When Peter III founded the 'Consulate of the Sea' at Valencia in 1283–4, he referred to Barcelona's existing *Consolat del Mar* as his model. The consulates were guild courts devised to expedite maritime cases at law. A similar consulate was established in Majorca in 1326; but men of Barcelona had long since organized consulates or colonies in Italian, African, and Levantine towns. The wars of Sicily and Greece were fought chiefly by the *almogàvers*, whose speech was Catalan. Even when the Aragonese had a hand in campaigns, as notably in Sardinia, the settlers who followed spoke Catalan. What is more, the leading figures in culture and learning were also Catalans writing in Catalan: the Franciscan writer and missionary Ramon Lull (*c.*1232–1315), the physician Arnau de Vilanova (*c.*1238–40–1311), the chroniclers Desclot (d. 1288) and Muntaner (1265–1336). James II seems to have patronized Lull and Vilanova chiefly for their usefulness in his affairs at the papal

court, although he was surely influenced by Lull's religious views
and probably encouraged the friar's flickering scheme to convert
the Muslims of Tunis. Lull also served in the royal court of
Majorca. Arnau de Vilanova was especially valued for his
knowledge of medicine, a subject to which James II was
passionately devoted; the count-king encouraged the study of
Avicenna and translations of other medical works from Arabic.
The king's cultural interests were not exclusively Catalan, it is
true. He sponsored a Latin translation of his grandfather's
chronicle and we happen to know that in 1314–15 he sought a
copy of Livy (presumably in Latin) of which he had heard as well
as a book of crusading legends translated from French into
Castilian. Earlier he had read and written verses in Provençal.
Lull and Vilanova wrote in Latin as well as Catalan, and in other
languages. The university at Lérida was promoted vigorously as
a multinational centre for the Latin curricula in arts, the two
laws, and medicine.

Nevertheless, Catalan had come to be the common vernacular
of the confederation, an expression of Catalonian dominance in
diplomacy and trade as much as of royal patronage. So it is not
surprising that the count-kings began to identify themselves
dynastically as Catalans. James I, his son, and his grandsons
were all buried in Catalonia, and James II took special pains in
building his father's tomb at Santes Creus. Moreover, there is
some indication that he came in his later years to share in the
dynastic pride exuded by Muntaner, a pride not so much
politically as culturally Catalan. James had spent his life in the
international lists. He had married into the houses of Anjou and
Cyprus. He had struggled to reconcile his dynastic interest with
Castile's. When at last he planned the conquest of Sardinia he
appears to have felt new confidence in his achievements and
prospects. In 1322 he took for his fourth bride no foreign princess
but Elicsenda de Montcada, a scion of the prestigious baronial
lineage identified with the valorous conquest of Majorca a
century before. It was a programmatic assertion of Catalonian
patriotism. Elicsenda stood beside the king at Portfangós as he
sent forth his fleet to another conquest.

Alphonse IV (III in Catalonia, 1327–1336)

Seldom had a king a worthier or more accomplished son to

succeed him than had James II in Alphonse. The hero of
Sardinia had demonstrated piety and fidelity as well as competence, he was well married to Teresa d'Entença who had
already borne him the sons with whom the future lay, and his
accession was greeted with singular enthusiasm. Muntaner
attended the coronation at Zaragoza as a citizen-deputy for
Valencia and left an incomparable description of the celebration
to close his chronicle. Yet the short reign of this 'good Alphonse'
was filled with disappointment.

It was not for lack of vision or energy on his part. When his
wife died in 1327 (a few days before the old king's death),
Alphonse arranged to marry Leonor of Castile, the very lady
formerly spurned by his brother Jaume on his wedding day. The
marriage, celebrated at Tarazona in 1329, was connected with a
renewal of the Castilian alliance directed to the conquest of
Granada. An international campaign was concerted with the
pope, the kings of France and Bohemia, and other princes. But
it came to nothing. Alphonse hesitated when Alfonso XI of
Castile negotiated a peace with Muhammad IV of Granada in
1331 and when he saw that the pope was willing to commit a
much more lucrative crusading tithe to France than to Aragon.
The count-king's own health was deteriorating, while the first
signs of economic troubles in his lands were becoming evident
(see below, p. 183). Perhaps most disruptive was the behaviour
of Leonor of Castile, who tried to endow her own sons by
Alphonse IV at the expense of her stepson Pere. To evade the act
of union, which prohibited the partition of the realms, the king
was induced to create a marquisate of Tortosa for Leonor's son
Fernando, a cession soon amplified by additional domains in
Valencia. The Infant Pere, who was already thirteen, became the
focus of a strong reaction that led his father to reconsider.
Following a dramatic confrontation between the Valencians and
the king and queen, the donations were revoked. But the seeds of
new conflict with Castile had been sown.

The Conqueror's dynasty had done well. In the time of his
grandson James II, the Crown of Aragon became the foremost
power in the Mediterranean. Its polity was defined and was
accepted by foreign principalities, it prospered economically and
culturally. But the *rayonnement* was the work of all these kings, of

James's father, brothers, sons, and cousins as well as himself;
there was, one might almost say, not a bad apple among them. If
James of Majorca and Frederick of Sicily were crown-starved
eccentrics, they were none the less men of character who won the
loyalties of their peoples and the trust of James of Aragon. There
is a sense in which the meridional ideal of patrimonial
condominium can be said to have persisted in these grand years
when the kings of Majorca contributed to expeditions against
Almería and Sardinia or the impetuous Frederick of Sicily
carried on ungrateful struggles against old dynastic enemies with
whom James II had felt compelled to compromise. Such was
evidently Muntaner's perspective when he traced the merits of
the kings of Aragon, Majorca, and Sicily to their descent from
James the Conqueror.

But there is another perspective on the age to be found in this
most ingratiating and observant of patriots. Muntaner's life
perfectly spanned the years since the marriage of Constance of
Hohenstaufen to the Infant Pere had opened a new destiny to the
Crown of Aragon. The chronicler knew at first hand almost every
imposing event and enterprise of his years. Born in Old
Catalonia where his house at Peralada may have been destroyed
by the French in 1285, he travelled with the Infant Pere's Sicilian
admirals as a young man. He was at Montpellier in 1281, in
Majorca when the campaign of 1286–7 was carried out, then
again as citizen in 1298–1300, before going to Sicily. From there
he accompanied the Catalan Company to Greece, acting as their
manager, and fighting with them. Returning to Sicily he served
King Frederick as governor of the Tunisian islands of Gharbi
and Kerkenna (1309–15), with an intervening furlough to marry
in Valencia (1311); then settled in Valencia in 1316, whence he
organized a local contingent for the Sardinian expedition.
Having begun his chronicle at his Valencian farm of Xirivella in
1325, Muntaner engaged in the cloth trade and was elected (and
re-elected) jurate of Valencia. In 1332 he and his wife moved to
Majorca, where he served as chamberlain to James III and as
bailiff of Ibiza. He died in Ibiza in 1336.

Of such a wanderer we may conclude that he seldom if ever left
home. His world was an expanded Catalonia, a tidewater Crown
of Aragon, in which he never lacked for agreeable employers in
need of his managerial skills. Among the foreigners Muntaner

admired were Ruggiero di Loria and his companions, of whom people said (he noted) that they spoke 'the most beautiful Catalan . . . in the world'. It was distance—and the sea—that nurtured such an outlook, a colonial outlook doubtless widely shared by the merchants whom the count-kings and the island-kings protected and taxed. Muntaner retired to Valencia, yet he was too engaging and lively to be left alone. In the end he returned to his beloved islands. The Crown of Aragon was made for men like him.

V

Peter the Ceremonious and his Sons
(1336–1410)

DURING the long reign of Peter IV (III in Catalonia, 1336–87), the Crown of Aragon reached it apogee as a federative state. The achievement owed much to the ruler once again, for it required a stubborn insistence on dynastic right to prevent Majorca, Sardinia, and Sicily from spinning off into irreversible and abrasive independence. More clearly than his ancestors Peter IV came to view these lands as integrally bound up with Catalonia, Aragon, and Valencia, which he inhabited and traversed as a composite homeland. Yet if it proved the strength people then allowed to dynastic fortune, Peter's reign none the less illustrated its fragility. Every perilous event of the reign was connected with marriage and its issue, with familial claims to land, with the want of heirs when needed or (in the case of Majorca) with their unwelcome survival. That Peter overcame his more tangible difficulties was not, however, due solely to dynastic luck. His settlements with his subjects and enemies confirmed a new order of privileged societies in his peninsular realms as well as a *convivencia* that his sons John I and Martin were fortunate to inherit. Other difficulties—social and economic—lay deeper, beyond the means if not entirely out of sight of these rulers.

The Reconquest of Majorca (1341–1349)

Born at Balaguer in 1319, Peter was the second son of the Infant Alfons, then count (-consort) of Urgell, and Teresa d'Entença. He was weaned on his father's pre-regnal triumphs and educated by his subsequent struggles and set-backs. Peter had clashed with his stepmother at the age of thirteen. So he began to reign, at sixteen, with lofty aspirations. He insisted on crowning himself in an otherwise traditional ceremony at Zaragoza, thus rejecting papal pretensions founded on the precedent of 1204, and disappointing the archbishop of Zaragoza. But it was a characteristic gesture, and the king no doubt spoke truthfully when he later recorded that it had cost him some distress. On the eve of the second-longest reign in their history, the peoples of the Crown of Aragon had a resolute and reflective king to obey.

Peter had first to face the pressures of privilege. By convoking his inaugural Cort for the Catalans at Lérida, he offended the men of Barcelona, who protested that 'it had been customary at all times to swear and confirm the *Usatges* and *Constitucions* there'. The king's excuse was that Lérida was on his way to Valencia, where he felt equally obliged to hold court, confirm the customs, and receive the fealties. He was even more concerned, we may be sure, about his stepmother's machinations in Valencia and Aragon. When pressed by the Castilians to confirm his father's donations to her sons, Peter had temporized; then in Valencia he moved to confiscate the queen's revenues and to prosecute her protector, Pedro de Ejérica. The latter, however, had Aragonese supporters who could only be overcome by an effort Peter could not then make. It would have antagonized Castile at a moment when Valencia and Castile alike were threatened by a new Moorish invasion from Morocco. In 1338 Peter agreed to leave the dowager-queen and his half-brothers in possession of their domains. In 1339 he allied with Castile against the Moroccans, contributing a fleet to the cause, but he had no direct part in the defeat of Abū al-Ḥassan at the Salado in October 1340. By that time Peter was distracted by disorders in Sardinia and, more urgently, by the matter of Majorca.

James III (1324–43, d. 1349), having succeeded his uncle Sanç as king of Majorca, had married a sister of Peter IV. He had done homage for his lands to James II and Alphonse IV according to the old protocol. But when his brother-in-law came to power in Aragon and Catalonia James balked, twice postponing his obligatory profession of vassalage before performing it, as nearly on his own terms as possible, in 1339. These refusals angered Peter more than is easily understood, but perhaps fundamentally because the *de facto* independence of Majorca was becoming diplomatically and economically burdensome to Catalonia. James had allied with Morocco among other enemies of the count-king. The merchants of Majorca were prospering at the expense of Barcelona, developing markets and colonies throughout the western Mediterranean and securing independent privileges for them. With her own gold coinage

Majorca could pretend to a prestigious parity with the city-states of Italy and with France. Peter IV could not easily abide signs that the pope and the king of France treated Majorca, with its flourishing annexes of Roussillon-Cerdanya and Montpellier, as an independent power.

Having alienated Peter, James III was foolish enough to anger his other overlord—and only effective ally against Peter—Philip VI of France. He disputed French suzerainty over Montpellier, and when the French threatened to attack, was obliged to call on Peter for aid. The latter astutely seized the moment to summon James to a Cort at Barcelona, and when James failed to appear—and it is clear from his own account that Peter expected this failure—he lost the protection of feudal custom. A process at law was carefully and cynically prepared; it alleged James's coinage in Roussillon as infringing on the exclusive right of the ternal money of Barcelona to circulate in the principality of Catalonia. Pope Clement VI secured for James a hearing at Barcelona in the presence of papal emissaries, while Peter encouraged people to think that his brother-in-law was plotting to dispossess him. In February 1343 Peter solemnly proclaimed James a contumacious vassal; the kingdom of Majorca and the counties of Roussillon and Cerdanya were declared confiscate; and James was to be regarded as an enemy of the realm. In May a Catalonian fleet, well supported by Barcelona, landed in Majorca, which soon capitulated. It is clear that James's unpopularity in the islands contributed to this result: he had taxed so heavily that Peter could pretend to have come 'like a doctor, to heal and cure the wounds of injured and afflicted men'. But there were many who resisted, while in Roussillon and Cerdanya an altogether more stubborn opposition prolonged the confiscation for another year. James and the pope pleaded with Peter to no avail. In 1344 James surrendered to Peter, only to discover that nothing remained to him but harsh captivity or the status of a minor noble. Escaping, he continued to resist, sold the lordship of Montpellier to France, and was killed in 1349 in a vain attempt to recover Majorca.

The reconquest had, in a sense, come none too soon. Ceasing to be an apanage, Majorca had become a realm in the fourteenth century, with her stately palaces at Majorca city and Perpignan. Her kings, whatever their failings, had learned to govern rather than exploit. Peter IV himself understood this, making the remarkable admission in 1347 that 'most of the men of Roussillon and Conflent and of all the other land that we have taken from him [James III] love and desire him'. A vassal kingdom was thus revealed to be an impossibility: one responded to one's 'natural lord', not to an overlord. So Peter took seriously the task of re-integrating the confiscated lands in his Crown of Aragon. He confirmed the privileges of Majorca city as these had been first granted by James I. He assumed ceremoniously the crown of Majorca rather than suppressing it. And he declared with the approval of general assemblies that the kingdom of Majorca together with Roussillon and Cerdanya was inseparably annexed to 'our crown'.

The Crisis of the Unions

Title to this crown, however, remained clouded as long as Peter IV lacked a son to inherit. His first wife, María of Navarre, had borne him only daughters, encouraging his brother Jaume to hope that he might succeed. In 1347 Peter muddied the waters by proposing to designate his daughter Constança heiress, winning some but by no means unanimous support from a conference of lawyers and prelates at Valencia. When María then gave birth to a son there was great rejoicing, but this sentiment turned at once to sorrow when the infant died, followed a few days later by his mother. Peter understandably lost no time arranging a second marriage, this time with Leonor of Portugal, but the genie of intrigue was out. Prince Jaume, having been forced to resign his procuratorship, formed a baronial party in Aragon to which his half-brothers adhered, a party that professed to unite in defence of the laws of the realm. King Peter thereupon prevailed on Pedro de Ejérica, at that time his governor of Valencia, to mobilize a royalist movement in opposition. But the revived *Unión* gained momentum, enlisting most of the Aragonese towns as well as a Valencian union, and this formidable coalition pressed the king to meet them in Cortes at Zaragoza.

When this assembly met in late summer 1347, Peter was forced, rather like his great namesake in 1283, to capitulate completely. His own subsequent account of the proceedings makes fascinating reading, not least for its revelation that the

estates were so wary of his political finesse as to prohibit all
negotiations between individuals and the king. They could not
prevent Peter's Catalan minister Bernat de Cabrera from
organizing on the king's behalf, and for a time it seemed that a
royalist reaction in Catalonia might be the king's salvation. This
prospect collapsed in a bitter confrontation, wherein Peter
accused Jaume of treachery. To escape imprisonment the king
yielded to the unionist demands, adjourned the Cortes, and
returned to Catalonia delighted, as he put it, to be 'delivered [by
God] out of a rebellious and wicked country'.

Worse storms lay ahead. Jaume's sudden death in Barcelona
in November was of little help to Peter, not so much because
rumour attributed the event to poison as because Jaume's
leadership of the rebels passed to the disaffected half-brother
Fernando, who could muster Castilian support. Before the year
1347 was out the reinforced royalists in Valencia had suffered
military defeat. As civil war spread in the western realms Peter
was obliged again to yield, recognizing Fernando as his heir,
appointing him governor in Valencia, and consenting to institute
a Valencian *justicia* on the Aragonese model. But the moral force
of the revolt was spent. Defeated and virtually imprisoned in
Valencia, Peter IV none the less managed to turn the tables on
his foes in the summer of 1348. When the Black Death struck in
May, the unionists, themselves dispersing in alarm, left the king
free to leave Valencia. Cabrera had roused the Catalans to
support him, Alfonso XI of Castile proved sympathetic, and in
July Peter combined his forces under Lope de Luna and won a
decisive victory over the *Unión*. Many of the rebel leaders were
killed or imprisoned, Prince Fernando himself was wounded and
taken to Castile by Peter's Castilian auxiliaries, and the banners
of the *Unión* were displayed in Epila as trophies.

The *Uniónes* thereupon dissolved in a powerful reaction. The
men of Zaragoza put themselves at the king's service, joined by
others from Calatayud, Daroca, and Teruel, inviting the king to
do justice in a general pacification. In a Cortes held at Zaragoza
in October the king not only reaffirmed his authority in Aragon
but expressed his emotion in a ritual savaging of the *Unión's*
records and seal, the documents being publicly burnt in the
Dominicans' refectory. Peter then swore to uphold the *fueros*
and privileges of Aragon. He granted amnesty (with some

exceptions), recognized that the governor of Aragon should be an Aragonese of knightly rank, and defined more precisely the powers of the *Justicia*, who was from this time forward effectively the defender of Aragonese liberties. It remained to deal with Valencia, where the rebels held out until defeated by a royalist force on 10 December. Here Peter's anger was less easily appeased. Valencian privileges were revoked, some rebel leaders were cruelly executed (being forced, by the king's account, to swallow the molten metal of the unionists' melted bell), and Peter destroyed the unionist records as he had done in Aragon.

It was a troubled victory. Peter's first wife had died in childbirth in 1347, his second died of plague barely a year later. Only in 1350 was the consolidation of the Crown of Aragon completed (and a main cause of the past revolt removed) by the birth of a male heir to the king's third wife Eleanor of Sicily. Economic misfortune had preceded the Black Death: the 'first bad year' in 1333, then the 'year of the great hunger' (1347) which conceivably weakened resistance to the appalling disease that struck Majorca, Barcelona, and Valencia in May 1348 and swept inland. The Plague diminished later that year, but revived each summer until 1351, and hit yet again—especially children —in 1362.

Wars Against Genoa

Peter IV was soon caught up in more costly and less successful wars. In Sardinia trouble had smouldered since the conquest. The native Judges of Arborea struggled to establish an autonomous sphere of power while Catalan officials imposed themselves heavy-handedly on the populace and the Judges alike. In 1347 they had suffered a defeat at the hands of Mariano IV of Arborea, who allied with the Oria and Malaspina families and called in the Genoese. In 1351 Peter IV raised the stakes by allying with the Venetians against Genoa. In 1352 a massive coalition, including Byzantine forces and Catalans in Greece, defeated the Genoese in the Bosphorus, but at excessive cost. When Pope Clement VI intervened to make peace, Peter insisted that the overlordship of Corsica be effectively restored to the pope. The war continued in 1353, when a massive new campaign was led by Bernat de Cabrera. The Catalans won a major victory in Sardinian waters in August, virtually destroying the Genoese

fleet; yet the effort to secure Alghero foundered in a new revolt by
Mariano IV. Only in 1354 did yet another expedition, led this
time by King Peter himself, succeed in capturing Alghero after a
long siege. But Peter's return to Barcelona was a hollower
triumph than his father's had been. Mariano IV was now
irremediably antagonized, and while he would give in to force, he
maintained his pretensions until his death in 1368. The years of
disorder had ruined northern Sardinia. Catalan settlers were
lured to Alghero in large numbers after the campaign of
1354—their language is still spoken there—but the count-king
had great difficulty in resettling the rest of Sardinia or even
mobilizing sufficient force to secure his administration. After
1368 successive Judges, often aided by the Genoese, made life
miserable for the Catalans. Exports of wheat declined, leaving
salt the main source of profit to a colonial administration
virtually reduced to Alghero and Cagliari.

The inability to secure Sardinia or, worse, to make it profitable
undercut Peter's whole Mediterranean policy. Sardinia and
Sicily were granaries for Majorca and Barcelona, and we know
from the king's own words that he believed in 1380 that the loss
of Sardinia would be an economic disaster. Better to hold it at all
costs than not, and if the Sardinians themselves had replaced the
Genoese as Peter's west Mediterranean foes, the exchange was
not unwelcome to Catalan merchants and mariners. With Sicily
Peter IV was more fortunate and arguably more canny. Here he
had little more to work with than a reversionary claim in the
event of failure in the male line of royal descent. He was aware of
Catalanist factional sentiment when he married Eleanor of Sicily
in 1349, but was too distracted elsewhere to exploit the
favourable opening thus offered. Not even the marriage of
his daughter Constança to King Frederick (1361) seemed to
improve Catalonian prospects, for Frederick took some interest
in preventing the devolution of Sicily and Romania to Aragon.
When subsequently Constança's daughter Maria was declared
heiress to Sicily and the duchies, the question of her marriage
became criticial. Peter had attempted to circumvent the problem by claiming the whole inheritance for himself, but there
were by this time too many precedents for female succession, to
say nothing of anti-Catalanist sentiment among the Sicilian
barons, for this to come about. Sending his own naval force to

Sicily in 1378, Peter was induced by the turmoil and resistance he encountered to transfer his claim to his second son, Martí, who would serve as viceroy in Sicily; but it required a second expedition in 1382 and the defeat of a Milanese fleet to discourage a proposed Visconti marriage for Maria. She was sent to Catalonia, where Peter hoped in his last years to see her married to his son Joan, thereby reuniting Sicily with his Crown lands. In the end she married Martí, the son of Peter's second son Martí, with consequences to which we shall return.

The *rapprochement* with Sicily entailed a new relation with the Catalan duchies in Greece. Nominally subject to the crown of Sicily, these had proved of little economic value to their western compatriots, who left them increasingly isolated. They were ill-governed and vulnerable when in 1379–80 Peter IV assumed their direction and protection. By then it was too late for anything less than a vigorous intervention such as Peter was unwilling to make. The duchies collapsed during the next decade, Athens falling into Florentine hands in 1386–8, while Neopatria and Salona held out to 1391 and 1394 respectively. Only the island of Aegina remained under Catalan rule until 1451. Failure to insist on the Romanian domination was quite in keeping with Peter's stress on the western Mediterranean. While not neglecting Catalan-speaking merchants in Egypt and the Levant and mindful of the needs of Christians, the count-king was none the less careful to avoid active commitments to their protection in eastern waters.

The Castilian War

The redirection and limiting of Mediterranean interests was in some part the result of new problems in Spain. One might almost contend that the second marriage of Alphonse IV had put an end to any possibility of basing the Crown of Aragon on insular resources and maritime power. It revived the dynastic involvement with Castile that had been essayed in previous centuries with mixed results. It created apanages for Castilian princes in Catalonia and Valencia and, when these were resisted by powerful elements in the eastern peninsula, the prospect of renewed conflict in the borderlands. Even more ominously, it encouraged strong kings of Castile to try and re-establish the quasi-imperial domination of Spain first projected by Alfonso VI in the eleventh century. Castile had never reconciled itself to the Aragonese possession of Alicante and Murcia in 1304. Alfonso XI regarded his sister Leonor's Aragonese marriage as a useful wedge for Castilian expansion in the south-east, and later encouraged his nephew Fernando's aggressions. Peter IV continued to insist on his Murcian rights even as Fernando and Alfonso XI sided with the unionists in 1347–8. Peter IV's struggle with his Castilian kin was virtually repeated in reverse when Pedro ('the Cruel', 1350–69) succeeded his father in Castile at the expense of his own half-brothers. Pedro pressed his inherited ambitions with unscrupulous and pitiless energy. The war that broke out in 1356 consumed his reign and destroyed him in the end; yet it cannot be maintained that this terrible war of the two Peters was any less catastrophic for the Crown of Aragon than for Castile.

It was touched off by a characteristically virulent exchange between the kings. Having witnessed a Catalan assault on ships bearing Genoese goods, Pedro demanded reparation from Peter IV, who promptly rejected the bid and gathered his forces. As Castilian galleys attacked the Balearics, Peter IV negotiated for the service of Enrique de Trastámara (Pedro's bastard brother) to whom he ceded an important complex of domains in Catalonia and Valencia. At the outset both kings overestimated their resources and capabilities. The first fighting took place in March 1357, when Pedro of Castile seized Tarazona. The count-king viewed this as a betrayal, not only because his lieutenant did little to resist the Castilian attack, but also because the cardinal-legate Guillaume de la Jugie had already tried to arrange peace with the kings at Zaragoza. Peter IV executed several of the Tarazonans who came to him, but in the face of a threat to Zaragoza he agreed to a truce (May 1357) whereby title to Tarazona would be decided by the legate. During this respite the count-king moved shrewdly to strengthen his position in Valencia, enticing his half-brother Fernando into his own service against Castile and appointing him procurator-general of his realms 'as is customary to do with the crown-prince of Aragon'. Fernando lost no time recovering Murcian lands previously seized by his cousin, the frontier of Valencia and Murcia having been omitted from the truce. Meanwhile, the dowager-queen Leonor's party in Castile had been caught in machinations that so enraged Pedro that he ordered her nephews Frederick and Tello executed, and finally executed Leonor herself.

The truce (such as it was) gave way in 1358 to an exchange of thrusts in the borderlands of Aragon and Valencia. Pedro of Castile tried to establish naval superiority without much success, while his foe pressed into Castile as far as Medinaceli (January 1359), lifting the siege for lack of fire-power and victuals. Returning to Zaragoza, Peter IV learned of a Castilian fleet preparing to attack Majorca. He organized a frontier garrison under Prince Fernando, Enrique de Trastámara, and Pedro d'Ejérica, and arrived himself in Barcelona none too soon to rally the townspeople to defend the city against a bold attack commanded by Pedro in person. The Castilian fleet numbered some forty ships and thirty galleys. Peter IV himself told vividly of one of the historic sieges in the Crown's annals. Invoking the *usatge Princeps namque*, the count-king called out the guildsmen and territorial villagers; his men fired with bows and trebuchets from their ships drawn up in the sand-bar, while the shore-folk beached their boats keels outward against the invaders. Unable to break the defences, Pedro of Castile withdrew to Tortosa, whence a ravaging expedition to Ibiza was all his fleet could salvage of the expedition.

This ill-conceived exploit was a gift to Peter IV's cause. It proved the war's urgency in his Catalonian heartlands at a time when the western borderland fighting was proving the count-king a poor match for Castile in manpower and wealth. In autumn 1359 Peter IV prevailed on a Corts at Barcelona to offer an important financial subsidy for the war. For his part Enrique de Trastámara was having mixed success on the frontier, but he succeeded in recapturing Tarazona. By 1361 Peter IV had mustered force enough to think of neutralizing Enrique and Fernando, his overpowerful allies. In the peace of Deca (18 May 1361) the Catalan minister Bernat de Cabrera agreed with Pedro that all conquests to date be restored, stipulating that Peter IV withhold further support from Enrique and Fernando. Pedro of Castile put the truce to good use, overthrowing his adversary's ally Abū-Saʿīd of Granada in 1362.

By this time the White Companies of France, thrown out of work by the peace of Brétigny (1360), threatened to cross the Pyrenees, giving Pedro the excuse for a complicated new alliance with the kings of Portugal and Navarre, the count of Foix, and Gascon lords; but instead of defending Spain he invaded Aragon over much of its frontier. Catalayud fell after a long siege in September 1362. Caught unprepared, Peter IV mobilized with difficulty, while his enemies continued to advance in 1363, threatening Zaragoza. Once again the count-king rallied a Corts (Monzón, February 1363) in brave words: 'while God has not made us great in person, yet we are as great in heart and will as any knight in the world, to die or to live to defend our crown and our realm'. We now face such a disaster, he added, that 'what took 500 years to conquer we may lose in fifteen days!' The Catalans voted a subsidy of 270,000 l. and organized another army, an effort sufficient to deflect the Castilians southward, where they menaced Valencia again. It was time for a fresh intervention by the papal envoy, leading to the peace of Murviedro (July 1363). Peter IV felt obliged to concede most of the Castilian seizures in Aragon, recovering only Calatayud, Teruel, and Tarazona in the form of a dowry for a projected marriage between Pedro of Castile and the Infanta Joana of Aragon. The Valencian conquests were to pass to Peter IV's (infant) son Alfonso if he would marry Isabel of Castile.

This 'peace', depending so much as it did on the good intentions of faithless kings, was worthless. It required Enrique de Trastámara and Fernando of Aragon (again) to set aside their pretensions, although the former had lately secured Peter IV's promise of support for a full-scale conquest of the crown of Castile. Amidst the intrigues that followed the count-king lost control of a situation he could restore only by doing to death both Fernando and his minister Bernat de Cabrera. Pedro threatened Valencia yet again, but was driven off in April 1364. He continued to harass Aragon, recapturing Teruel among other places. At this time Peter IV was organizing a more stable coalition including Enrique, Charles the Bad of Navarre, and the White Companies led by Bertrand du Guesclin. The stakes shifted as the Castilian alliance with England effectively brought the dynastic war in France to the peninsula. The suspicious death of Pedro's queen Isabel of Bourbon in 1361 encouraged the French to support Peter IV, whose grand campaign in 1366 had almost the aura of a crusade. Joined by many French knights and financed by Charles V and Pope Urban V, who were doubtless even more interested in the pacification of France than in punishing Pedro, the Companies were sumptuously received in Barcelona by Peter IV, who paid them himself to continue into Castilian lands. The campaign became a triumphant military procession, forcing Pedro to take refuge in Seville, and then to flee to Bordeaux. For the Aragonese it was enough to reclaim the frontier lands their enemies had come to call 'New Castile'. Enrique de Trastámara was proclaimed king of Castile at Burgos on 5 April 1366.

It was a costly way to rid Aragon of the Castilians, for Enrique refused then and later to honour the terms by which Peter IV should have certain Castilian lands in return for his support. Murcia was irretrievably lost. Having paid and fought to exhaustion, the Aragonese, Catalans, and Valencians could only stand by while the Castilian drama was played out. The ousted Pedro struck up his own bargain for mercenary support from the Black Prince, whose campaign in 1367 drove Enrique in turn from Spain. The danger that Pedro might turn against Aragon was ended when he foolishly antagonized his allies; and when the Prince and Charles of Navarre joined the Aragonese the way was cleared for Enrique to return to Castile. Pedro retained strongholds, however, and the land was disputed for a time between his forces and those of Aragon, with both sides bargaining for external support, when in March 1369 Enrique defeated his brother at Montiel and murdered him. Hostilities dragged on, for Peter IV clung to the Castilian border town of Molina like a last straw, and later allied with Portugal and Navarre against Enrique II. He had also to contend with another head of the Majorcan hydra in the person of Jaume (IV), whom he had long held in captivity after his father's death in 1349, but who had escaped in 1362, married Joanne of Naples, and sided with Pedro of Castile against Aragon. Having been captured by Enrique at Burgos, he was ransomed by his wife, and in 1374 was stirring up support among dissident knights in Catalonia. His attempt to reconquer Roussillon and Cerdanya failed in 1375 and Jaume escaped to Castile, dying at Soria soon afterwards. A final settlement with Castile was reached in treaties at Almazán (12 April 1374) and Lérida (10 May 1375). Peter IV gave up Molina (as well as Murcia, of which nothing was said) in exchange for an indemnity of 180,000 florins and Aragonese territorial integrity.

In a further stipulation of transcendent if unforeseen importance, the Infanta Elionor of Aragon was betrothed to Juan of Trastámara.

With this settlement Peter IV's worst troubles were past. His chronicle virtually ended with the Castilian wars, although he lived for many years after the last events he recorded. His third wife, Eleanor of Sicily, having borne him the sons who would succeed him, died in 1375. She was a forceful presence in the court, becoming the king's chief adviser after the fall of Bernat de Cabrera, whom she had pitilessly opposed. Her marriage, like Peter's previous ones, had been arranged with dynastic politics in view, and it was some indication of the king's own sense of having reached tranquil waters that he neither hurried to remarry after her death nor aimed high when he chose. Yet his fourth marriage proved no less eventful than his third. He took as mistress Sibilla de Fortià, the widowed daughter of a minor baron of the Empordà, then married her solemnly in October 1377. She had already borne him a daughter, she had set up her own *casa* with her endowment and servants; and as she rose to queenly respectability in her domineering way, the seeds of renewed courtly dissension were sown. Her fondness for the lately amplified palaces made Barcelona the king's preferred residence in his last years. There Sibilla de Fortià invited her friends and relatives, placing the sons of penurious Empordan gentry in administrative and ecclesiastical posts. She used her mother and especially her brother Bernat, who became the king's chamberlain, to wrest influence from the older aristocracy of court. This behaviour antagonized the princes Joan and Martí, who absented themselves conspicuously from the ceremonious Cortes at Zaragoza (January 1381) where Sibilla was crowned queen—an unprecedented consecration of her social 'arrival' and that, accordingly, of her class.

These events likewise fanned the discontent of Count Joan of Empordà, at once the king's cousin and son-in-law, into a virtual civil war. No holder of a county that had so long and proudly kept its autonomy could easily defer to insolent knights who were his natural vassals; and when Bernat de Fortià was charged to break his resistance, Joan of Empúries called on Gascon and Provençal barons, and even the king's son Joan, to battle the

A. Acts of the synod of Jaca
(1063). Archivo Capitular, Huesca.
(Photograph: Instituto Amatller de
Arte Hispánico.)

B. San Juan de la Peña, portal
the upper church (ninth and
eleventh centuries).

II. A. Sant Quirze de Pedret (tenth to twelfth centuries).

II. B. Chapel of Bernat Marcús, Barcelona (*c.*1166–1170). (Photograph: Instituto Amatller de Arte Hispánico.)

III. A. Musicians: capital sculpture, cloister of Santa Maria de l'Estany (twelfth century).

III. B. Poblet, cloister (twelfth and thirteenth centuries). (Photograph: Instituto Amatller de Arte Hispánico.)

IV. A. King James I and the conquest of Majorca (thirteenth century). Museu d'Art de Catalunya.

IV. B. King James I and his men capture Valencia (late thirteenth or early fourteenth century). Alcañiz castle.

V. Santa Maria del Mar, Barcelona (fourteenth century).

VI. Major Palace (*Palau Reial Major*) of Barcelona (fourteenth to sixteenth centuries). (Photograph: Reuss.)

A. Billon diner of Alfonso I of Aragon (1104–1134). Wt. 0.73 g. The obverse shows the royal bust in profile, with ANFVS REX as legend. The reverse shows a cross on a foliate base, symbolizing the 'living wood' of the cross, with ARA GON across.

B. Billon diner of Peter II (I of Barcelona, 1196–1213). Wt. 1.02 g. The obverse shows a long cross with an annulet in each quarter, and PETR' RE:X: as legend. The reverse shows a cross, with a circle at its centre, and the legend BAR-CINONA.

C. Silver croat of Alphonse III (II of Barcelona, 1285–1291). Wt. 3.15 g. The obverse shows the royal bust in profile, with ALFOSVS DEI GRACIA REX as legend. The reverse shows a long cross, with an annulet and three pellets in alternate quarters, and the legend CIVITAS BACKNONA.

D. Gold florin of Peter IV (III of Barcelona, 1336–1387) minted at Perpignan. Wt. 3.46 g. Both the obverse and reverse types copy those of the gold florin of Florence, a city having Saint John as its patron saint and the lily (*flos*) as a punning allusion to its name. But while the obverse legend remains S IOHAN-NES B (for *Baptista*) the reverse one has ARAGO REX P instead of FLOREN-TIA. The privy mark by Saint John's head, a helmet, indicates the mint of Perpignan.

VII. Coins

VIII. A. Sant Vicent Ferrer at prayer: attributed to Pere Huguet or to Pedro Garcia de Benabarre among others

VIII. B. Petitions to the king, *Llibre del Consolat del Mar.* Valencia, Arxiu Municipal. (Photograph: Instituto Amatller

king. Joan's refusal, and finally the queen's as well, to play the part of Leonor of Castile eased the crisis. But the ceremonious king who celebrated his jubilee at Barcelona in 1386 was all but deserted by the old nobles. His plan to annex Sicily had failed when the Infant Joan refused to marry the heiress. Sardinia remained turbulent, the Romanian duchies were collapsing. The royal family could not even agree which of the schismatic popes to recognize, although the king for his part lost nothing in withholding his favour from both claimants. Yet when he died on 5 January 1387 Peter I of Majorca, Sardinia, and Romania, II of Valencia, III of Catalonia, and IV of Aragon was a more numerously titled king than any of his predecessors.

The Reign and the King

Peter IV worked hard at government, if perhaps less compulsively than his grandfather. His vision of an expanding Crown found clear expression in the multiplying registers of his chancery. The governors-general for each land, henceforth retaining authority even in the count-king's presence, assumed bureaucratic character. Early in the reign Peter ordained for the royal household and the chancery, and in 1346 he instituted an archivist whose functions, little changed from those pioneered by Ramon de Caldes in the twelfth century, were now defined explicitly. To these impulses we owe the preservation of one of the greatest secular archives of medieval Europe. Other ordinances dealt with the Crown's naval forces (1354) and fiscal accountancy (1358), the latter serving to strengthen the function of the *Mestre Racional*. Peter IV built new walls at Valencia (1356) and Barcelona (1374), and he rebuilt the palaces at Barcelona, Zaragoza, and Valencia. He promoted universities at Huesca and Perpignan, while taking other steps as well to regain the loyalty of Roussillon after the Majorcan war. Emulating Alfonso the Wise of Castile, he patronized scientific, legal, and historical writing, directing Catalan translations of the *Siete Partidas* and *General estoria*, and improving on the astronomical observations in the *Tablas Alfonsíes*. He also promoted poetical writing, cartography, the revision of maritime law, and translations from Latin, Castilian, French, and other languages into Catalan. Notaries, secretaries, and translators were among his most valued servants. He ruled through *familiares*—knights, prelates and clerks, Jews; seldom barons, save those of his own blood—commended personally to him.

Peter's authoritarian impulses were evident early. He resisted all efforts of the church to impose on him, insisting on control over clerical appointments as well as crowning himself. He proposed to legislate on the Romanist pattern of the *Partidas*, which specified a stronger royal control of castles than was customary in Catalonia. Yet the king's real power declined in the course of the reign. The customs of the original realms made no provision for extended military service or expansionist wars against Christian realms. Unable to match his foes' ability to pay professional soldiers, Peter IV became so reliant on the Corts and Cortes during the Castilian war that he lost the initiative in policy and finance. In 1359 he was obliged to cede judicial supremacy to the Corts of Catalonia in return for a subsidy, and from that time on the *Diputació del General* (as it was later called) functioned as an administrative committee of the Corts. The latter assembly convened some eighteen times during the reign, the Cortes of Aragon fifteen times after 1350, with general Corts of the three peninsular realms meeting three times at Monzón; the sessions often extended to months or even years. Peter's promotion of lesser knights and dependants after 1375 may be understood as a reaction to the preponderance of baronial influence in the Cort(e)s. Similarly motivated by dissatisfaction with the urban oligarchs were the count-king's reforms of the electoral regime in Majorca city (1373) and Barcelona (1386), admitting lesser merchants and artisans to representation in the councils. But these policies were doubtless little more than symptomatic. By the end of the Castilian war the royal patrimony had been dissipated in sales, pledges, and gifts. Thus the ruler who had begun his reign attempting to enhance his prerogative with Castilian law ended up bound by constitutions balanced by foral rights in his peninsular realms.

It is not an easy reign to judge. Measured by his main intentions Peter IV failed in most of his undertakings. Measured by his achievements he was conspicuously successful. Both measures are necessary, together pointing to a singularly complicated interplay of power, circumstance, and ambition—and to the inestimable importance of royal policy and decision-making in this reign. Could Peter have avoided conflict in Aragon had he been more patient or prudent? Could he have avoided the Castilian wars by compromising on Murcia?—or was any such vision of geopolitical reality incompatible with his aggressive nature? The questions epitomize two wars which Peter neither wholly won nor wholly lost, wars of which the first defined a lasting structure of Aragonese aristocratic privilege while the second reduced the crown to financial dependence on the Corts of Catalonia. Neither result being intended, Peter IV was less father than midwife to the mature Cort(e)s of the Crown of Aragon. None before him had 'used' the assemblies as he did; he was one of the great parliamentary speakers of the Middle Ages. And because he claimed such demonstrative responsibility for the events of his reign, Peter and his affairs may be characterized in his own tendentious words and works.

He was moulded curiously of past and present: assiduous, cultivated, pompous, vindictive, militant without a personal taste for combat, he took pride in his divine and dynastic destiny and his public obligation. We owe his *Chronicle* to Peter's passion for self-celebration, although it is not hard to find in it a more specifically justificatory purpose. It was composed mostly in the 1370s, when hostilities with Castile were winding down and when Peter could see (as we have seen) the problems of Majorca, Aragon, Sardinia, and Castile as central matters of his reign. Some of these events, and incidents arising from them, burdened the king's conscience—or might have done so. James III is represented as seditious although it was Peter himself who goaded him to war. The treatment of Bernat de Cabrera's fall is full of dissembling; others shared the private remorse which brought Peter in the end to restore his former minister's confiscated estates to Bernat's grandson in 1381. Perhaps Bernat's least forgivable failing had been to oppose the war with Castile. This war like the others was providential in Peter's view: brought on by the wickedness of Pedro of Castile, it was vindicated by his fall, however unfortunate for Aragon the subsequent betrayals by Enrique de Trastámara. Peter IV wrote for the edification of his successors: that seeing how he had 'passed through divers perils and many wars with powerful enemies, and had been delivered with great honour and victory, [they] should take this as an example'.

Equally revealing of this commemorative inspiration were Peter's patronage and political style. He was the first of his line to conceive of Poblet as a dynastic mausoleum, directing the construction of his own tomb there early in his reign, and later rebuilding the tombs of Alphonse II and James I to form a grandiose setting for his own monument and those of his wives. In 1342 he ordered alabaster statues for the palace at Barcelona representing eleven of the early counts of Barcelona and eight of the count-kings who had reigned in Catalonia down to himself. But Peter IV was less openly Catalanophile than some of his predecessors, promoting something more like a pan-regnal patriotism. The dynastic story, prelude to his *Chronicle*, was told in a *Chronicle of the kings of Aragon and the counts of Barcelona* which, for the first time, attempted to represent the rise of Aragon and Catalonia impartially; the work was produced in Latin, Catalan, and Aragonese. There were ringing appeals to history and destiny in Peter's speeches to the Catalonian Corts, often on the eve of critical decisions. The self-justifying pageantry of his Cort(e)s remained a form of persuasion in itself, although the royalist proposition now figured as an element of debate.

For Peter IV more distinctly than for his predecessors the Cort(e)s gave focus to power, his councils to wisdom. Nothing in his *Chronicle* is more vividly expressed than the record of counsel and consultation; of advisers, *parlaments*, and opinions. We are shown something approaching ministerial responsibility (and loyalty) in the behaviour of the Infant Pere, Bernat de Cabrera, and Queen Eleanor. Among these, only Bernat was genuinely devoted to the royal prerogative, which Peter habitually wielded politically, not arbitrarily; ever insistent on having his way, ever needing to have his way conceded. He was none the less temperamental in action, his manner stemming partly from an imagined sense of physical inferiority, partly from genuine impatience with the interests of others; those who waited on him can have had no illusions as to his cunning, which Peter tried betimes to conceal with legalism. Law served him psychologically, perhaps abstractly: a prop for efficiency not to be confused with associative rights.

John I (1387–1396)

Peter IV was succeeded by well-seasoned sons, ruling in turn. Of

John I it might be said that his reign was half over when it began. Born at Perpignan in 1350, appointed duke of Girona by a grateful father from infancy, he was lieutenant-general at thirteen, in which capacity he was forced (at fourteen) to preside over the trial and execution of his tutor Bernat de Cabrera. It is hardly surprising that so worldly a youth proved difficult for his father to direct as he came of age nor even, perhaps, that John once king—at the age of thirty-six—took less interest in government than his father. He was well educated in a fashionable courtly mould that suited him perfectly. He learned early to read and write in several languages and to practice with discerning craft the élite art of the hunt. John took no very active part in the war of the two Peters, owing possibly to some ineradicable anxiety about the succession on his father's part.

Such anxiety in any case was in no way allayed by the Infant John's marriages. He was first promised to Joanne of Valois, who died in Béziers on her way to the wedding in 1371. This marriage had been arranged in France by John's counsellors with the king's full approval; it opened the gates to Francophile tendencies that would dominate John to the end. In 1373 he married Mata of Armagnac at Barcelona. It was her fate to be always pregnant, always mourning. The couple had five children, four of whom, including three boys, died in infancy. Only Elionor, who was born in 1375, survived her parents, not apparently without some genetic defect. Mata was unambitious and deferential, accepting the *arriviste* queen Sibilla de Fortià and her excesses with patience. When she died in 1378 her husband, like his father before him, was approaching the middle age of thirty without a male heir. His remarriage became, in the words of Tasis i Marca, 'a veritable affair of State'.

It was at this juncture that King Peter imagined a marriage between the Infant and Maria of Sicily, hoping thus to solve two problems at once. But John now responded to different signals. Without experience of the Sicilians, who supported Pope Urban VI against the clementists, increasingly put off by Queen Sibilla, he welcomed proposals from Charles V of France; even Clement VII, whom John now favoured, suggested a candidate for his hand. In the spring of 1380, having resisted every blandishment of his father and stepmother short of violence, John married Yolande of Bar ceremoniously at Perpignan. Despite ritual attempts at conciliation, this event sealed the breach between the Infant and his father. Very unlike Mata, Yolanda, then aged fifteen, was pampered, vivacious, and ambitious. She soon threatened Sibilla's ascendancy. Introducing fine vestments, jewellery, feasts, and balls, she created a court *à la française* that rendered the duchy of Girona an apanage comparable to those glittering ones of her homeland. Yet the new couple had no better fortune as parents than the last. Of their six children, only the first lived, to become in time titular queen of Naples. It was left to her mother to play an increasingly political role, none the less accentuated by her husband's alarming illnesses. In 1386 it appeared more than once that Peter IV would survive his son.

John's malady, perhaps epilepsy, persisted into his own reign. Physicians, including Moorish and Jewish ones, were summoned to Barcelona, together with learned men from Paris and Avignon; Yolande renounced her luxury while her weakened husband struggled up to Montserrat priory to commend himself to the Virgin. In these circumstances, the reaction following the great king's death was mercifully mild. Sibilla de Fortià fled to Sant Martí Sarroca, where she was captured, on John's order, by his brother Martí; two of her advisers were executed, but the dowager-queen herself, following an intervention by the Aragonese cardinal Pedro de Luna, was allowed a pension in return for giving up her endowments. John acted promptly to establish his authority, swearing to uphold the Catalonian privileges and receiving sworn fealties at Barcelona in March 1387. Convoking the Aragonese several months later, he was reminded by the *Consell de Cent* of Barcelona that the general Corts of Monzón prorogued by his father in 1385 were still legally in session, which meant that a general summons of the several realms was required. It was a sign of Catalan influence over a new king singularly attached to Old Catalonia. The great Corts that met at Monzón in November 1388 was to be the first (of its kind) and last of the reign. In it the urban deputies—they came from some twenty cities and towns of Aragon, thirteen of Valencia, and nineteen of Catalonia and Majorca—pressed for administrative reforms in such manner as to require a careful political response. This was something John could not give. Having announced new uprisings in Sardinia and a threatened invasion of Roussillon by the count of Armagnac, the king was obliged to wait on a Corts bent on reorganizing the royal household and reforming the judicial apparatus. It was not simply reaction to his father's reign, for John was already well known and dissatisfaction was expressed with his courtly extravagance and devotion to the chase. Giving vent to ineffectual impatience instead of wrath, threatening to dissolve the assembly, John merely unified the resistance; and it was his wife Yolande who presented compromise proposals on judicial administration that prevented political disaster. In a further confrontation months later John rejected charges of an excess of curial officials, deploring in turn the unwonted number of deputies from the urban estate (or *Braç reial*); still other complaints about royal favourites followed. Not until December 1389 was the assembly suspended, having done little more than prove that John had not inherited his father's parliamentary skills.

Yet John I was not incapable of statesmanship. For all his self-indulgence, he had a sense of Mediterranean order that was realistic in its own way. Was it such a mistake to prefer a French alliance to the Castilian after what had happened? If little came of the threatened invasion of Catalonia, that was partly because the chimerical pretensions of Bernard of Armagnac to the inheritance of Majorca made no more sense to the French than to the Catalans. Moreover, John dealt with it energetically. He dispatched his brother Martí, whom he had created duke of Montblanc, with a defensive force before which the Gascon mercenaries melted away. John had dealt with the Schism from the first days of the reign, sounding the opinion of jurists and theologians in Barcelona (February 1387) before pronouncing firmly in favour of Clement VII. He settled the frontier with Navarre by treaty in 1388 and reconciled his realms with the house of Anjou-Naples through negotiations at the court of Avignon; these were confirmed by the promise of the Infanta Violant to Louis II of Naples.

Of John's policies elsewhere it is harder to speak well. Toward Castile he acted feebly when at all, nor was he much concerned to defend Valencia against Granada's thrusts. In Sicily he carried on his father's intentions, if we may credit him with securing his nephew Martí's marriage to Maria of Sicily. But it was quite another matter to secure Maria's inheritance politically. Sicilian barons opposed to the resumption of Catalan rule found an excuse for resisting in their adherence to Pope Boniface IX. Duke Martí led a Catalan fleet to Sicily in 1392, capturing Trapani and Palermo, but failed to break a resistance that stiffened in 1393. In the same year the duchies of Athens and Neopatria were lost. As for Sardinia, while John had treated in 1390 to neutralize the Genoese, he did little to discourage anti-Catalan sentiment in the island. Having been freed from captivity, Brancaleo de Oria joined his bellicose wife Eleanor to drive the Catalans from their properties, fomenting a revolt at Sassari. John tried to organize a punitive expedition, only to be distracted repeatedly, and finally to abandon the project. There were financial obstacles, to be sure, but in this matter John proved indecisive and negligent. Only an outbreak of plague in 1395 induced him and his wife to take ship to Majorca, where the hunting was not up to John's standard.

The worst of John's distractions was a terrible outbreak of violence against the Jews. It began in Castile, where in June 1391 one archdeacon Martínez incited an attack on the Jewish quarter of Seville. By July the agitation had reached Valencia, where some 250 Jews were killed, and massacres soon followed in Majorca city and Barcelona. These clashes revealed a deep chasm between the tolerance generally shared by the kings, the higher clergy, and the aristocracy, and the distrust felt by the lower classes, often in debt, and incapable of accepting those who failed to share in their credulous Christianity or even scorned it. John I, like his ancestors, drew on the services of Jews and protected them. He was in Zaragoza when word of the riots reached him, a circumstance that spared the jewries there. Denouncing the violence, he ordered that Jews everywhere be protected.

Troubles multiplied in John's last years. The death of Clement VII resulted in the election of the Aragonese Pedro de Luna (as Benedict XIII), an event not in itself unwelcome, but at once productive of foreign complications. For a French protégé seemed to be substituted an Aragonese one, and it was no accident that the doctors of Paris were soon recommending resignation as the way out of the crisis; the French court urged this solution on King John. Accusations of misgovernment persisted. The men of Valencia and Barcelona complained that their privileges were violated, and it was alleged that favourites were mismanaging the castles and fiscal domains. The king, not wishing to face the Cort(e)s again, fell into debt, notably to the Genoese financier Luigi Scarampo, whose loyalty was dubious. In May 1396 John fell from his horse, perhaps as the result of a seizure or stroke, while hunting near Girona, and could not be revived.

John I was a ruler of whose character we may be sure. His registers are full of revealing letters, many of them addressed to his remarkable wife, who shared his tastes, even that for hunting. But the correspondence points to a lethargy John could neither remedy nor, perhaps, even quite recognize. He acted or, more often, reacted, but he was too devoted to the royal estate to grasp its incompatibility with the dawning conception of public order that had formed in the Cort(e)s. While exhibiting distaste for certain privileges, including the *mals usos* suffered by the Old Catalonian peasantry, he none the less restored the oligarchical electoral regime in Barcelona. He too easily mistook criticism for disloyalty. Such a man's culture could not be programmatic, like that of Peter IV; it tended to 'lose touch' and so to become vulnerable. In the proscription that followed John's death, his secretary Bernat Metge was imprisoned together with other cronies of the king. Yet Metge's *Lo Somni* (1399) points not only to the breadth of his lamented patron's culture but also to its humanity. Thus the king so devoted to his wife could appreciate, in the guise of a refutation of Tiresias, the qualities of the queens of Aragon in a sympathetically rendered series from Elicsenda de Montcada down to Yolande of Bar.

John was a thoroughly Catalonian king, although in a sense quite new in his line. Having inherited an uneasy federation, he felt content to secure his Pyrenean boundaries while postponing the rest. Yet he failed to grasp the real problems even of the Catalans, transcending the parochial only in his culture. He never quite outgrew the duchy of Girona.

Martin I (1396–1410)

It was a sign of the reigning court's unpopularity that no claim for Yolande or for John's daughters was raised at the moment of John's death. The Infant Martí was proclaimed king, even though he was then in Sicily, and his wife María de Luna assumed power in Barcelona as regent. She presided over a Catalonian *parlament* that dealt correctly with Yolande's claim to be pregnant, organized a commission of investigation into affairs of the late king's advisers, and dispatched an embassy to notify Martí, offering a subsidy of 40,000 florins conditioned on the king's acceptance of the crown and his promise to return promptly to Catalonia.

The second son of Peter IV and Eleanor of Sicily, Martin was forty years old at his accession. His first endowment was the county of Besalú and he was entitled seneschal of Catalonia in 1368; from 1378 he was his father's lieutenant in Valencia. He married María de Luna in 1372; of their four children only the oldest, another Martí, survived infancy. Like his brother John for the paternal inheritance, Martin and his son were charged to maintain the maternal tie with Sicily. Designated his mother's heir, the elder Martin led the Catalan expeditions (1378–84) intended to secure the succession to Frederick III through his daughter Maria, Martin's niece. When the Infant Joan refused to marry her, Peter set his hopes on the younger Martí, a scheme that was fulfilled with his marriage to Maria in 1390. The elder Martin, like his brother John, distanced himself from Queen Sibilla's ménage while carefully avoiding hostility; he served under King John in various capacities, as we have seen, with competence and loyalty. When proclaimed king he had been in Sicily for several years trying to dominate that seething cockpit, and it was not until 1398 that he managed to secure the island for Martí (the younger) and his wife.

María de Luna governed effectively before her husband's return to the peninsula in 1397. There were rumblings of mercenary companies in Occitania while Count Mathieu of Foix tried to organize an invasion to enforce his wife's right to her late father's realm. Count Pere of Urgell mobilized Catalonian forces to repel the invaders, thus establishing some claim to be dynastic lieutenant in his nephew's reign. The investigation of John's counsellors, having been made a major process at law, resulted in imprisonments and fines. For his part the new king exhibited at once a sort of political vision mixed with piety very unlike his brother's. On his way back from Sicily he visited Pope Benedict XIII (his wife's kinsman) in Avignon, where he remained for some weeks. It was a critical moment in the history of the

Schism, for although Pedro de Luna had promised to resign as a means to ending the impasse, he refused to do so once elected. Martin I offered sympathetic and prestigious support just when the old prelate's allies were dwindling. After spending some weeks with the pope the king arrived in Barcelona in May 1397 bearing part of the True Cross from the pontifical court.

He was received enthusiastically by the Catalans, although for the moment he simply confirmed the privileges of Barcelona. He remained attentive to Sicily, appointing Joan of Cardona admiral of his fleet and seeking financial support for his son's regime. Martin's political responsiveness is shown by his intention of spending time (and holding Cort(e)s) in each of his realms, although he was to take years doing so. After some months in Barcelona he went to Aragon, where he resided for more than two years. At his ceremonial reception in Zaragoza he swore to uphold the *fueros* confirmed by Peter IV in 1348 together with all other *fueros* and privileges of Aragon and, for such places where Aragonese custom applied, of Valencia. His entry to Valencia, postponed by a new outbreak of pestilence, took place in April 1402, by which time he was thinking of making Barcelona his preferred residence. His letters tell of detailed projects for improving the Plaça del Rei at Barcelona and his rural retreat at Valldaura. Not until 1405 were the Catalans convoked in Corts, but this event was to be the political climax of the reign. Having issued the summons to Perpignan some months in advance, Martin moved ceremoniously through the towns of Old Catalonia, including notably Castelló d'Empúries. This was the capital of the old county of Empúries which, having proved more rebellious as a royal apanage than it had ever been in its independence, had been annexed to the crown when Count Joan II died in 1401. The Corts of Perpignan, perhaps the most brilliant assembly in Catalan history, opened on 26 January 1406, remained in session for two months, and was subsequently reconvened more than once.

Two problems of internal governance preoccupied Martin I. First, there was chronic disorder created by the ambitions and violence of noble families and their adherents. The trouble they caused had become as bad in the peninsular realms as it had long been in Sicily and Sardinia. Around Cervera were the obstreperous families of Oluga and Cirera; in Aragon the Luna and Urrea; in Valencia the Centelles, Vilaragut, and Soler. Once again, as in ages past, the local peace was threatened by the regalian pretensions of exploitative rural lords or by military retinues or by the oppressive demands of urban oligarchs. When his first appointed lieutenant in Aragon proved unfit for this struggle, Martin replaced him with a tougher man. His ablest deputy continued to be his wife, who applied herself tirelessly in Valencia and Barcelona to enforce the king's order. One hindrance to this work was the ever-mounting insistence on privilege in constituted corporations, such as the *Diputació del General* and, in Barcelona, the *Consell de Cent*.

The other problem was that of restoring the fiscal domains. Archival research has shown not only how alarmingly the comital-royal patrimonies had been dissipated in sales and pledges by Peter IV and John but also how diligently Martin I laboured to restore the domain. In 1399 he decreed the patrimony inalienable while strengthening the earlier constitutions on the indivisibility of the Crown's constituent realms. He recovered jurisdictional rights and restored direct administration and tenancies in the comital-royal domains, especially in Old Catalonia. This was no gentle effort, for the inhabitants of alienated domains were often required to pay for their restoration; both lords and peasants resisted. In Aragon and Valencia the redemptions were negotiated through the Cort(e)s, with less troubled results.

But the time had passed when count-kings could 'live of their own'. Martin's external enterprises, while hardly extravagant, required incessant bargaining with the Cort(e)s and towns, which seldom failed to demand assignments of jurisdiction or revenue in return. Martin was undaunted by such demands. He recognized the assemblies to be an indispensable if imperfect mechanism of his government. In the Cortes where he received the fealties of Aragon for himself and his son (1398) he exhibited just the sort of political tact his brother had lacked. The expeditions against the Moorish pirates became a collaboration between the count-king and his maritime cities. In the Corts of Perpignan (1406), the syndic of Lérida speaking for the *Braç reial* objected to the attendance of lesser knights as a fourth estate created by John I in 1389; coming under extended debate, the matter was finally turned over to a commission, at the king's request, for study.

Abroad, Martin remained firmly supportive of Benedict XIII. In 1398 Catalan forces had to defend their schismatic pope in Avignon against the French. More years of fruitless negotiation ensued. Benedict had taken refuge in Roussillon when in 1409 the Council of Pisa declared him and his rival deposed and elected Petrus Filargo as Alexander V. Martin opposed this election through his ambassadors, as did many other powers; and it was but a final step—as appropriate as it was desperate— for Pedro de Luna to move his court, by the count-king's invitation, to the Major Palace in Barcelona (September 1409).

With Benedict's support the Valencian campaigns against the Moors (1398–1400) were promoted as crusades. These ventures were the reaction to the sacking and sacrilege perpetrated at Torre blanca by pirates from the Maghrib. A first expedition ravaged Dellys in Tlemcen; a second, against Bône, was unsuccessful. We know from a directive to the Valencians that the king sought not only to recover 'the holy Eucharists the infidels hold in Barbary' but more generally to establish new footholds for the expansion of Christianity against Islam. Little came of this, and in 1403 Martin made peace with Tunis. He confirmed peace with Navarre in 1399, then negotiated his son's second marriage with Blanche of Navarre in 1402. A treaty over reprisals was passed with France in 1406, a dispute with Castile over a customs tax settled in 1409.

The Mediterranean islands continued to pose troublesome problems. Martin I had visited Sardinia and even Corsica in 1396–7 and he undertook seriously to reinforce the Sardinian garrisons and castles. But his policy produced Genoese reprisals on Catalonian shipping; and when faced with the demand to expel Italian merchants from peninsular cities, he balked and made peace with Genoa (1402), only to see the Genoese persist in supporting Sardinian rebels. For a time Catalan positions in the island were reduced to Cagliari, Alghero, and Longosardo. The situation worsened in 1408 when Brancaleo de Oria allied with Viscount Guilhem of Narbonne, a scion of the Arborea, who was chosen Judge. In 1409 Martí the younger led a major expedition from Sicily, supported by men and ships from the peninsula, and won a decisive victory over the rebels at Sanduri (30 June). But Martí of Sicily died of malaria a month later, once again leaving Sardinia incompletely pacified—and leaving the Crown of Aragon in an alarming crisis of succession.

Sicily had been more nearly dominated than Sardinia. But there, too, some barons remained hostile to the Catalans and therefore supportive of the schismatic pope at Rome; and the younger Martí remained simply his father's heir and viceroy. Nevertheless, the Catalan-Aragonese title was not called into question when Maria of Sicily died in 1401, and many loyal Sicilian barons went on the Sardinian expedition in 1408. But the elder Martin, a widower since 1406, had placed every hope for the future on his son, who had only illegitimate children when he died. In desperation Martin married Margarita de Prades without ceremony in September 1409. The marriage bore no fruit other than cruel gossip; the king was ailing, and he died on 31 May 1410.

Martin I ranks among the more impressive rulers of the Crown of Aragon. Deeply cultivated like his father and brother, he was more civilized than either, well versed in the records and history of his house, responsive to the prevailing sentiments of his peoples. Physically incapable of the close attention required to deal with the factional conflicts that persisted, he was fortunate in his energetic wife. He was also more pious than his predecessors, given to contemplative reading and private devotion, influenced by the fervent Dominican Saint Vicent Ferrer, and regarding himself the defender of the churches (as well as of the pope) in his realms. He proposed to set up Celestine friars as a kind of palace-chapel in Barcelona, and he secured for the monks of Montserrat the privileged status of an abbey. Yet he was hardly a crowned monk: Martin's piety had a political and humanist dimension that enabled this king, like few of his ancestors, to move his subjects. His great 'proposition' to the Corts of Perpignan in 1406, ranging through a vast classical, biblical, and dynastic literature, was a political sermon of compelling force—the serene and unchauvinistic vision of a ruler who knew how to celebrate one of his peoples without prejudice to the others. Martin's personal preference for Barcelona and his popularity in Catalonia did not blind him to problems of the federation. His attempt to set up faculties at Barcelona was balanced by his effort to render the university at Lérida better representative of the three peninsular realms. Yet Martin's political success was that of one forced to compromise with baronial and oligarchical privilege—it was a seriously flawed success. His worst failure was to die the last of his dynastic line.

The reigns of John I and Martin confirmed the new balance of political forces that had emerged under Peter the Ceremonious. The king's power had become that of one privileged estate among several, a power that for most public purposes could only be exercised through negotiation with the nobles and urban patricians. John's failure with his Cort(e)s and Martin's success afforded experimental proof that the Crown of Aragon had become (after the late medieval fashion) a parliamentary monarchy. Yet it was the estates that imposed themselves rather than the assemblies. Peter IV sounded opinion and probed for means in diversely constituted *parlaments* and his sons did the same; in Martin's time the towns of Catalonia and Valencia supported or even initiated expeditions the count-king rightly believed they would find useful. Such practices together with the kings' assertions of dynastic and foreign interests tended, however feebly, to promote pan-regnal identity. But there could be no insistence on such identity against the aristocracies and urban oligarchies. Their privileges were defined in regional or local charters increasingly associated with the customs or constitutions of the national Cort(e)s, a process that accentuated the inherited distinctness of Catalonia from Aragon. These realms together with Valencia and Majorca gained less and less from the costly ties with Sardinia and Sicily, where the count-kings struggled in vain to translate their rights into rule. Everywhere in the federation these rulers were obliged to deal with the powerful, hardly anywhere could they rule the many, a menacing reality that seems to have troubled Peter IV toward the end but that his successors accepted without demur. The power of the estates did have the salutary effect of ensuring that public authority would assume the institutional form of a condominium between curial officers and agents of the estates, such as the *Justicia* in Aragon or the deputations of the Cort(e)s. The rulers of the later medieval Crown of Aragon might be capricious but they could not be tyrannical. Their means and institutions, moreover, were dependent on fiscal exploitation and taxation such as placed the nascent state at the mercy of economic and demographic realities largely beyond anyone's grasp or control. It had required the peninsular wars to prove that the Crown of Aragon, for all its splendour, could not match Castile or France in military might or wealth. By the end of the fourteenth century her rulers, limited by a variety of constraints, clung to a dynastic vision of west Mediterranean hegemony stripped of wider expansionist designs.

VI

The Trastámaras
(1412–1479)

WITH the passing of Martin the Humanist was extinguished the oldest line of direct princely descent in Europe. The fate of Germany in 1268, of France in 1328, and of England in 1399 was now to befall the Crown of Aragon at a time when the mysterious potency of dynastic right remained undiminished. People were conscious of the crisis before Martin's death, as we have seen, and there can be no doubt that in the fifteenth century they looked back to the deliberations of 1410–12 as the beginning of a new epoch, and wondered—as modern historians have wondered —about what might have been. Yet the resolution of the crisis was compatible with new tendencies in political outlook and constitutional law; it provided for a dynastic *rapprochement* between Aragon and Castile that had been in the wind for centuries and that arguably made sense in geopolitical terms. What might have seemed disturbing about this *rapprochement* to those who cherished the privileges of Aragon and Catalonia was that it came at a time when the socio-economic preponderance of Castile was bound to influence the relationship deeply. This, however, was less evident to contemporaries than it is to us; nor could they have noticed any better than their dynastic rulers what deep fissures were forming in the underlying terrain of social and institutional order. There was progress in the fifteenth century, even creativity, but there were no solutions to structural problems. A federative outlook shared by the count-kings with their subjects seemed ever more difficult to sustain. So the history of the Crown of Aragon becomes increasingly that of its peoples and their institutions: as Vicens Vives put it, referring to one of these peoples, after 1412 no ruler but only Catalonia itself could properly form the subject of a biography. It is a history of absorbing if somewhat melancholy interest, one in which constructive impulses were repeatedly lost sight of in futile

conflicts over unrealistic ambitions; one in which a busy corner of
the Mediterranean world lost its way as the shadows lengthened.

The Compromise of Caspe (1412)

The main difficulty in 1410 was that the late king had failed to
express his will firmly. If he had pronounced in favour of Count
Jaume of Urgell, this great-grandson of Alphonse IV would
almost certainly have succeeded Martin. His claim was strong
and he was the most visible of the claimants; he had acquired the
lieutenancy, a post normally reserved for the principal heir, in
1409; and he had proceeded to act as governor-general in
Aragon. But the Aragonese had resisted his exercise of power as
contrary to their privileges, and the troubled king had done
nothing to support Jaume. In his last months Martin seems to
have placed his hopes on his illegitimate grandchild Frederick of
Luna. When pressed to declare himself he refused, although a
party favouring Louis of Anjou, grandson of John I through the
latter's daughter, claimed to have elicited the dying king's
approval to the formula that the succession should go to
'whomever justice should decide'. This and other partisan moves
effectively undermined Jaume's strength, preventing a coup on
his part, and opening the matter to general deliberation if not
even, as some hoped, to the vote of the realms including the
islands.

The Catalans' wish to proceed in parliamentary fashion could
only have aided Jaume if it had been accomplished without
delay. But it meant having to persuade the Aragonese and
Valencians to join in representative deliberation at a moment
when both peoples were torn by conflicts. In the spring of
1411 Aragonese allies of Jaume murdered Archbishop García
Fernández de Heredia, who had favoured the Angevin cause;
and when from this point the governor of Aragon, Gil Ruiz de
Lihori, threw his support to Fernando 'de Antequera' the balance
of forces shifted decisively. Fernando was the grandson of Peter
IV through his mother Elionor, who had married Juan of Castile;
he was the uncle and sometime regent of King Juan II. He was
thirty years old in 1410, experienced, immensely wealthy from
his Castilian apanages—and ambitious. He had lately won a
gaudy victory over the Granadan Moors, capturing their
stronghold at Antequera. His claim to the Crown of Aragon was

represented cautiously to a Catalonian *parlament* in 1411, and to Pope Benedict XIII, whom he had previously supported. Benedict had first favoured Frederick of Luna, whose election would have entailed a papal tutelage; when this prospect failed Fernando must have seemed to the embattled pope his best hope for a politically useful succession. So when Benedict urged that a commission representative of the peninsular realms decide between the claims, and when the Catalans accepted a list of Aragonese electors (*compromisarios*) put forward by known opponents of Jaume of Urgell, a decision for Fernando was assured. The electors, chosen by parliaments in each realm, met at Caspe in Aragon (a place geographically central to the three realms) from 29 March to 29 June 1412. The vote in favour of Fernando de Antequera was announced by the friar Vicent Ferrer, himself an elector for Valencia and a convert to Fernando, at the end of a long sermon. Two of the Catalan electors had held out for succession through the male line, but their inability to agree on Jaume of Urgell sealed his fate. Jaume retained support to the end, notably in the towns. Had he acted resolutely against the decision at Caspe he might conceivably have undone it. But the election of Fernando was seen generally and was defended by powerful voices (including that of Vicent Ferrer) as a deliverance from intolerable disorder. When Jaume tried belatedly to rebel, blandished by Antón de Luna who spoke of Gascon, even English, military support, he failed even his homeland adherents, secluding himself at Balaguer, where he was besieged and at length captured by Fernando I (1 November 1413). Deprived of Urgell together with the viscounty of Ager, which were again annexed to the crown, Jaume continued to plot for some years, but remained a prisoner until his death in 1433.

Few events in medieval history have evoked such heated judgements as the Compromise of Caspe. Much of the debate has engaged modern historians, among whom Catalanophiles, with notable exceptions, have deplored it as a betrayal of national interest and tradition. But the greater historical importance of the issue lies in the fact that contemporaries themselves, including the electors, anguished over the options that confronted them. This means that even for contemporaries the issue was (or became) political rather than simply legal, a utilitarian question of which candidate with *some* dynastic claim would make the best king. Thus had the progress of parliamentary thought brought electoral practice full circle from those distant days in 1131 or 1213, when in narrower counsels it had seemed imperative to defend strictly dynastic succession against all other interests. But it means, too, that patriotic considerations were not necessarily foremost. In Aragon the nobles and Jews had already found advantage in negotiating the marketing of Castilian wool; in Valencia the burghers obtained commercial favours from Fernando I. Even in Catalonia the *estaments* were divided, the lesser knights and urban patricians tending to oppose Jaume of Urgell. On the other hand, the chronicle *Li fi del comte d'Urgell*, which comes close to sounding the poignant note of national despair, accused the *majors* of Barcelona of introducing 'a strange and new man' to their lordship and of 'exterminating their natural [lord]'. The Catalans, as such, had no candidate, so in the genuine interest of peace they agreed to negotiate without one. That was their contribution to Caspe. They represented faithfully the spirit of the federative constitution, they settled for a just compromise, and they cannot be condemned for failing to see the distant consequences of not uniting behind Jaume of Urgell. Yet if the overriding issue at Caspe was pacification and justice, the compromise was none the less a dynastic decision that would bind future generations.

Ferdinand I (of Antequera, 1412–1416)

The new king assumed power in the summer of 1412. Received ceremonially in Zaragoza in August, Ferdinand reappointed some of Martin's officials, convoked the Cortes, and in September swore to the assembled Aragonese to uphold their privileges in the comprehensive package that had become customary. When Jaume of Urgell and Antón de Luna failed to appear, they were branded contumacious, so it was a decisive event of the accession that in January 1413 the Catalonian Corts voted the new count-king supplies. The prosecution of Jaume, legal and military, took most of another year during which time Ferdinand consolidated his power. His coronation took place in January 1414 at Zaragoza in grand pomp and splendour. There the king created vast endowments in his new lands for his sons: the duchy of Girona for Alfonso, the elder; that of Peñafiel for Juan, the second.

The major problem in the peninsular realms continued to be that of the royal patrimony. In Aragon the Cortes found that while ordinary revenues amounted to some 26,000 fl. yearly, the royal pensions and charges alone came to 33,700 fl. A commission was appointed to recommend a reform. In Valencia as in Aragon the restoration and enforcement of order were very urgently required, and Ferdinand worked with deputies of the Cortes to provide for a statute of pacification. In Catalonia he had more difficulty, for the financial offer of the Corts in 1413 was conditioned on far-reaching demands that could not, for the moment, be resisted. With a major vassal in revolt, without adequate landed revenue or natural allies, Ferdinand was at first precariously situated in Catalonia. The greater lords found it easier to resist him than his predecessor in the matter of restoring the patrimony; those who had benefited from alienations included barons and churches, who were joined by those whose purposes it suited to keep the Crown dependent on the Corts. Equally symptomatic was the Corts' vote to annul the royal privilege that had given the lesser knights a place in the Corts: from 1413 no fourth estate was to be admissible in the assembly. Nor was Ferdinand permitted to carry on the crown's effort to mitigate the harsher practices of lordship over *remença* peasants in Old Catalonia. Finally, and most momentous, Ferdinand confirmed and strengthened the position of the *Diputació del General* as a standing committee of the Corts. Retaining its power to administer extraordinary taxation, the *Diputació* now received custody of the privileges and constitutions of Catalonia. In the following years the *diputats* established themselves as a coordinate administration with the count-king's. By 1414, however, the political situation had changed and Ferdinand refused to be pushed further. When the Corts of Montblanc demanded additional concessions concerning the patrimony and the *Diputació*, he was content to let it disband without result.

Ferdinand was more successful in his foreign enterprises. In the Mediterranean he managed to restore the heritage of the two Martins, opening up new possibilities of expansion for his successor. He first secured investiture of Sicily, Sardinia, and Corsica from Benedict XIII (1412), thereby confirming the old dynastic title he had acquired. Sicily had been divided during the

Interregnum between partisans of Queen Blanche and Bernat de Cahors. Ferdinand's envoys succeeded in confirming Blanche's regency and restoring ties with the crown. When the Sicilians characteristically asked for the king's son as their own king, Ferdinand obliged to the extent of sending his second son Juan as viceroy while declaring Sicily united to the Crown of Aragon (1414). The Sicilians failed to persuade Juan to assume an independent title, and it may not be accidental that he was the last royal prince sent out to tempt them to revive their historic monarchy. The administration and finances were reorganized, while Catalans, Aragonese, and Castilians assumed the principal offices.

Juan was also appointed viceroy in Sardinia and Majorca (and potentially Naples, as we shall see). In Sardinia the problems were, as usual, even worse than in Sicily. It is true that Viscount Guilhem had failed in an attempt to capture Alghero in 1412, leaving the Catalans in nominal control. But there was no pacification, the Catalan garrisons remaining weak and unprincipled. Ferdinand treated with Leonardo de Cubello, whose title Marquis of Oristano was intended to compensate him for discouraging rebellion beyond the castellans' control. The viceroy Juan made a stop at Cagliari in 1415, but took little interest in Sardinia.

In Naples King Ladislas had negotiated with Ferdinand over a number of issues since 1412, although the idea of a marriage alliance went back to Martin's time. In 1414 a marriage was projected between Ladislas's sister Giovanna and Juan, and then celebrated by proxy at Valencia (January 1415) on condition that Juan would succeed Giovanna, who was much older than he, if she died without heirs. But the Neapolitans reacted angrily, their parliament refused to confirm the marriage, and when Giovanna was compelled to marry Jacques de Bourbon, Ferdinand's bid for Naples collapsed. He did better when he followed precedent, his usual course. Generally protective of Catalan trade, he set out to restore Catalan sea power; he made a new truce with Genoa in 1413. Following embassies to Egypt in 1413–14 Ferdinand secured a peace with the sultan and restored the consulate of Barcelona in Alexandria. In the western Mediterranean he was content to renew truces with Granada while negotiating peace with Morocco, a policy that suggests how thoroughly this Castilian had assumed the interests and outlook of his acquired realms.

Finally and by no means least, it was Ferdinand I who effectively put an end to the Great Schism. The matter was delicate, for Benedict XIII had been a powerful, perhaps decisive, intermediary in Ferdinand's election. The king had continued to support Benedict and, in the matter of the investiture, to use him. By this time sovereign allies were the Aragonese pope's last resource. Giovanna of Naples' French marriage ended hopes of Italian support at the very time when the Council of Constance was requiring all three popes to renounce their titles and pretensions. When Benedict alone of these failed to respond or to acknowledge deposition, Ferdinand made a last vain bid for foreign support, then abandoned Benedict in 1416. The old prelate held out, obdurate and alone, in Peñíscola until his death in 1422. He had played an astonishing part in the history of the Crown of Aragon—to which he was chaplain, king-maker, and protégé—but one can hardly fault his last protector for rejoining the universal church.

Ferdinand I died in 1416, too soon to have carried out his purposes, not too soon to have changed the course of his acquired lands. A rich Castilian prince who became a poor count-king, he reigned conscious of this unfortunate irony that lay at the root of future problems. He is said to have complained that Catalonia, compared with Castile, was not a monarchy but an agency (*procuratio*). He was a faithful husband and a devoted father, but his family remained Castilian in taste as well as opulence; his children learned to think of Castile as their homeland and most of them married accordingly. Yet for the Catalans even moderate displays of their new ruler's identity, such as his appointing Castilians to some advisory or curial functions, were excessive. The men of Barcelona made a loud fuss over Ferdinand's unwillingness to pay a tax on provisions from which the clergy and nobles seemed to be exempt, then regretted his departure— for the presence of the royal entourage was no mean stimulus to local profits—when the king grimly paid and silently left the city. Ferdinand's experience with Catalonia—the liberal yet penurious ruler facing a prospering yet suspicious people—was a temperamental misunderstanding that might have been resolved in time.

Alphonse V (IV in Catalonia, 1416–1458)

The misunderstanding hardened into constitutional conflict under Ferdinand's son. Alphonse V came to power an experienced prince of twenty, well educated in military pursuits, the chase, and the arts, with tastes for French dress and Castilian wealth. Married to his cousin María of Castile at Valencia in 1415, he was fortunate in her political sagacity. She was to act as lieutenant in Catalonia for long periods (1421–36, 1438–45); a woman of admirable patience and fidelity, she hardly deserves blame for failing to bear the heir whose existence might have spared future trouble. Alphonse likewise relied on his brother Juan, whose willingness to give up Sicily to take charge of the count-king's Castilian affairs served Alphonse's Mediterranean ambitions but rendered the Crown of Aragon vulnerable to conflicts in its alien dynasty's homelands. Later he succeeded to his sister-in-law's lieutenancy in one or more of the Aragonese realms. For the first time in their history these realms were to be ruled in the name of an absentee king.

Alphonse dealt first with Catalonia, holding Corts in the fall of 1416 and confirming the Catalonian customs even before assuming the crown in Aragon. The Aragonese bore this affront patiently. They joined the Catalans and Valencians in protesting the king's appointment of Castilian courtiers, but as Alphonse spared Aragon in his first requests for financial subsidy his troubles there were postponed. In 1423 a Cortes of Aragon met in the king's absence, an unprecedented convocation by the queen-lieutenant permitted 'for this one time'. It was the first of a long series of meetings, many in the king's absence, in which appeals for financial or military aid, first for the Genoese war and then for the king's Neapolitan campaigns, were negotiated on the basis of fiscal contrivances—the charge of rents (*censals*) on royal patrimony—and demands for the king's return from Naples. The history of Aragon under Alphonse V and his lieutenants is a parliamentary history, above all; it was characteristic that the Cortes of Alcañiz (1441) provided for collecting the records of previous Cortes of Aragon. When the Aragonese wished to protest the appointment of Castilians, they did so through justiciars, two of whom Alphonse summarily deposed. These anti-foral measures led to a reaction in 1442 when the king was obliged to accept regulations strengthening the *Justicia's* position and prohibiting the sale of offices. In Valencia as in Aragon the worst days of factional strife were past. The Valencians acquiesced to financial demands of the king in his first years, then continued to support the Neapolitan campaigns. It was a time of increasing prosperity in a land scarcely touched by the turmoil elsewhere.

In Catalonia, however, Alphonse had little but trouble. In his first Corts (1416) the royal proposition was badly received, and although the clerical and urban *estaments* were disposed to grant a subsidy, the greater barons refused. Objecting to the king's choice of retainers and to the restoration of the royal patrimony, Roger Bernat of Pallars, Bernat de Cabrera, and others induced the estates to designate a commission of reformers whose sweeping programme would have drastically reduced the king's already eroded prerogative. Moreover, the 'pactist' magnates strove to establish themselves as a legitimate (and sufficient) representation of the principality while seeking political allies in Barcelona, Valencia, and Zaragoza. Alphonse was obliged to defend his administrative policy as having reasonable precedents while attempting to divide his opponents. As he insisted on support for a Mediterranean campaign while resisting 'reforms' that threatened an inherited royal programme, the lines hardened. In the Corts of Sant Cugat and Tortosa (1419–20) Alphonse reached agreement with the clergy on customary aids while conceding articles reserving benefices for Catalans and providing for a new reforming commission; only then was he voted a gift of 50,000 florins (less than one-third the grant made by Valencia city alone). At Tortosa a new series of resolutions amounted to a veritable constitutional programme: the king's council was to be chosen with consent of the Corts, the royal *Audiència* should judge independently of the king, while royal orders in contravention of the *Usatges* or *Constitucions* of Catalonia were to be held null. Other articles expressed aristocratic opposition to peasant syndicates and the recovery of royal patrimony. It was incessantly alleged that the king was abusing the patrimony through gifts to rapacious Castilians, but the deeper issue was the royal prerogative and the limitations to be set upon it. No élite in Europe pretended to such power as the Catalonian pactists. This Corts ended in stalemate and was dissolved with bad will on both sides.

To a ruler thus tried the prospect of Mediterranean enterprise was more than usually appealing. Yet Alphonse's Italian policy began as a Catalan undertaking on traditional lines, and it was supported by Catalan men, money, and ships. Its object was to end the Genoese menace by seizing Corsica and securing the Crown's administration in Sicily and Sardinia. Alphonse's accession had been greeted by new uprisings in Sardinia, where disease and social unrest had undermined the old rebel leadership. Landing in Alghero (June 1420) the count-king easily prevailed; Guilhem III of Narbonne renounced all claims to Sardinia in exchange for the payment of 100,000 fl. In September 1420, having allied with the Corsican foes of Genoa, Alphonse seized Calvi and besieged Bonifaci before the Genoese rallied and forced him to withdraw. That this operation was not renewed was a result of events in Naples.

By this time Giovanna II was a puppet of the Neapolitan magnates and *condottieri*. While Sforza de Tennebello supported Louis III of Anjou for the succession, Gianni Caracciolo came to agreement with the queen in favouring Alphonse V. In August 1420 their ambassadors offered him the succession to Naples and its dependencies on condition of his military aid. Alphonse dispatched ships, but avoided all other appearance of haste, proceeding deliberately with operations in Sardinia and Corsica before sailing to Naples himself in July 1421. On 8 July he was received there as the son and heir of Queen Giovanna. It was the beginning of his life-work—and a characteristically deceptive beginning. The queen and her allies were perfectly incapable of steadfast support. Within a year Caracciolo joined forces with Sforza against 'the Catalans' and in June 1423 the city of Naples went over to them in a surprise coup. Alphonse used a Catalan fleet mobilized against the Genoese to blockade Naples, and then to assault (Angevin) Marseille: 'the last great feat of Catalonian arms in the western Mediterranean' (Vicens Vives). The count-king had displayed resourceful energy in his first campaign, which ended even so with disturbingly mixed results.

Meanwhile, the Catalonian pactists continued to press their programme in the Corts of Barcelona (1421–3). But the pressures of special interests were increasing, thereby dimming the prospect of a constitutional union against the king. In fact, the higher nobility was already aligned in factions anticipating the battle lines of 1462, while the knights, excluded from power in 1413, divided in siding either with the more radical count of Pallars or the more royalist viscount of Cardona. Constitutions providing for the absolute supremacy of the *Usatges, Constitucions*, and *Chapters of the Corts* as well as for the reservation of jurisdictional offices for Catalans were approved in April 1422.

Returning to the peninsula in 1423, Alphonse remained there for nearly a decade. The ambitions of his brothers to dominate their cousin Juan II had thrown Castile into turmoil. When Juan of Aragon and his ally Álvaro de Luna imprisoned the Infante Enrique (Master of Santiago), the latter's party took refuge in Valencia and called on Alphonse for aid. In 1425 a treaty with Juan of Aragon secured the release of Enrique and the restoration of his property, but dissension then arose between Juan and Álvaro. By 1429 Alphonse and Juan were ready to invade Castile to secure a settlement on their terms when Queen María, her tents pitched between drawn-up armies, prevented a violent clash. King Juan remained dissatisfied with an arrangement that left the Infantes of Aragon free to pursue their Castilian ambitions; while on the other side Alphonse and Juan of Aragon found their Cort(e)s unwilling to support the war any longer. In July 1430, they agreed to a truce of five years, on terms favourable to Álvaro de Luna. The Infantes of Aragon were to withdraw from Castile, a condition that Juan could accept—he was now prince-consort of Navarre—but not Enrique. That the count-king could accept it was a sign of his well-considered inclination to give up his dynastic interest in Castile.

For he was now faced with worsening problems in Catalonia—and with the opportunity to escape them. In 1421–3 the Corts had secured important elements of the pactist programme, as we have seen, and during the Castilian war they had presumed to negotiate directly with Juan II to the count-king's disadvantage. Economic difficulties were coming to be felt. Revenues from the customs and from taxes on cloth plummeted after 1426, threatening the whole edifice of credit. In the Corts of Barcelona in 1431 the magnates and knights set aside their differences to reject demands for severe penalties against debtors.

In May 1435 Alphonse V left these troubles to his wife and sailed for the islands. Few can have supposed that he would never return. He dealt first with Sicily, where he spent two years, but was drawn progressively into the intrigues surrounding the succession to Giovanna of Naples. She had in the end pronounced in favour of René of Anjou, some of whose adherents together with other foes of Alphonse held Naples against him. Defeated catastrophically by the Genoese in a naval battle off Gaeta in 1435, Alphonse was imprisoned by the Milanese; but the situation changed when he persuaded his captor Duke Filippo Maria that in view of threats by the French he should be content with hegemony in northern Italy while leaving the South to Alphonse (October 1435). Giving up Corsica and dispatching his brother Juan to manage the peninsular realms, Alphonse committed himself in 1435–6 to the conquest of Naples. This required years of fighting and negotiating for the Neapolitans continued irresolute, the Genoese hostile, and the pope unsympathetic. When Eugenius IV inclined toward René, the old Angevin-Aragonese rivalry was revived in effect, with Naples in the place of Sicily. In 1438 Alphonse besieged Naples, but not until 1442 could he force entry to the city, where his quasi-imperial triumph was celebrated in February 1443. Alphonse strove to pacify his adversaries and to establish a political base. His bastard son Ferrante was recognized as his heir. The pope's recognition was secured by threats to oppose him in the Council of Basle. But this investiture entailed the count-king's support of papal ambitions elsewhere in Italy, while Alphonse himself could not resist the temptation of adding Milan to his possessions. Years more of fighting and intrigue followed, while the Catalans and Aragonese pleaded incessantly for their ruler to return. By 1450 Alphonse had become an Italian potentate, the successful *condottiere*-king who ruled Naples in a courtly magnificence such as had eluded him in his homelands.

So for the first time the Mediterranean took precedence over the peninsular realms in the Crown of Aragon. Alphonse V sought to dominate Italy, but his position even in Naples was precarious enough to recommend caution in his wider Mediterranean projects. His efforts to check Tunisian piracy were as constant as their results were slight. He was willing to attack Egypt and to defend Balkan lands from the Turks, but not to take a crusading initiative befitting his station either before or after the fall of Constantinople in 1453. What Alphonse did well enough was to protect and promote maritime trade. He instituted consulates at Modó in the Morea (1416), Candia (1433), and Ragusa (1443); he protected the Knights of St. John at Rhodes. His was, in Carrère's words, 'the last great epoch of Catalonian trade in the East'.

Alphonse never ceased to govern. In Naples he made some effort to revive Hohenstaufen administrative efficiency. But he was fatally incapable of making the old patrimony profitable, having to depend almost everywhere on corrupt officials and extortionate creditors. Only an independent fiscal base in Italy could have enabled him to govern the peninsular realms effectively. As it was, he was obliged to make those realms pay for Italy, thereby weakening the crown's real power in them; it was increasingly for financial reasons that he kept in touch with his lieutenants and the Cort(e)s. Only in his last years, when his mistress Lucrezia d'Alagno gave birth to the son for whom Alphonse staked everything, did the administrative correspondence fall silent. Only then was completed an emotional metamorphosis by which, for a few heady years, a precarious periphery became the centre of the Crown of Aragon.

It was a desperate diversion, made worse by the count-king's inability either to support his lieutenants consistently or to restrain the Infante Juan from further Castilian adventures at the expense of Aragon. Complaining that payments for ransoms alone were ruining the economy, the Cortes of Aragon forced Juan to make peace in 1454. Majorca was badly set back by the renewed war with Genoa and suffered a rebellion of peasants from 1450 to 1454. Only Valencia seems to have escaped the worst of social unrest and economic dislocation that afflicted the other realms, and Catalonia above all.

Here there would have been trouble under a responsive ruler in residence; Alphonse's prolonged absence was disastrous. Without firm direction the Corts of Catalonia had fallen prey to searing antagonisms: of the knights against the old nobility, of merchants and artisans against the urban patriciate, of greater landlords against the *remença* peasants or against royal agents trying to recover alienated domains. At first Alphonse sided with the pactist magnates who controlled the Corts; thus in 1432 he consented to their measure sanctioning the recovery of escaped peasants or their lands by rural lords. But as time passed and their financial support dwindled he revived—opportunistically—

the traditional royal programme of agrarian reform. In the 1440s he negotiated with a syndicate of peasants in the Gironès, offering them freedom for a grant of 100,000 florins, only to suspend the concession in 1455 when the Corts voted 400,000. When this grant was delayed Alphonse revived the *remença* decree, proving that his interest in fiscal reform was for sale; the matter remained unresolved as peasant agitation continued. In the towns the count-king tried to mitigate social conflict by imposing the *insaculació*, or electoral lottery, which spread widely in the peninsular realms from the 1440s. The patricians resisted this threat to their control of offices. In Barcelona the problem was compounded by economic troubles so as to create a split between the 'honoured citizens' and landlords (known as the *Biga*), on one side, and the merchants, artisans, and labourers (the *Busca*), on the other. Supported by the deputy governor Galceran de Requesens the *Busca* organized a 'syndicate of the three estates', and in 1454–5 gained control of the city councils. Once in power the *Busca* tried to devalue the coinage and to protect the shipping and textile industries, delicate matters over which their leaders themselves soon split. Not quite concealed by these issues was that of whether the syndicate could be allowed to dominate the municipality. In the Corts of 1454–8 the king's support of the *Busca* and the *remences* together with an effort to enlarge the representation of the urban estate galvanized the opposition of nobles, prelates, and patricians. There could be no compromise—and no grant of financial subsidy—in the king's absence.

In Naples Alphonse V stayed—and there he died in June 1458. Unresponsive to his peninsular subjects who were united on nothing but their urgent need of him, he ceased in the end to understand them. He made no attempt to integrate Naples with his other realms. Conventionally pious like most of his predecessors in the Crown of Aragon, intellectually lively, even learned, and shrewd, he none the less failed in his inherited task. What he created in his foreign lordship was a self-celebrating microcosm in which appearances became preferable to bleak reality. In one telling respect the court reflected Alphonse's nature and his wounds. Although he patronized Latin, Catalan, and Italian writers, humanists among them, artists, and musicians, he remained Castilian at heart, preferring the company of Castilian-speaking prelates and friars. It was symptomatic that Castilian writers could now think of Aragon as part of Spain and of Alphonse as their own. But there was nothing partisan about the triumphant tone: writing in Catalan the Valencian poet Ausiès March predicted that Alphonse would 'soon have the monarchy of the world'. Catalonia and Aragon were no doubt meant to have a place in such a polity, but hardly the easy centrality of Muntaner's day.

John II (1458–1479) and the Catalonian Civil War

With the death of Alphonse V the peninsular realms of the Crown of Aragon once again had a king. John II succeeded his brother at the age of sixty. Behind him lay a long and uneasy career of administration, ambition, intrigue, and war. First charged with managing dynastic affairs in Castile, later married to the heiress of Navarre, he had struggled for his own vision of Hispanic hegemony. For all his obsession with Castile (and because of it) he had retained his brother's confidence, serving as lieutenant in 1436–8 and again in 1454–8, when he succeeded the controversial Requesens in Catalonia. He knew the acrid temper of the Cort(e)s as well as anyone, and his peoples, however relieved to have once again a visible ruler, can have had few illusions as to what lay ahead. Only John himself failed to see that his own ambitions were dangerously irrelevant to the urgent needs of his new realms. Catalonia lurched toward civil war.

John promptly rearranged the alliances to serve his Castilian purpose. He abandoned the war with Genoa in hopes of breaking the Franco-Castilian *entente*, but this seems to have achieved little more than to anger maritime interests in Barcelona. He rejected bids to intervene in Italy or the East, leaving Ferrante I (1458–94) with a desperate struggle to secure Naples against the local barons and other foes. In short, John began to reign as he had already ruled in Catalonia, and if he made changes in his father's policies he made none in his own. His worst blunder was to allow an old quarrel with his son Carlos to escalate into political opposition beyond his power to destroy.

Born in 1421 of John's marriage to Blanche of Navarre, Carlos Prince of Viana could have been expected to succeed his mother in Navarre when she died in 1441. But Blanche's will had enabled John to forestall this succession, thereby preserving for himself the influence of a widower-consort while allowing his son to act as lieutenant. This scheme could only have worked if John had shared purposes with his son, but the prince had been brought up with French manners and intellectual inclinations uncongenial to his father; nor could he be persuaded to support John in Castile. This point became crucial when John chose for his second wife Juana Enriquez of Castile, the birth of whose son in 1451 gave his father new options. What John could not do was mobilize Navarre without antagonizing the Beaumont allies of Carlos. In an increasingly bitter war fought in the 1450s Carlos was captured and released, John frustrated in his Castilian aims, and Carlos disinherited by his father in favour of a sister married to the count of Foix. This last act, legally preposterous, forced Carlos to flee Navarre, but it had also the unintended effect of enlarging his cause to his father's discomfiture; he sought support in France, even from his uncle Alphonse in Naples, and in 1459–60 the Sicilian parliament appealed to old precedents in requesting the first-born Carlos for their viceroy.

This request John II understandably rejected, but it was time for a new tack. Carlos was ready for reconciliation, having no resources outside Navarre; his father would have been content to marry him to a Portuguese princess to the disadvantage of Castile; but the critical (one may say, fatal) stumbling-block to an accord was John's refusal to recognize Carlos publicly as 'first born', thereby preventing his son from exercising the royal powers customarily accorded to the heir-designate. No one knew better than John the extent of those powers. But if the king and queen meant to reserve such status for Fernando, they could hardly withhold Navarre from its prince without forcing Carlos into renewed hostility at a moment when his following elsewhere was growing. The Catalans had welcomed him joyously when he returned from the islands in 1460. When the Prince was discovered negotiating with Enrique IV of Castile, he was arrested at Lérida on 2 December 1460.

This was to light a fuse. The Corts, then in session in Lérida, immediately branded the arrest a violation of Catalonian privilege. Before disbanding they conferred emergency powers on the *Diputació* in Barcelona, where as early as 8 December a 'Council representing the principality of Barcelona' was appointed to work with the *diputats*. In all the realms were heard demands for Carlos's release, but in Catalonia these demands were easily transformed into the pactist issue of the prerogative. By arresting Carlos and rejecting protests of the *Diputació* and the new Council, as Hillgarth puts it, '[John] performed the miracle of uniting (against him[self]) a bitterly divided country'. The *Diputació*, the *Biga*, and the *Busca* joined in outspoken defiance. Winning support throughout the Crown of Aragon, raising armed force of their own, the Council not only secured Carlos's release (25 February 1461) but also imposed a 'Capitulation' by which King John had to concede the *Diputació*'s authority and promise to recognize his elder son's right of universal succession. Enacted at Vilafranca del Penedès on 21 June 1461, this Capitulation marked a triumph for the Catalanists as such, besides validating the extreme claims of the pactists and foralists. Only the prince of Viana had made it possible, only his exercise of authority could secure it. But John prevented him from acting as lieutenant, forcing Carlos to cast about once more for allies; and when he died on 23 September, probably of tuberculosis, the unanimity he had inspired soon collapsed. Only the rise of a legend and cult of Carlos (*Sant Karles de Cathalunya*) marked the tenuous survival of an idea of Catalonian revolutionary unity. The pactist programme, for its part, was again seen to be partisan. While landlords and patricians took the opportunity to put down syndicates in the countrysides and towns, Queen Juana managed to win support for the king and their son Fernando. When the *remença* peasants revolted in February 1462, a general civil war broke out.

The causes of this war were complex. Some contemporaries thought that the *remença* problem was chiefly to blame. Modern historians were formerly inclined to cite economic difficulties. Modern research has disposed of both these views, showing that powerful elements in Catalonian society were very divided in their views of the *remences* and that the chronology of economic change is out of phase with that of the war. Nor was the conflict primarily a matter of social antagonism, the partisan interests—such as *Busca* and *remença*—failing conspicuously to unite against common enemies. More than any other cause one may perhaps argue for the arrogance of the pactist–*Biga* reaction following the Capitulation of Vilafranca: if the price of a compliant king was to be the crushing of peasant and artisan aspirations, those of the

peasants seeming by this time so close to realization, compromise
was at an end. 'The leaders of 1461', observed Vicens Vives,
'became the demagogues of 1462.' The war was, in this sense,
fundamentally political. It was a struggle over the rightful place
of the count-king, the greater landlords, and the lesser tenants
and workers in Catalonian society.

In the winter of 1462 the queen worked to create royalist
sentiment in Barcelona, thereby reviving an anti-*Busca entente*.
Unable to prevent the Council of Catalonia from recruiting an
army to repress the *remences*, she and Prince Fernando left
Barcelona for Girona on 11 March, probably hoping to impose
peace herself in the *remença* lands, certainly fearing for their safety
in Barcelona. They left a poisoned atmosphere, in which former
Busca councillors of Barcelona said to have plotted with the
queen were condemned and executed in May 1462. The violent
elimination of potential mediators worsened the conflict. Queen
Juana undertook to negotiate with the *remences* through their
leader Francesch Verntallat. This resulted in a new wave of
suspicion of the queen, the landlords looking in vain for signs
that she meant to put down the rising. Meanwhile, King John
had entered into negotiation with Louis XI of France, who
characteristically saw events in Catalonia and Navarre serving
his own expansionist aims. Late in 1461 Louis had gathered a
military force at Narbonne. In April 1462 at Olite he confirmed
John's scheme to vest the succession to Navarre in his younger
daughter married to Gaston of Foix and their heir, a wicked
scheme that entailed delivering John's elder daughter Blanca to
the beneficiaries of her disinheritment. They let her die in prison.
Having thus solved one of John's problems, Louis found it easier
to impose his own terms for military aid. By treaties passed at
Sauveterre (3 May) and Bayonne (9 May) Louis agreed to
provide 700 lances (4,200 mounted men plus retainers and
weapons) in exchange for the payment of 200,000 *écus*. It was a
high price for service that proved of doubtful quality, all
the higher because it was stipulated that Louis should appropriate the revenues, castles, and jurisdiction of Roussillon and
Cerdanya until the payment was made.

As word of these treaties got out, all hope of settlement
vanished. In May the count of Pallars led forces of the *Generalitat*
against Girona; they entered the city on 6 June while the queen

and the prince took refuge in the 'old castle'. The king had entered Catalonia from the west, seizing Balaguer on 5 June, but was in no position to relieve the queen; as his invasion violated the Capitulation the *Generalitat* branded him and his wife alike as 'enemies of the public interest' (9 June 1462). On 23 July French forces led by Gaston of Foix rescued Juana and Fernando while King John defeated a Catalan army at Rubinat, near Cervera, and seized Tàrrega. Joining the French at Montcada in September, John besieged Barcelona without success. Tarragona fell to him on 31 October, but the year ended with the king in control of only two cities and his foes casting about for new allies. Neither side had more than a few hundred men at its disposal, morale was low, and desertions frequent. The king raised little more than token support in Aragon and Valencia. He did better in Sardinia and Sicily, having made costly concessions to the Sicilian magnates in 1460; after 1462 Sicilian grain and money were a life-line to the royal cause.

The king's perilous appeal to France and his early successes drove his enemy to equally desperate bids for foreign support. In August 1462 the Catalans (so to call them) summoned Enrique IV of Castile, proclaiming him Count of Barcelona and John and Juana deposed. No one gained from this except Louis XI. Enrique approached Barcelona by sea but refused to intervene further, while agents of John II and Louis XI persuaded him to give up Catalonia for the cession of Estella in Navarre (April 1463). It seemed for the moment that this Louis, like another, might become the arbiter of a civil war: an embassy of the Catalans sounded him out at Abbeville (November 1463) but decided he was no Saint Louis. Put off by his claim to be of Catalan dynastic descent and his opinion that 'there are no mountains' between Catalonia and France, they returned to find their compatriots in touch with Pedro, constable of Portugal. Descended from Jaume of Urgell, the claimant of 1410, Pedro was more to the pactists' liking, a foreign *condottiere* whom they might easily control in a quasi-republican state. He arrived at Barcelona in January 1464, showed some desire to act independently of the *Diputació* and Council, but failed to create his own following or to win in the field. John prepared a new offensive, conquered Lérida in July 1464, Vilafranca del Penedès in August, and defeated Pedro near Prats de Rei in February

1465, capturing the count of Pallars among others. When Pedro of Portugal died in June 1466, the rebels' cause was in serious disarray. King John had long since promised to respect the *Constitucions* of Catalonia and the privileges of the cities; he had offered a general pardon of his foes that helped turn several places to his cause. Even the *Generalitat* was wavering in 1466. But when John proposed peace after Pedro's death, a radical minority of the opposition forced yet another defiance on the shattered country. Deciding to deal harshly with royalists as traitors, on 30 July 1466 they offered their sovereignty to Alphonse V's old rival, René of Anjou, duke of Provence.

This was the boldest and most desperate stroke of the war. One may view it as a perversion of national tradition or as a resourceful revival of Catalan Mediterranean ambitions; one cannot defend it as serving the interest of Catalonia. No potential in Provence or Naples could justify the virtual renunciation of Roussillon and Cerdanya; and if it was expected that René would rely on Louis XI, as he did, it was folly to imagine that Louis would serve the principality any better than he had done the king. Nor did he, in the end. But for a time John II's cause was seriously set back—and the war went on. René of Anjou was better equipped than his predecessors, and his son Jean of Lorraine proved a capable military leader. John himself had gone blind, his son Fernando was only fourteen, and his wife Juana died in 1468. Girona held out for the king in 1467–8, then surrendered to Jean of Lorraine and the French in June 1469. Could some lingering memory of 1285 have been stirred? Once again the fall of Girona was to mark the limit of French penetration. The tide turned as a resilient septuagenarian king, his sight restored by a skilful Jewish physician, opened a new diplomatic front against France.

Resourcefully and deliberately John II detached France from her allies. He began by working toward an alliance between Aragon, England, and Burgundy. He encouraged a league of French barons against Louis XI. All this followed logically from the diplomatic reversal of 1466. But the fortuitous death of Alfonso of Castile in 1468 offered John a more dramatic prospect of embarrassing France while realizing his fondest ambition. He proposed a marriage between his son Fernando and the princess Isabella, half-sister of Enrique IV and widely accepted as heiress to Castile; and—more difficult—won acceptance of the proposal. The marriage celebrated at Valladolid in October 1469 did little to settle disorder in Castile, but it gave the king of Aragon new leverage against his own opposition. René's offensive foundered as French support fell away, nor did his Catalonian allies treat him more respectfully than Pedro of Portugal. King John by contrast prevailed on a general Cort(e)s at Monzón to grant the subsidy required to expel the French from Catalonia.

A war-torn country could now reasonably hope for peace. The death of René (16 December 1470) removed the *Diputació*'s last useful ally. As barons and knights of Old Catalonia returned to the king's allegiance, the royalists recovered Girona (October 1471), leaving Barcelona the last vulnerable bastion of the rebellion. Its last months were a nightmare as rations were short and the water supply cut off; the people were demoralized, even terrorized. Besieged by the king, the city fell in early October. In the Capitulation of Pedralbes (10 October 1472) John offered lenient terms: a general pardon without recrimination, exception being made for the count of Pallars, and recognition of the *Constitucions* and other privileges of Catalonia; he excluded only the Capitulation of Vilafranca, which the royalists viewed to the last as the provocation of the war.

The war created and ignored as many problems as it solved. It did at least determine that Catalonia should have a king, whatever limitations Catalonian privilege might place upon the king. Most Catalans had come to fear anarchy more than arbitrary rule, few seem to have worried that John's Castilian heir might misgovern. John himself strove to undo his most politically costly concession: the assignment of Roussillon and Cerdanya as security for advances of war subsidy by the French. The men of those counties had already driven out most of the French when John himself was received joyously at Perpignan on 1 February 1473. His Catalan forces garrisoned castles there and at Bellegarde, Collioure, and Salses. But this political solution did nothing to fulfil the treaty of Bayonne. Louis XI counter-attacked a few weeks later. John resisted with the aid of Castilian forces brought up by his son Fernando, then entered into negotiations leading to a truce in July and to a settlement at Perpignan on 17 September 1473. John recognized the treaty of Bayonne and won his adversary's recognition of his sovereignty in Roussillon and Cerdanya; he conceded that these counties be neutralized until the payment stipulated in 1462—200,000 *écus*, now raised by the French to 300,000—was effected.

Once again the Crown of Aragon was revealed prostrate before France. John returned to a triumphant welcome at Barcelona, but his resolve and his allies alike then failed. With no payment forthcoming, the French overran Roussillon in the summer of 1474 and recaptured Perpignan the following March. While Castile lapsed into a new civil war and Burgundy and Naples were committed elsewhere, John could not even oppose French raids into the Empordà, and as far as Girona, in 1476. In October 1478 he settled more feebly than ever, leaving Roussillon and Cerdanya to France until he could raise the money to redeem them. Meanwhile, he had lost control of the peace in Aragon and Valencia, where factional violence flared again. Only in Sardinia did John II succeed in putting down rebellion in his last years.

The potential loss of Catalonia's dynastic homeland was matched by the king's failure to grasp the social and economic problems that the constitutional conflict had obscured. It was a failure of sympathy as much as of understanding. For all his astonishing vitality, the ageing John II remained insensitive to the plight of *remença* peasants or misgoverned townspeople. He lost sight of the more general interest represented by the royalist programme his father and brother (and he himself) had advocated in the past. The Corts pressed on him one partial solution after another. Property lost or sequestered in the fighting had to be restored or titles determined, yet claims at law and settlements lagged in hopeless confusion. And these problems were bound to others that would have defied even resolute policy to resolve. Contemporaries themselves knew only that Catalonia had been ruined by the civil war. Merchants of Barcelona, even artisans, had moved to Valencia and Naples to carry on more securely. Barcelona's population was severely reduced. Trade was depressed, the coinage of Barcelona slipping in value of account.

Not all the disorder can be charged to John II, nor was Catalonia the only victim of his policies. The royal patrimony in Sicily as well as in Catalonia had been squandered. It was the refusal of the foralist magnates to compromise in the 1460s as much as John's desperation that had lured a menacing French genie out of its box. The *Biga* had succeeded no better than the *Busca* in governing Barcelona. Yet it was characteristic of John II that his ambitions were always elsewhere, and costly to his own realms. Insisting relentlessly on his personal Castilian destiny, fighting yet another Castilian war to secure his daughter-in-law's succession in 1475–6, he had opened the way to a historic union of Hispanic kingdoms. A cruel streak in this dogged ruler was shown by his brutal substitution of Fernando for Carlos of Viana, but the ultimate acceptance of Fernando in Catalonia as well as in Aragon, Valencia, and the other realms marked a significant shift in political opinion. Internal disorder came to seem worse than alien rule. Everywhere people were ready for his son when John II died at Barcelona in January 1479.

Institutional Maturity

The Trastámara count-kings governed the Crown of Aragon—or left its realms to govern themselves—through institutions already in place. They imposed little that was new, least of all any theory of kingship (absolute or otherwise), their modifications of curial and local administration resulting more from bureaucratic logic than from any sovereign disposition to control. Only perhaps in Naples was there innovation, but that only means that even Alphonse V thought of this acquired realm as distinct from the confederation. In all the other realms institutional and legal change owed much to the requirements of delegated administration and territorial representation. So in Catalonia the Corts of 1413 began the work completed in those of Alphonse V of organizing the *usatges*, constitutions, and privileges in a coherent body of written law—a territorial law of the principality. In Aragon the *Observancias* of Jacobo del Hospital and his successors put the customs of that realm in a quasi-official form. In these realms and elsewhere Romanist principles figured in the codified customs, not uncommonly in ways serving to strengthen seigneurial rights. The fact that Ferdinand I acceded by election undoubtedly strengthened older foralist notions of limited kingship. Jurists like Jaume Callis and Tomas Mieres in Catalonia and Pere Belluga in Valencia spoke for a constitutional order balancing the rights of monarchy with those of estates and constituted bodies of the land.

The practical difficulty of managing affairs centrally became very apparent under Alphonse V. It was easier to supervise the islands from the peninsular mainland than to do the reverse. So while the royal court and its maintenance continued to be regulated as laid down in the ordinances of Peter IV, Alphonse V instituted a *Mestre Racional* exclusively for the Kingdom of Valencia in 1419, and the process of decentralizing the fiscal audit was later extended to Catalonia and Aragon. Whatever the utility of this change it badly suited the needs of a king habitually absent from the peoples whose money he wanted, so in 1456 Alphonse tried to restore central accountability under a *Mestre Racional* at Naples, less a reform, perhaps, than an experiment that met with opposition from local treasurers everywhere.

Delegated royal authority was exercised chiefly by governors and lieutenants. The governorship was the older function, associated since the thirteenth century with the claim of the count-king's heir to share in his powers from the age of majority and normally appointed to this purpose from the later fourteenth century. It bore ordinary powers of jurisdiction in the several realms and the superintendance of local officials, but might also be empowered specially *ad hoc*. In the fifteenth century the governor was commonly supplemented by lieutenants whose function had evolved from temporary procurations, but who now often served even when the king was present. This development resulted from the increasingly honorific nature of the governor's unspecialized office and from the need to deal politically with the barons, towns, and their representative bodies in Sicily, Sardinia, and Majorca as well as in the peninsula. The viceroyalties organized in Sicily and Sardinia early in the fifteenth century met this need and may have been the models for the peninsular posts whose holders came later, in their turn, to be called viceroys (*virreis*). Alphonse V having no children, the governorship fell vacant during his long reign, leaving the lieutenancy, held by Queen María and later by Prince Juan, the chief delegacy. The claims on behalf of Prince Carlos showed to what point Catalans regarded the governorship an institution and wanted it revived. The power assumed by lieutenants to convoke the Cort(e)s rendered them virtually the equals of the old governors in authority.

Almost everywhere the lieutenants or, when present, the king now dealt continuously with their peoples through the Cort(e)s and parliaments and their standing deputations. These bodies having assumed custody of the privileges and their observance, their inaugural sessions became political confrontations in which the amiable celebration of the sovereign's estate gave way to more or less partisan demonstrations of the demands and pretensions of privilege. It is unnecessary to review here the ways in which these confrontations in Catalonia and Aragon powerfully influenced events in each Trastámara reign, forcing Ferdinand's sons to cultivate new or distant resources to compensate for dwindling patrimonies or evade troubling demands. In Catalonia the exclusion of the lesser knights consolidated the formidable alliance of landed magnates and urban oligarchs through which a pactist programme hostile to reform was institutionalized. The instrument of this privileged representation was henceforth the *Diputació del General* (or *Generalitat*), whose autonomous powers were recognized definitively in 1413. Three *diputats* and three auditors of account (*oidors*) were to be chosen triennially by co-optation, forming a cosy committee prone to lose sight of interests wider than those of its members. A Valencian *Diputació* was similarly organized in 1418, but soon thereafter reconstituted so as to admit of balloting. In Catalonia various experiments to liberalize the selection of *diputats* culminated in the adoption of an electoral process resembling Valencia's in 1455. The crown had not lost all initiative, to be sure, not even in Catalonia. If the *estaments* protested convocations in the count-king's absence, they none the less learned to live with them. They could bully lieutenants at least as well as the king. The summons and attendance tended to become fixed in customary forms and numbers, which did not prevent (and may have encouraged) the estates to divide among themselves: for example, the military *braç* in the Corts of 1419–20 and 1421–3 over the extent of limitations to be set on the prerogative, or the clergy in those of 1436 over a question of the Peace and Truce. Alphonse V extended the summons of Catalonian towns from some twelve to fifteen, as was customary, to forty in the sessions of 1449 and 1454.

In Aragon too the *Diputación* was constituted permanently from the accession of Ferdinand I. The construction of its own edifice at Zaragoza was authorized in 1427 and carried out from

1437 to 1450, when sessions of the Cortes were held in the 'houses of the kingdom, commonly known as houses of the deputation'. The Cortes of Aragon, constituted in four estates (that of the nobility being divided), supported Alphonse V with less acrimony than the Corts of Catalonia, but after 1445 they tired of John's insatiable appetite for fighting in Castile. Since every decision of the Cortes—such as on matters of internal security and order—required a negotiated concession, sessions lengthened to such a point that attendance fell off or was maintained perfunctorily through procurators. The constitutional powers of the Aragonese were now vested so fully in the Cortes that the weakening of the justiciarship under Alphonse V (see p. 140) had little practical consequence.

In local government the older vicariates and bailiwicks persisted in Catalonia, the *merinados* in Aragon, etc. We still know too little about the effects of war and contraction of royal domain on these offices. The overriding problem of the fifteenth century was the oppressive dominance of a patrician oligarchy in municipal offices. Rejecting all bids to widen the franchise or spread more equally the fiscal obligations, such men clung to power gained by co-optation. This is why Alphonse V's interest in a new system of balloting by lot for administrative and conciliar posts (*insaculació*) was so important, for it gave impetus to a movement of natural appeal to a growing class of men whose power lagged behind their means. Possibly tried first in Majorca, this reform spread from Valencian towns (Játiva, 1427; Castellon de la Plana, 1444) to Vic in 1450, Barbastro in 1454, and Girona in 1465. Election to the Catalonian *Generalitat* was reformed on the same model in 1455. But there was no dogmatic insistence on the idea: at Barcelona, also in 1455, the king tried simply to institute a fair representation of the *estaments* in the municipal council, including for the first time those of artisans and labourers. The appearance of the *mostassaf* as supervisor of commercial affairs and the market in many towns signalled a spreading recognition of labour as a matter of public interest.

The commercial and industrial guilds of the towns reached their apogee of influence and ceremonial vigour. Consulates of foreign trade multiplied only in places of secondary importance, in Tortosa (1401) and Sant Feliu de Guíxols (1446), among others. The major consulates, founded much earlier, expanded

and codified their regulations: for example, at Valencia in 1418
and 1420. The jurisdiction of Barcelona's Consulate of the Sea
was strengthened by royal decree 1443–4. Deposit banking dated
from the establishment of the *Taula de Canvi* at Barcelona in 1401
and at Valencia in 1407. Barcelona's bank operated by ordinance
from 1412, but ran into trouble during the civil war when
payments were suspended. Valencia's bank had already ceased
to function in 1418, to be re-established only a century afterward.
Queen María chartered a new bank at Girona in 1443.

The election of Fernando de Antequera at Caspe in 1412 appears
in retrospect a fateful turning-point, the dynastic ratification of
Castile's demographic and military superiority to the Crown of
Aragon. Ferdinand and his sons ruling after him were Castilians
who married Castilians and appointed Castilians; they were
rulers in real and constant danger of losing touch with their
subjects. This was evident in their time. It sufficiently explains
why Ferdinand I and Alphonse V met strenuous opposition in
their efforts to lay down the fiscal and political basis for a
monarchy independent of magnate and urban factions; in other
words, although few perhaps admitted or remembered as much
to re-establish the monarchy as James II or Peter IV had known
it. In view of this opposition, notably that in Catalonia, it would
have been astonishing if they had succeeded; they are not alone
to blame for having failed. The political history of the later
medieval Crown of Aragon was not one of embattled nationalists
against foreign rulers but of patriots too narrowly interested, too
divided against themselves, to animate Cort(e)s or armies in a
common cause. The euphoria over Carlos of Viana in 1460–1
was a sentimental flash of enlarged identity—but it would surely
have collapsed even if the prince had lived. The maintenance of
estate by the old nobles, prelates, chapters, and urban lords in a
faltering economy was too perilously competitive to admit of a
widened consensus such as would have rendered Cort(e)s and
Diputacions effective representations of society. In this respect the
constitutional theories of fifteenth-century jurists were too
idealistic to describe the real motives of pactist magnates and
diputats.

Yet the overriding need of effective monarchy had come to be
admitted by all. The extraordinary tenacity of John II hd served

the federation well, had perhaps even preserved it from dismemberment or subjugation to France. But to have salvaged the old monarchy at the cost of wrecking Catalonia was a sadly mixed success—and such was the inheritance of Ferdinand II when he succeeded his father in 1479. Under Ferdinand and Isabella arose a new monarchy embracing most of the Iberian peninsula. Within a few years the Reconquista would be completed, a New World discovered, and a consolidated Hispanic power launched toward hegemony in Europe. The Crown of Aragon formed no small part of the New Spain, but it was a part none the less, no longer a proud whole. Its Middle Ages were over. Our story ends here.

Yet not precisely in 1479. Dynastic union with Castile did not of itself put an end to unfinished business nor disrupt the deeper continuities of institutional life in the realms of the old federation. The king would come less often, but he would come. Ferdinand II visited Barcelona only six times (and would spend fewer than four of his thirty-seven years in Catalonia), but the first two of these visits, in 1479 and again in 1480–1 to celebrate the Corts, showed that he recognized the need of general reform in Catalonia. He provided for the restitution of property, the repayment of war debts, and the protection of trade and industry, and he reorganized the *Generalitat* and *Audiència*. He received a healthy subsidy from the Corts and it may have been for financial reasons that he temporized on the *remença* problem. First allowing the *mals usos* to be reinstated, he soon faced a new peasant uprising even more disagreeable to the landlords than to himself, whereupon Ferdinand acted firmly to abolish servitude altogether in rural Catalonia. By his Sentence of Guadalupe (April 1486) the peasants redeemed their freedom at a price of 50,000 l. to be raised during a period of years; the arbitrary rights of landlords were abolished. At a stroke the oppressed tenant-farmers of Catalonia thus achieved freedoms that peasants in Aragon would envy for centuries more. There were renewed efforts to reform municipal government in the 1490s, when signs of economic recovery appeared in Catalonia. Ferdinand II completed a political restoration by treating with France (Barcelona 1493) for the return of Roussillon and Cerdanya.

In such ways the new king acted vigorously on behalf of his inheritance. In such ways, it must be added, he conserved far more than he changed. He set up a new Council of Aragon (1494) comprising regents from the several realms, but he also established the old viceroyalties of the major realms as a permanent feature of the Crown of Aragon preserved as such. He imposed himself rather more arbitrarily on Aragon and Valencia, seldom convoking their Cort(e)s; and he neglected Majorca, where agrarian tensions and the public debt increased. Even in Catalonia his reforms were seldom other than compromises with the privileged orders, calculated efforts to restore the medieval constitution. So too, in a more curious way, was his foreign policy restorative, for having first encouraged the French in Naples as the price of redeeming the old Pyrenean counties, Ferdinand later contrived brilliantly to oust them and his cadet-line nephew alike, thereby incorporating Naples for the first time with Sardinia and Sicily under Aragonese rule (1504). There was something poignantly ironic about this energetic Castilian wrestling with Catalonian problems together with so much else. Was not Ferdinand II fulfilling his father's dream? The first modern king of Spain was the last medieval king of the Crown of Aragon.

VII

Prosperity and Crisis in the Later Middle Ages

IT cannot be said that war, dynastic failure, and political strife were reserved for the Crown of Aragon in the later Middle Ages. France, England, and even Castile suffered these scourges, too, and—until about 1460—arguably in more acute forms. Catalonia, which fared worst among the Crown's lands, experienced little violence at home until the civil war (1462–72), while her knights, mariners, and merchants seldom lacked the freedom to decide which foreign wars they thought worth fighting. Yet the civil war when it came left the land reeling from maladies political, social, and economic; maladies so compounded as to place the Catalans and their confederates virtually at the mercy of powerful neighbours well on the way to recovery at the dawn of the modern era. Only Valencia presented a different picture, but her relative prosperity could hardly brighten the sombre colours in which the larger canvas was painted.

Historians of the past half century have taught us that political narration will not sufficiently explain these troubles. Led by Jaume Vicens Vives and Pierre Vilar, they have introduced new concepts—structure, conjuncture, crisis—to focus a more penetrating analysis on social order, disorder, and change. They have found that the rhythms of social and economic life by no means necessarily coincide with those of political change, nor even with each other. They have discovered the paradox that prosperity may coexist with crisis in the complexity of historical experience; and have rediscovered the truth that culture may thrive in adversity. Above all, they have helped us to conceive of a long period extending from the later thirteenth century to the end of the fifteenth in terms of structural continuity and disruption. In this perspective it becomes clear that the troubles in fifteenth-century Catalonia, while in some respects the result of peculiar circumstances and mistaken policies, were symp-

tomatic of deeper and often older problems characteristic of the
Crown of Aragon.

Demography and Society

Possibly the most fundamental of these problems was demographic. There were simply not enough people to compete on
economic, financial, and military terms with the vast new
monarchies taking shape to the west and north of Aragon. This
may seem surprising in view of the enormous growth of Aragon
and Catalonia, which since the eleventh century had sent forth
wave after wave of colonists to their frontiers and to foreign
lands. But the very bulk of this emigration may itself be a clue to
the limitations of the old lands, in which the fertile belts were
offset by an abundance of arid or otherwise unyielding and
undeveloped habitats. Despite indications of increasing longevity
in the thirteenth century, it looks as if continued emigration
drained away the natural increment in Catalonia's population
down to 1350 or so.

The population of the peninsular crown of Aragon (including
Majorca) has been estimated by Vicens Vives at around 900,000
before the Black Death. This figure, drawn chiefly from fiscal
registers of hearths post-dating 1348, is almost certainly too low.
It was the calculation of a scholar quite justifiably rejecting
exaggerated notions of the importance of the Catalan-Aragonese
realms in late medieval Spain but perhaps allowing too little for
the incompleteness of the records. Yet even if the composite
population is set at more than one million—even if, say, as high
as 1,200,000—such a figure alone, when compared to Castile's
six million people, goes far to explain the rise of Castile to
peninsular dominance. Catalonia with perhaps 500,000 was for
long the most populous and prosperous of the realms, having
many more people than lived in Aragon (about 250,000) and
Valencia (200,000) combined in the early fourteenth century. As
late as the 1450s Alphonse V saw fit to request 400,000 florins
from Catalonia, 120,000 from Valencia, and 80,000 from Aragon.

The composition and conditions of these populations continued to reflect their origin in expansion from the mountains
and in conquests. Old Catalonia and Old Aragon remained
overwhelmingly peasant societies dominated by barons, knights,
bishops, and the old regular clergy. Since the constitution of 1283

binding rural tenants to the land except by payment for release (redemption, or *remença*), the freedoms of peasants in the Old Catalonian lands (plus the old frontier) had been progressively curtailed; the *remença* peasants, numbering some 80,000 to 100,000 in the early fourteenth century, made up at least one-fifth of the principality's population. In the crescent formed by New Catalonia, the frontiers of Aragon, and Valencia, the Mudejars were a vast element of peasants and artisans, amounting to some 200,000 persons about 1400—over one-fifth of the entire confederation's population. Most of the Mudejars were in Valencia, only some 3 per cent (about 6,000) in Catalonia. In these former frontier zones the Cistercians and Hospitallers were the principal landlords. Having incorporated Templar holdings after 1317 and having been reorganized as a Grand Priory of Catalonia, the Knights of the Hospital of Saint John of Jerusalem were the richest lords among the regular clergy, dominating 1000 hearths in the principality and, together with the seculars, two-thirds of the land in the dioceses of Tarragona and Tortosa. The monks of Poblet held some 600 hearths; those of Santes Creus, 400. Counting secular and regular jurisdictions together, the church dominated some 100,000 peasants throughout Catalonia; the lay aristocracy perhaps 150,000. These figures include 150,000 non-*remença* peasants in Catalonia, mostly in old-frontier zones, to which should be added about 75,000 Christian peasants in Aragon, Valencia, and Majorca to account for the agrarian population of the Crown of Aragon. People living in cities and towns numbered perhaps as many as 250,000 or about 25 per cent of the aggregate. Of this number the 'little people' (*poble menut*) everywhere formed the mass, day-labourers and *menestrals* aspiring to the minimal security afforded by acceptance in a guild. The merchants, master craftsmen, notaries, and lawyers formed a fluid élite of initiative and new wealth; but they lacked the political power of the patricians, or 'honoured citizens'.

Two other elements were characteristic of the Crown of Aragon as a whole. The Jews are thought to have numbered about 60,000 in the thirteenth century, or perhaps (then) as much as 6.5 per cent of the total population. Artisans, physicians, and money-lenders, they lived mostly in the old cities and towns of Catalonia and Aragon, forming a cultured non-

Christian society radically different from the Mudejars. Finally, there were slaves in astonishing numbers: possibly as many as 30,000 around 1400. Purchased in Mediterranean port-markets or from pirates and including Greeks, Turks, and Tartars as well as Africans ('Moors'), they were not estate-hands but domestics serving in the houses of burghers and patricians. They were particularly numerous at Barcelona.

What chiefly weakened the demographic and social fabric was the Black Death, which first struck the confederation with devastating force in 1348. A mortality of two-thirds has been discovered in the Plain of Vic! In Barcelona four of the five councillors died together with almost all of the *Consell de Cent*. At Santa Maria of Ribes the lone surviving monk elected himself prior. Men in the Balearic Islands, finding themselves at the mercy of pirates, pleaded with the king for reinforcements. The ordinary administration of contracts was suspended at Puigcerdà, Prades (Baix Camp), Montblanc, and elsewhere for want of notaries; lands and houses were abandoned. Up to half the people may have died in some Catalan-speaking zones by 1351, although a mortality of 25 to 35 per cent seems more likely for the confederation as a whole. It is possible that Catalonia recovered strongly in the 1350s before falling victim to new scourges: a devastation of crops by locusts in 1358, another outbreak of plague at Barcelona in 1362–3, followed by further epidemics, not always confined to Barcelona, in 1375, 1381, 1396, 1410, 1429, 1439, 1448, 1465, 1476, and so on as late as 1521. Reduced by war and emigration as well as by disease, the population of Catalonia is thought to have fallen to about 350,000 by 1378 and to fewer than 300,000 by 1497. The city of Barcelona was reduced from 50,000 inhabitants in 1340 to 20,000 in 1477; Perpignan from 18,000 to 15,000; etc. The other realms, having likewise suffered waves of plague, experienced demographic recovery in the fifteenth century. Aragon's population rose from some 200,000 to 250,000. Valencia surged past Catalonia during the civil war, her capital of 75,000 becoming the largest city in the Crown of Aragon.

How the recurrent epidemics affected the social order in the several realms is far from clear, for their impact was seldom divorced from the influence of other factors. The royal patrimony, for example, was surely wasted more by alienations than by deaths; in Catalonia it had encompassed some 31 per cent of registered hearths toward 1350, of which the rural component (only one-fourth) had been much reduced since the twelfth century. We still know too little about the higher clergy to see very well how they rode out the storm. But with lordship over some 16,000 rural hearths, they can hardly have escaped damage to their incomes. Presumably the lay aristocracy suffered—or changed—most, but not simply because disease is a leveller. In Catalonia the nobility of arms remained an open and diversely constituted class, perhaps 1 to 1.5 per cent of the population. Barons and knights (*cavallers, donzells*) dominated some 38 per cent of recorded hearths, almost all of them peasant hearths. This means that the rural mortality struck at the roots of their power, leaving many hundreds of manses unoccupied, cutting seigneurial revenues, and creating a sellers' market for wage labour. Peasants fled to the towns. In the later fourteenth century a newly prospering element of *remença* farmers entered into negotiation with lawyers and townsmen to press for reforms. In Aragón the Cortes of Zaragoza in 1350 tried to regulate prices and wages in a vain effort to protect clergy, nobles, and patricians. Over several decades the weakening or flight of the silver coinage and the emigration of knights likewise depleted the aristocracy. Threatened everywhere, in Catalonia the old baronial élite was decimated. Only two distinguished families, the Cardona and the Rocabertí, survived the fifteenth century, while by a more inclusive reckoning half of all knightly families in the fifteenth century were new ones. In Aragon the greater families fared better, although they failed in efforts to close ranks against the new rich and king's favourites not of their own. The lesser rural lords were impoverished.

The Mudejars in Aragon were fortunate to have the protection of the king and other lords; those of Valencia, more than half the population and less assimilated, declined in numbers and were persecuted in the fifteenth century. The Jews were doubly afflicted by plague, which not only took its toll of dead in their urban *calls* but aroused suspicions among frightened Christians of their having poisoned the wells. Already before the massacres of 1391 the economic position of Jews had weakened, as royal taxation continued to bear heavily on them and as new forms of credit and finance were devised. Some 5 per cent of the Jews may have died in the riots, leaving (by the estimate of Vicens Vives) about 50,000 Jews in worsening circumstances, a number reduced to 30,000 by the end of the fifteenth century. The breakdown of religious *convivencia* was fomented by Vicent Ferrer and other friars, resulting in conversions as well as persecutions of Jews and Moors. Around 1400, moreover, Jews were coming from France and they were not the only immigrants. Gascon peasants and shepherds crossed the Pyrenees to take up abandoned lands while Italians moved in considerable numbers to Catalonian cities, followed by German merchants. The social consequences of this immigration were mixed, for while the Italian colony in Barcelona was productive and wealthy, the Gascons were a rootless and unsettling element in the country-sides. The *remença* conflict was none the easier for the intrusion.

Chronic underpopulation thus contributed to social unrest and dislocation. Contemporaries lamented the strife that weakened traditional order. But their very values were in conflict: sumptuousness for the ruling classes, poverty for the rest. It is true that Eiximenis, writing in 1383, spoke of public order (*la cosa publica*) as 'composed basically of three *estaments* of persons, that is, of the lesser [people], the middling, and the greater', and went on to define their organic coherence by the old metaphor of the human body. But the political reality was different. Everywhere society was oligarchic and jealous of the 'liberties' by which it defended the incomparable advantages of birth and inheritance. Neither in Cort(e)s nor in municipalities were merchants, artisans, or peasants adequately represented; in Catalonia even the lesser nobles were politically excluded. Yet the federation as a whole was remarkably urbanized, as we have seen: in Catalonia and Valencia some 30 per cent of the people lived in towns or cities. Only in Aragon, where Zaragoza with some 15,000 inhabitants in the fifteenth century was by far the largest place, formed an exception to this pattern. So it happened that the most dynamic social class, whose wealth the kings sought most urgently to tap, was also the most restricted and most vulnerable in its power and rights. Everywhere the nobility, including the estate of 'honoured citizens', was thought to possess an innate right to command, an ancient presumption that lent credibility even to political groups like the *Biga* without a viable cause. Eagerly grasped by the new rich, this debilitating élitism was hardly less important than depopulation and social conflict as a factor impeding national consensus.

Economy

Oligarchy was a product of wealth in the Crown of Aragon and, indeed, of economic prosperity. In earlier centuries prosperity had been founded on increasing agrarian productivity and the growth of population in the old realms; by 1300 at latest these movements had been overtaken by an expanding commerce and the beginnings of homeland industries that made possible a genuinely international economy. Whether this possibility was ever fully realized is doubtful, for the count-kings, municipalities, and merchants, if equally avid for profit, can seldom have thought of, let alone agreed upon, schemes of common economic benefit. Even in the grand days of Mediterranean expansion, there seems to have been no commonly held idea of empire. Not unlike the old castellans, one exploited, at home as abroad, rather than nurturing or 'developing' economic opportunities. For men of such outlook plagues and famines were small deterrent: fortunes do not die and may even be improved by concentration or dissolution. It is no paradox that economic prosperity survived the social disasters of the fourteenth century before succumbing in other circumstances.

The agrarian basis of this economy was little changed from the past and inadequate to mounting demands put upon it. Its tooling was archaic, its cultivation unprogressive, save only in parts of Aragon and Valencia where irrigation had been adopted from the Moors. Wheat and barley were the principal cereal crops in Aragon and Catalonia, where wine and olives were also produced. Rice was cultivated particularly in Valencia, as was saffron, which the Moors had developed as an export crop; in Catalonia the cultivation of saffron spread from Tortosa and Ager to Urgell in the fourteenth century. Sheep continued to be raised in Catalonia and Aragon, producing an ordinary grade of wool that tended to replace the finer product of England in supply to a new textile industry in Catalonia. Among natural resources, iron from the Pyrenees and coral from the coasts were especially valued.

Industrial production, though diverse, seems in general to have developed rather modestly in the later Middle Ages.

Metallurgy prospered in two directions: weaponry and military supplies and the working of silver. The silversmiths of Barcelona came to dominate Hispanic markets for jewellery. Clothiers, leather-workers, and builders flourished at Barcelona. Textiles were even more important. Woollen manufactures had been a local industry until the French war beginning in 1285 cut off supplies of high-grade wools from the North. By 1300 a new industry was booming at Barcelona with an influx of immigrant workers and commercial capital. Once the economic potential of this industry became clear, old centres of production in hinterland Catalonia were rehabilitated. Girona expanded enormously on cloth-working in the fourteenth century; there were important factories also in Valencia and Majorca. The bulk of Catalonian and Valencian produce consisted of cheap woollens and fustians, although fine black cloths came from Perpignan, Vic, and Majorca.

All these products continued to figure in a lively mainland trade conducted in local markets. But the real potential lay in an overseas trade that was dominated from its beginnings by Barcelona; it was well developed by 1300, and attained a vigorous maturity by 1350. This trade was organized in several routes. The route of Languedoc–Provence had originated in the twelfth century and persisted vigorously for 300 years. Its principal ports were Barcelona, Perpignan, Montpellier, and Marseille; its goods chiefly cereals, wine, and spices. The 'route of the islands' linked Sicily, Sardinia, and Corsica with Majorca and Barcelona. Textiles and coral from Catalonia, silver and salt from Sardinia, and wheat from Sicily were the staples of this route, largely controlled by Catalans in Sicily. An Italian route, highly competitive and insecure, featured the export of Catalonian cloths and Sicilian grain to Naples. The more easterly Mediterranean routes centred on Venice, where the import of Sicilian wheat enabled Catalan merchants to tap Adriatic markets for Balkan and Russian products, including slaves, for sale in the western Mediterranean; and on Constantinople, the greatest entrepôt for a lucrative far eastern trade in silk, gold, spices, and slaves. In the Greek zone the Catalans suffered from the ill repute of the *almogàvers* and still more from the competition of Genoa and Venice; but despite costly naval conflicts, especially in the 1380s, Catalan traders held on in

Constantinople until 1453. They had a more profitable foothold in Egypt, where a valuable market in exotic dyestuffs, drugs, and spices was concentrated at Alexandria; but this traffic, weakened by Catalan piracy and violence, declined in the fifteenth century. The African routes were dominated by Catalans and they were profitable. In Tunis and Bougie entrepreneurs of Barcelona and Majorca exploited a virtually colonial market, collecting customs on a favourably balanced trade of Catalonian iron and textiles for gold and coral. In the Maghrib Catalans had again to compete, here with the Portuguese, Andalusians, and Genoese; the capture of Ceuta by Portugal in 1415 put an end to Catalan trade there. Finally, the Atlantic routes developed with imports of tin and wool from England and fish and textiles from Flanders. There was a Catalan colony in Bruges until the early fifteenth century. At about that time, too, an old Catalan interest in Seville declined before Genoese competition. Majorcan mariners pioneered west African routes in quest of gold and slaves in the fourteenth century, but their explorations had no lasting result.

These routes were more or less prosperous depending on political and economic circumstances. In the long run the peninsular Crown lands lacked the productive capacity to compensate for its own demands. Imports of wheat, spices, fine cloths, and slaves tended to outweigh exports of common textiles. saffron, wines, and manufactured goods. Valencia parlayed the export of rice to its own advantage after 1400. The 'routes', indeed, formed a complex of decentralized interests, earning profits more or less 'Catalan' in a vast Mediterranean world and beyond. The need to protect merchants and trade resulted in the multiplication of consulates that has been mentioned (p. 158); but these promotions, even considered in their excesses, hardly amounted to an imperial policy. The count-kings nevertheless encouraged marine vocations and industries, old Catalan interests that were vastly expanded in the later Middle Ages. Barcelona became the great shipbuilding centre of the western Mediterranean. As late as 1378 Peter IV and the municipal authorities proposed to spend 17,000 florins in rebuilding the *drassanes* shipyard of the city.

Commercial techniques improved apace. Barcelona was no innovator in this matter but a keen pupil of the Florentines and Genoese. Alongside the old commenda contracts arose the 'society of the sea', by which several persons undertook to ship, sell, buy, and divide the profits. A contract of 1336 shows merchants in Barcelona and Majorca working with the money of twenty-one others, including a tailor and a fisherman of Barcelona and their relatives. Maritime insurance is attested from the 1350s, attaining considerable importance in the fifteenth century. Bills of exchange appear by the end of the fourteenth century, such as that of 1400 in form of a draft written in Bruges and payable in Barcelona.

That Barcelona became a major centre of banking and finance owed as much to overseas trade as to the king's and others' fiscal and public needs. Already in 1300 the rights and functions of money-changers were regulated by the Corts. But the practice of lending money from private tables developed enormously, so that by 1380 a large sum of credit was outstanding. Meanwhile, the municipality of Barcelona had assumed control of local taxes, the income from which was used to secure annuities sold to raise money when needed. By the *censal* the lender and his heirs could collect indefinitely at 7 per cent per annum; the *violari* was a lifetime annuity at 15 per cent. But just when the generation of money was becoming easy, the contraction of 1381 caught the private lenders over-extended, with the result that many in Barcelona, Girona, and Perpignan went bankrupt. Out of the crisis came reforms leading to the founding of a municipal bank, the *Taula de Canvi*, in 1401. This institution, while it proved capable of managing the city's revenues, bore some marks of financial immaturity. By limiting its base to municipal credit and obligatory deposits, its founders tied up much-needed private capital. 'A period of financial conservatism was inaugurated which did not bode well for the future of Catalonia' (Vicens Vives).

The most palpable indices of commercial prosperity in the Crown of Aragon may be found in money and prices. For a long time the silver croat was the basis of an expanding economy; it had been minted in large amounts well into the fourteenth century without having to be protected or devalued—the symbol of a triumphant merchant class. What best marked the economic ascendancy of Barcelona and the Crown lands was Peter IV's order of 1346 to mint a new gold coin on the standards of the famous Florentine coinage. But at 22 carats the Catalan—

Aragonese florin almost at once proved insupportable at prevailing rates of military expenditure and a weakening balance of
trade. The standards were reduced in 1351, 1363, and 1365,
when the florin contained barely 75 per cent of its former gold
content. At this standard it would long remain; but the refusal to
devalue the croat in stringent times caused the flight of silver and
opened a rift between merchants and *rentiers*.

The movement of prices and wages may now be seen to
correspond to social, commercial, and monetary trends. From
about 1340 to 1380 prices and wages rose sharply, led by wages.
Only after 1380 did the effects of depopulation and financial
disorder combine to bring on a period of instability lasting until
the 1420s. From then on prices and wages tended to fall, prices
first in Aragon, then in Valencia and elsewhere. The years of
political and social crisis were marked by oscillations and, in
1454, by the devaluation of the croat.

In view of the structural difficulties in society, economic
resources, and finance, it is a remarkable fact that commercial
prosperity persisted in the fifteenth century. Despite periodic
setbacks such as were experienced in common with the great
Italian emporia, Catalan merchants and financiers managed to
carry on with some success until the crisis of the 1460s. Records
of port taxes suggest that the value of cargoes at Barcelona was
high in the years 1432–4. Contracts of marine insurance show
that confidence in Catalan shipping persisted. It was in the 1420s
that the old mercantile routes tended to become lines, organized
in regular sailings after the Venetian practice. The 'Sirvent
project' of 1443 proposed two annual sailings, one to the east and
the other to the north, with eastern spices to be re-exported to
northern ports; the scheme was in some part realized in 1436–44.
Moreover, Naples became a major stage in the Levantine trade
after the conquest, attracting Catalan investment. There the
Catalans, responding for once to Alphonse V, achieved the
favourably balanced trade that had so often eluded them
elsewhere.

Yet the prosperity had narrowed in its base and become
vulnerable. Barcelona's dependence on foreign grain worsened to
the point that she bought castles on the Ebro river to secure the
transport of wheat from Aragon, which was too poor for its part
to provide a compensating consumer demand. Even profitable

exchanges, as in Sicily and Naples, were too limited in volume to make up for losses and competition elsewhere. Nor could Catalonia's other Mediterranean markets match those of Venice in Germany and the North. Pressure on an over-valued silver coinage was constant down to the reform of 1454, while any weakening of demand for locally made textiles threw people out of work all over Catalonia. Whatever the value of foreign cargoes, customs and taxes on cloth had declined since 1426 and shipbuilding at Barcelona was badly depressed in the 1430s. Investment capital and entrepreneurial decisions fell increasingly into the hands of aliens, while some patricians whose ancestors had initiated capital ventures were now inclined to live from *censals* or rents or even to purchase rural lordships. Trade in Egypt and the Levant had been damaged by piracy and violence. *Busca* economic measures in the 1450s, promoting shipbuilding and protecting the cloth industry as well as devaluing the coinage, were a good indicator of problems that new opportunities in Naples only temporarily relieved. Barcelona's traders were already seeking better conditions in Valencia, which largely escaped the commercial dislocation brought on by the civil war by allying with Barcelona's competitors Genoa and Marseille. As for Majorca, once a proud and not always friendly rival to Barcelona with her superior harbour and imposing fleet, the later fourteenth century brought sorrow and trouble. Venetian and Genoese ships bound eastward stopped less often; the Jewish community, with more merchants and no less maritime expertise than Barcelona's, was virtually destroyed in 1391. Heavily dependent on imported grain and torn by social conflict, Majorca retained little but a share in the African trade she had pioneered. There, as in Barcelona, enterprise foundered in the partisan ambitions of short-sighted oligarchs.

Culture

Yet it was the prosperity of the urban élites, while it lasted, that generated the creations that tell us most about the spirit of the later medieval Crown of Aragon. In the carrer Montcada, shadowed by Santa Maria del Mar, arose fine houses, 'half bourgeois, half noble', as Vilar remarks, some of which still stand to reveal a sensibility less individual perhaps than in some contemporary Italian domestic architecture but none the less characteristic. King and municipal councils joined in the construction of imposing public edifices at Barcelona: the Sala Tinell in the palace, the *llotja*, the *drassanes* shipworks, all projects of the fourteenth century; and in the early fifteenth the *Generalitat* palaces at Barcelona and Valencia and the great *llonjes* at Majorca and Valencia. As the chronology suggests, these projects tended to lag behind phases of economic prosperity, their very completion in some cases telling of the brave assurance with which proud men viewed their future.

Their cultures were not, of course, solely bourgeois. Their inheritance was an amalgam of traditions and interests, some of them religious, others courtly or royal, still others popular or practical. Ideals of the Christian Church ran in deep and unoriginal veins. The clergy of the Crown of Aragon, like those everywhere else, were hard pressed to hold to legislated standards of celibacy and pastoral competence. None doubted that their material endowments were superior to their spirituality, few lamented their troubles after the Plague. Learned men were not lacking, notably in the cathedral chapters of Catalonia, which were required to depute canons to study theology or canon law, but their reading was seldom pertinent to pastoral needs. Parish Christianity may have functioned best in Valencia, where priests laboured with unencumbered zeal in a challenging mission. In the Pyrenees the friars seem to have worked efficaciously against the Cathar heresy, which threatened greater Catalonia in the later thirteenth century before collapsing in the fourteenth. Among houses of regulars Poblet prospered in the later Middle Ages by holding tenaciously to the system of farming by lay brothers; from such administrative strength was supported an enormous congregation (ninety-two choir monks in 1316) and a splendid practice of the choral office. In most Benedictine houses the old monastic life persisted without fervour, although some, like Ripoll, had the libraries with which to sustain an interest in learning. Poblet among others sent monks to universities.

Reforming traditions stemmed chiefly from Ramon de Penyafort and the Dominican bishops who followed him. Probably the most influential figure was the Franciscan Ramon Lull, who learned his way about Majorca, Catalonia, Valencia, and Aragon as a knight-courtier in the mid-thirteenth century, and later wrote voluminously of their peoples and their failings and needs. His mind was critical, literary, and visionary. He could think of the clergy as rightfully set by God above all men, including kings; yet he satirized their worldliness mercilessly in his novel *Blanquerna*. In more original ways Lull's interest in founding hospitals and preaching conversion to the Moors answered to practical needs in his society. The idea of equipping Christian missionaries with Arabic was pioneered by Ramon de Penyafort; the Dominicans founded schools of Arabic at Tunis as early as 1250 and, together with Hebrew, at Murcia, Valencia, and Játiva. The friars, Lull among them, preached in mosques and synagogues, promoting public disputations of the faith. Lull's early *Book of the gentiles and the three wise men*, composed in Arabic at Majorca about 1272, presents allegorized expositions of the faiths in engagingly unpolemical form. It cannot be said that such exercises were very successful; yet if the colleges failed in the fourteenth century something of their spirit lingered in the commercial ties forged with Africa and Egypt.

A century later Christian attitudes had hardened. In his fiery sermons the Dominican theologian Vicent Ferrer was less concerned to persuade than to convert or condemn. It is true that he denounced the persecutions of Jews in 1391. But he spoke of Jews as enemies of Christians, likened them to prostitutes, and did nothing to dispel popular fears that he evidently shared. His relentless campaign to convert Jews and Moors undermined the sincerity of disputations at Tortosa (1413–14) in which his convert Joshua Halorki forced the Christian belief in the Messiah on Jewish spokesmen. But Ferrer was no less harshly critical of disorder in the Christian church—indeed, in his own order. He charged that friars buried or heard confessions for money alone, and he seems to have thought that the proportion of the damned among secular priests and lay men (99 per cent) was exceeded by that of monks who neglected the requirements of their Rule. What matters about such hyperbolic views is that they doubtless reflected as well as influenced popular attitudes. As elsewhere people were discouraged by the Schism, an anomaly that prevented reform; the enthusiasm of some for the friendly popes of Avignon soon waned. As elsewhere, baptized Christians in the late medieval Crown of Aragon found it ever harder to respond to the expression of God's service in an impersonal public liturgy,

seeking religious meaning preferably in processions, confrater-
nities, and private devotion. The Bible could be read in Catalan
by 1400; and the *Imitation of Christ* was translated into Catalan in
1482.

Other interests grew out of royal and baronial patronage.
Learned Jews had long served the count-kings as physicians and
fiscal managers before James II employed Arnau de Vilanova
(d. 1311), a polymath perhaps second only to Lull in his range of
passionate interests. More publicist than scholar, he had an
astonishing career in medicine, Hebrew and Arabic studies,
diplomacy, and apocalyptic theology; his more lasting fame
attached to his tracts and translations, from Arabic to Latin,
on medicine. History and genealogy, first cultivated in the
monasteries of Old Catalonia and Old Aragon, gave way to the
great series of vernacular memoirs by James the Conqueror,
Desclot, Muntaner, and Peter IV. These are no less ideological
than the old (Latin) *Deeds of the counts of Barcelona*, which was
revised at Ripoll toward 1303–14 in a faithful if somewhat
archaic way, but the vision is bigger and more assured. Peter
IV's passion for commemoration (above, p. 119) went easily with
his heightened sense of royal dignity and ceremony. He
decorated his palaces and gardens with paintings, tapestries, and
inscriptions. Hunting and dining became works of art in the
court of John I, in whose reign manners, dress, and literary and
musical tastes were much influenced by French courtly styles. Of
noble patronage and culture in Aragon and Catalonia we still
know too little, but traditions of amusement and reading—for
example, tastes for hunting and genealogy—surely went back to
the thirteenth century in great houses like the Montcada. The
troubadour Cerveri de Girona (see p. 178; cf. p. 71) found a
patron in Ramon Folc IV of Cardona. It was characteristic that
royal tastes influenced baronial pursuits and, indeed, those of the
count-kings' allies in the urban élite, many of whom aspired to a
share of nobility that only the king could confer.

Still other interests must be traced to the practical needs of
increasingly urbanized societies. The foundation of universities
and higher faculties by royal privilege—at Lérida (1300),
Perpignan (1350), and much later at Barcelona (1450, 1483) and
Valencia (1499)—may be counted in this category, for they were
usually under municipal control. Local schools of less renown

were probably important in developing a common literacy. A
better example may be found in the group or school of
cartographers that flourished in Majorca before the conquest by
Peter IV. This was a matter of technical expertise acquired by
Jews more immediately engaged in maritime trade than was
common in the mainland ports, who were in constant touch with
mariners, notably Italians, interested in exploring the western
limits of the Mediterranean and beyond, and whose activity
carried on older Majorcan traditions of literate concern with the
foreign and distant. What these men produced were not merely
maps but marine handbooks (*portolans*) full of detailed infor-
mation. One of the great surviving examples of this scientific art
is the 'Catalan Atlas' made probably by Cresques Abraham or
his son in 1375 and given by King John I to Charles VI of
France. The dispersion of Majorcan cartographers to Barcelona
and Portugal was a symptom of Majorca's decline. Others would
search a New World with Majorca's tools.

Vernacular literacy spread apace in aristocratic and urban
societies. Already in the eleventh century notaries were recording
oaths and peasant complaints in Catalan, and new strains of
utilitarian writing appeared in the twelfth century. A translation
of the *Liber iudiciorum* for use by the count's judges dates from
about 1140; while the *Homelies of Organyà* (*c.*1200) are a precious
relic of vernacular preaching in a remote mountain parish. Later
the *Libre dels feyts* and works of Ramon Lull boosted literary
Catalan to the common currency it enjoyed in the fourteenth
century. Tradesmen in particular had a penchant for moral
treatises. The Franciscan Francesch Eiximenis (1327?–1409),
protégé of Peter IV, and well schooled in theology, wrote about
civic functions as well as constitutional order. His major work
was *Lo crestià* (*The Christian, or the regimen of princes and the public
order*), an encyclopaedia of Christian moral philosophy in the
tradition of Vincent de Beauvais or Brunetto Latini, but of
which the anecdotal and learned content reveals a new interest in
classical and secular moralities. The part of Book 12 first
dedicated to the jurates of Valencia is an engaging treatise on
practical politics. Eiximenis also wrote a *Libre de les dones* (*Book of
women*), which is a moralizing discussion that deals with the
cultural attainments as well as the weaknesses of women; the
work had some currency in Castilian translation. The royal

secretary Bernat Metge (c.1340–6–1413), having started out writing in traditional style, produced the first work of humanist prose in Catalan, *Lo somni* (*The dream*, 1399). This was an ingeniously allegorized political defence of Bernat's and others' fidelity to the late king John I, full of passionate descriptions of male customs and dress and of feminine virtue; 'one of the finest and most intelligent manifestations of Catalan prose of any time' (Riquer). King Martin I's celebrated proposition to the Corts of Perpignan (1406; see above, p. 130), with its quotations from Horace, Ovid, Livy, Caesar, Sallust, Lucan, etc., marked a culmination of this early Catalonian civic humanism.

Poetry in Catalan developed more slowly than prose because the artificial Provençal (or Limousin) of the court-singers so long dominated creativity in verse. Catalan troubadours preferred the less obscure mode of conventional expression, the *trobar leu*, yet their thought is seldom easy or popular. Guillem de Berguedà (d. 1196) and Cerveri de Girona (d. after 1285) were outstanding figures in a rarified tribe that flourished for more than a century in the courts of southern France and the Catalonian Pyrenees. Catalanisms from vernacular speech begin to appear in the songs of Cerveri de Girona; and Ramon Lull, though a better moralist than poet, was one of the first to attempt purely Catalan verse. In the fourteenth century the weight of tradition and the beginning of thematic influences from Italy and France tended to repress spontaneity; and when the *Consistori de la Gaya Sciensa* was founded by John I in 1393, in imitation of the *Sobregaya Companha* of Toulouse, the concern was clearly to promote a congenial observance of rules rather than poetic originality. Breaking free of such constraints, the Valencian Ausies March (c.1397–1459) wrote a subtle and difficult lyric of love and death that lifted Catalan poetry to a new level of mature power. Something of the same sensibility may be seen in the chivalric novels *Tirant lo Blanch* and *Curial e Güelfa*, the former mostly by the Valencian knight Joanot Martorell (c.1413–68), the latter anonymous. In both, as indeed in March's poems, traces of old courtly or conventionally classicizing motifs linger, but the treatment of character and incident is transformed by a new realism full of irony and wit. A popular vernacular drama outgrowing the liturgy and focused on feast-day celebrations is known to us only from few and fragmentary texts.

No art was so international as music, which flourished in many forms. A purely popular music arose from Moorish and troubadour practice. Religious plainchant evolved towards polyphony under French influence; the Ars Nova was propagated from the 1340s by musicians from Avignon. There is little to show that native schools or composers had much importance; singers and instrumentalists as well as style came from abroad. Peter IV and his sons patronized minstrels from every land. John I sent his musicians to Germany or Flanders to study. Alphonse V likewise attracted musicians from all parts to his court at Naples.

In the representational arts as in letters stylistic change came slowly. The twelfth century had produced a flowering of romanesque art that not only survived for all to see but that seemed hard to improve upon. In some spheres—one thinks of the great rustic frescoes, such as at Santa Maria of Taüll; or the finely historiated cloister sculpture, such as at Elne, Estany, Girona, and Sant Cugat—it had no successors. The great portal of Ripoll (1131–70), drawing on local manuscript and biblical culture, is unique in its iconographic wealth. The cathedral of Urgell, begun in 1131 and exhibiting influences from Po valley churches, stood without alteration in the later Middle Ages. Castilian influences penetrated Aragon in the later twelfth century in buildings such as San Esteban at Sos and Santa Maria of Uncastillo. The Cistercians built in a severely proportioned modification of romanesque at Poblet and Santes Creus; while the cathedral building at Tarragona and Lérida after 1200 developed a more sumptuous and articulated style. Anonymous painters decorated apses and altar frontals: the master of Taüll, who worked in Aragon as well as in the Vall de Bohí; the Master of Bagües (Zaragoza), who painted gospel scenes; the brilliant traditionalist who decorated the old church in San Juan de la Peña as well as the Pantheon of the Kings at León and Berzé-la-Ville in Burgundy; and the incomparable Master of Cabestany, whose appealingly human sculpture at Sant Pere de Roda, now sadly ruined and dispersed, must have been among the glories of the later twelfth century. At about the same time the English artist who decorated the chapter house at Sigena introduced a powerfully original inspiration from abroad.

Everywhere rustic churches in romanesque styles survived

quietly (as many still do), leaving it to urban builders to adapt the new northern modes of articulation and vaulting to a doggedly original conception of breadth and space. The first 'gothic' churches are no earlier than the foundations of new cathedrals at Barcelona (1298) and Girona (1312). Here the exteriors were designed to stand without flying buttresses, while the interiors are marked by wide and high aisles and spaciously arched naves. This style achieved perfection in the mariners' and merchants' church of Santa Maria del Mar in Barcelona, begun in 1328. Meanwhile, a theoretically purer manifestation of this southern inspiration appeared in the 'single nave' churches, of which the dormitory at Poblet and the Dominican church of Santa Catalina in Barcelona seem to have been precursors. Santa Maria del Pi, begun by 1322, and Santa Maria of Montblanc are fine surviving examples; and it is striking to find this conception prevailing after long debates at Girona, where in Santa Maria the original three-nave edifice was replaced in the fifteenth century by that of a single nave which proved to be the widest (23 metres) ever built in the Middle Ages. In addition to the civil monuments already mentioned (p. 174), at Barcelona the civil hall for the *Consell de Cent* (begun in 1373) and the sick rooms in the *Hospital de la Santa Creu* (early fifteenth century) witness to the same meridional gothic inspiration in their original treatment of space.

The new and rebuilt cloisters of the later Middle Ages, such as at Santes Creus, Lérida, Pedralbes, and Vic, are notable less for sculptural decoration than for their graceful arching and lighting. Italian influences, manifest in Catalan painting from about 1330, appear in the work of Jaume Cascalls, who made the funerary monuments at Poblet for Peter IV. More distinctively Catalan was the sculpture of Jordi Johan, whose son Pere Johan (1398–after 1458) brought this art to high perfection in the portal of the *Generalitat* in Barcelona (1418), and later worked at Tarragona, Zaragoza, and Naples.

The painters Ferrer Bassa (fl. 1324–48) and his son Arnau effected a shift from fresco and altar-frontal working to the quasi-reliquary reredos that becomes usual in altars in the Crown of Aragon. One of the last important frescoes is Ferrer's work in the chapel of Sant Miquel at Pedralbes (1346), a perfectly realized adaptation of Giotto and the Lorenzetti. Jaume Serra painted the reredos for the Holy Sepulchre chapel in Zaragoza (1361). In Lluis Borassà (d. *c*.1424–6), who created a remarkable Lamentation of Christ (1410), now at Manresa, and altar-screens for Sant Pere of Egara (1411–13) and for the Poor Clares at Vic (1414–15), may be discerned the international influences then prevailing: richness of colour and decoration, realism of emotion. New talents of originality appeared in Bernat Martorell (d. 1452), who painted the great Transfiguration in the cathedral of Barcelona in 1447; Lluis Dalmau (d. 1460), probably Valencian, who was momentarily influenced by Jan van Eyck; and Jaume Huguet (d. 1492), whose works for Santa Maria of Egara (1460) and Santa Agatha of Barcelona (1464–65), and whose monumental Saint Augustine for the tanners' church in Barcelona, for all their quality, betray signs of an inspiration running dry.

The Moors and Jews influenced later medieval culture in more profound and ordinary ways. In Aragon the building arts and crafts fell so completely into Mudejar hands as to transform the décor of urban and village architecture, to this day marked with their distinctive motifs of geometric and hatchwork design. Of Moorish high culture we know far less, for the Mudejars, unlike the Jews, seldom attained élite status. Jewish artisans in Barcelona worked as bookbinders, silk-weavers, and silversmiths, and their crafts persisted in the hands of *conversos* in the fifteenth century. Jews composed in Catalan: for example, Jafudà Bonsenyor (d. *c*.1330), a physician and translator in the service of James II; and even expressed their spoken Catalan in Hebrew verse, as in songs by Rabbi Natan (possibly Mosse Natan of Tàrrega, d. 1361). Rabbinic and literary culture suffered after the persecutions of 1391–1414, faring worse if anything in Catalonia, where the old communities were badly reduced, than in Aragon.

It seems clear that the generation of 1400 marked an apogee of cultural achievement in the later medieval Crown of Aragon. It is also clear that no generation had a monopoly on inspiration; nor did the crests of creativity coincide with favourable conditions in society and economy. Courtly patronage happened to be strong and resourceful, perhaps even extravagant, just when plagues, social unrest, and financial crisis were most pressing. In vernacular letters and painting the fifteenth century proved a

grand epoch coinciding with the brave but threatened continuity
of Barcelona's maritime trade, and with the new ascendancy of
Valencia. High culture everywhere remained predominantly
Catalan.

The Problem of Decline

The historical experience of prosperity and crisis can
be postulated of concrete phenomena: growth of population,
expansion and continuity of trade, dispensation of artistic
patronage, for example; or on the other hand, disease and
depopulation, disruptions in trade, coinage, or finance. If these
disorders are viewed as threatening to structural continuity or
'normality' they may be spoken of as 'crises', a word used here
only in that sense. The evidence of disruption and disorder also
lends itself to what historians have agreed to refer to more
generally as 'decline' in the later medieval Crown of Aragon.
This is an evocative concept, but it is not free of difficulty, for in
the present case it is not necessarily clear what precisely may be
thought to have declined. No one doubts that Catalonia was
prostrate at the end of the civil war, so that land is a prime
suspect. Pierre Vilar spoke sweepingly of 'the decline of
Catalonia', showing that her difficulties in many spheres long
antedated the civil war. Jaume Vicens Vives argued more
pointedly for 'economic decline in Catalonia', but left no cogent
synthesis to clarify what he held to be the relative and total
importance of economic factors. J. H. Elliott altered the
perspective in describing 'the decline of the Crown of Aragon' as
a consequence of crises and structural problems in Catalonia;
while J. N. Hillgarth has called the whole concept of "decline (of
Catalonia")' into question on the basis of new researches
stressing crisis, recovery, and short-term factors at the expense of
structures and the *longue durée*.

Doubtless there is merit in all these views. They coincide on at
least one cardinal point: the primacy of Catalonia in the Crown
of Aragon and the consequent impact of her demise. There is
substantial agreement on other points of fact and interpretation.
There may even be some agreement that the very concept of
'decline' is problematical in reference to the later medieval
Crown of Aragon—but *this* recognition has seldom been made
explicit. It may not be quite enough to chart the objectively

attested shifts in 'economic indicators' when we know so little about the effects of such shifts on action and attitudes.

The difficulty becomes clear when one tries to isolate and interpret what may be called symptomatic events. One such event is of special interest: the famine attended by social disturbance at Barcelona in 1333–4. When the local chronicler Guillem Mascaró set out to revise the old annals toward 1390 he referred to the year 1333 as the *mal any primer* ('the first bad year'). Doubtless this was a popular idea that had originated much earlier, possibly soon after the first great outbreak of plague in 1348. People remembered that present afflictions were not unprecedented, that there had lately been, and had now ended, an untroubled time. Can such a recollection be verified? We learn from Barcelona's records that already in 1325 there had occurred such a severe shortage of grain that prices rose to exorbitant heights. Probably then, and certainly by 1331, the *Consell de Cent* was actively engaged in importing grain. But if Mascaró spoke of 1333 as the 'first bad year' it was surely because people remembered that only then was the shortage accompanied by social unrest: outcries against the rich incited by the friar Bernat Dezpuig, and perhaps even by a lethal epidemic. The combination was new and frightening—no one remembered the uprising of Berenguer Oller in 1285, which had been followed by military success and the rise of a new industry—because it was to recur, in 1339, in 1343, and after.

Was there some popular awareness that social order and economic prosperity had been set back, or ended, in these events? If so, was that awareness felt beyond the walls of Barcelona? Let us admit near perfect ignorance on both points. What can be said is that the contemporary consciousness of which Mascaró's chronicle seems to afford a trace was surely that of the urban élite. On its prosperity depended such contentment as the *poble menut* could hope for. Few would have contended that famine and dearness alone mattered much; such events were not uncommon nor were they confined to the Crown of Aragon. What mattered was their conjunction with social unrest: that is, with the demagogic incitation to upset the God-ordained social order. One wonders whether some of the 'honoured citizens' were not relieved when in May 1348 a frightened crowd attacked the Jewish *call* of Barcelona for the first time. That King Peter IV

wrote promptly to vicars and bailiffs directing them to protect
the Jewish communities in other Catalonian towns may be some
indication that disturbances in Barcelona were having an
unsettling effect elsewhere. Managers of cloth works dependent
on the export market would have watched the situation in
Barcelona with anxiety.

The patrician outlook immediately following the epidemic is
even harder to gauge. The Crown of Aragon, as many would
have known, was not alone in suffering this scourge; even before
it struck, the authorities at Girona had written for news of it to
those at Narbonne. Survivors of all classes may have been
temporarily at an advantage and, as we have seen, the hearth-
registers suggest a strong recovery from the first onslaught.
Moreover, what may be called the economic policies of Peter IV
suggest either that leading elements of the propertied and
mercantile classes retained considerable optimism during these
years, or else (perhaps less likely) that the count-king was acting
boldly to rebuild confidence. The issuance of a new gold florin at
an elevated standard in 1346 was a proud sign of prosperity and
cohesion; this was a coinage for all the Crown of Aragon. Then
there were the king's decisions in 1359 to build a vast new wall at
Barcelona and in 1378 to refurbish the *drassanes* shipyard at high
expense. The men who worked and financed these projects may
have had misgivings, but they cannot have foreseen that, as Vilar
points out, it was to take five centuries more to settle the space
enclosed by the new wall.

Two other events of these years bear on the question of
contemporary perceptions. As we have seen, the new florin
proved almost at once to be overvalued; declining in weight as
early as 1349 it was reduced by more than 25 per cent by 1365.
So for the first time merchants and proprietors in the peninsular
Crown-lands faced the economic reality of weakening currencies,
although it does not follow that they foresaw that the problem
would become chronic. Moreover, it was probably during the
inflationary cycle of about 1340 to 1380 that purchases of fiscal
annuities began to detract from commercial investment and
enterprise. Was trade already becoming too perilous, or competition too stiff? At any rate the financial crash of the 1380s
followed by the massacres of 1391 and peasant unrest surely
brought on the crisis of confidence that led to excessively

restrictive controls on money and investment in the early fifteenth century.

We are left to wonder whether business men and *rentiers* who looked back to 1333 as 'the first bad year' were aware that a golden age of strong money and strong markets had passed in the middle of the fourteenth century. What those people knew at least was that they had experienced a series of crises, some of which we may safely imagine were beginning to exert a depressive effect already before 1400. They continued to react to difficulties in the fifteenth century, not always successfully; those who stress the continuing volume of trade have not always taken due account of the continuing weakness of the coinage as well as the crisis of noble fortunes. Enterprise and finance were passing into foreign hands.

Moreover, by this time other circumstances and structural weaknesses were surely working to counter long-term growth and recovery. Commercial competition had turned so adverse that the Catalans were squeezed out of Andalusia and the eastern Mediterranean. Even in the western Mediterranean competitive pressures mounted, so that it is hard not to view Catalan piracy as counter-productive acts of desperation. Furthermore, sustained depopulation in Catalonia and Majorca together with peasant unrest contributed to the inability of these lands and Aragon to feed the lowland cities. Barcelona's purchase of Ebro castles to secure the passage of grain looks like an admission of economic defeat. A surprising defeat, on its face; one such as north European polities seldom faced. Here it may be well to attend to an acute observation of Yves Renouard: that we still know very little about agrarian techniques and tooling in the Crown of Aragon. It may be that as Catalans turned to the sea or emigrated and as the Aragonese were left to exploit Christian peasants on unyielding lands to which Mudejar irrigation could not be extended, the whole cycle of agrarian expansion and improvement known in the North simply bypassed the Crown's realms. Traction, tools, and yields seem to have been as archaic in the old Christian zones as the rubble churches that stood mute witness to more energetic days long past. The patricians of Barcelona who bought rural properties in the fifteenth century were among the first to employ more intensive methods of cultivation.

Underdeveloped, underpopulated, unfavourably situated in a
Mediterranean trade they could no longer dominate, and led by
insecure oligarchs incapable of agreeing on unselfish remedies,
the Catalans and their dynastic allies faced a bleak future even
before the civil war. If this was not quite palpably 'decline' it was
assuredly *échec*, the wearying effect of successive crises, partial
solutions, and incomplete recoveries. To argue thus is not to deny
that Barcelona's trade held up until the 1450s; or that, as
Dufourcq put it, if 'the causes of the civil war were perhaps not
economic, the consequences of it were grievously so'; or that, in
Hillgarth's words, 'No inevitable chain of events can be
discerned.' But the question here is not what caused the civil war
but why that war proved ruinous. If not the foregoing events
themselves, then at least the consequences of repeatedly adverse
events for vulnerable structures and adjustments may be said to
have become inevitable.

Yet it would be mistaken to equate social and economic
weakness with decline save in a purely notional and relative way.
Catalonia and Aragon were overtaken by their neighbours well
before the troubles of the fourteenth century. The concentration
of their energies in urban industries and trade merely completed
the age-old movement of descent from the mountains; the
fixation on adventure and profit perpetuated a mentality of the
old frontier. Perhaps this is why the old hinterlands were
neglected until it was too late—it had not been necessary to
'develop' them in times when the adjustment of rural forces
would have permitted it—but neglect is not decline. We are left
with evidence not so much of decline as of problematic and
troubled continuity. Continuity in institutional life, as the
organs devised to balance the élite interests of monarchs and
the *estaments*—consulates, Cort(e)s, *Diputacions*, etc.—achieved
maturity as the political expression of oligarchy; in patronage by
the rich, who were progressively deprived of other outlets; in
ecclesiastical life, where the inability of old institutions to meet
new religious needs was but a regional manifestation of a
universal phenomenon.

What declined in the later medieval Crown of Aragon was not
so much institutional and economic indicators as the psycho-
logical adjustment of political and social forces. Consensus,
energy and optimism, religious *convivencia*: these things, having

survived the crises of the mid-fourteenth century, weakened or failed only after about 1390. It is in this perspective that we may understand that recoveries from later epidemics were less vigorous than that from the first one; or that municipal taxes were progressively entailed in the support of a *rentier* class less disposed than its ancestors to invest capital; or that a deepening chasm between the old tolerance of the élites and the new religiosity of the masses should have contributed to the dispersion and conversion of Jews in unprecedented numbers. Options were fewer, lines drawn more clearly, conflict nearer the surface. That major conflict was postponed until the mid-fifteenth century may finally say as much for institutional strength as for commercial prosperity.

Historians have rightly stressed the primacy of Barcelona and its hinterland in their discussions of the later Middle Ages. Catalonian initiatives and enterprises were what chiefly drove the early confederation to the quasi-integrated status it achieved under James II and Peter IV. But centrifugal tendencies remained strong. The churches of Aragon and Catalonia had gone separate ways as early as 1318, when Zaragoza was erected an archbishopric. Majorca subjugated never matched the vitality of her days as a cadet kingdom, nor was she any less a rival to Barcelona. Valencia salvaged what she could by steering an independent course increasingly to Barcelona's disadvantage. Aragon clung to her constitution, her dynasty, her poverty,—and to Catalonia. So the Crown of Aragon survived, no longer quite intact, no longer quite a unity, but with all of Catalonia's problems for her own.

Epilogue

I el reialme pirenenc
fóra la flor dels reialmes . . .

Maragall

HISTORY played her customary tricks on the Crown of Aragon. It kept alive the memory of a golden age while allowing people to forget who enjoyed it and when. The Aragonese early took refuge in the myth of an ancient constitution, placing its genesis just before the beginnings of recorded (medieval) time. The Catalans likewise gloried in their privileges, which they associated with their Corts, the *Generalitat*, and resistance to Castile. Few anywhere long remembered the grim realities of the later Middle Ages, which were succeeded by recoveries, crises, and disasters of equally momentous impact; few entirely forgot that an age of independence (*sc.*, from Castile) had preceded their own. As late as 1760 the deputies of Barcelona, Palma, Valencia, and Zaragoza could defend an ancient federalism against the centralizing policy of Carlos III. But in truth this solidarity was limited to the mutual recognition of foral diversity. No tradition of bi-regnal dynastic solidarity survived the Middle Ages. This does not mean that all sense of community was lost. Just as Catalan enterprise had formerly crossed customary boundaries, so when the Romantic imagination found powerful Catalan expression in the nineteenth century it evoked a 'Pyrenean realm' that corresponded not so much to the historical Crown of Aragon as to the somewhat eccentric vision of thirteenth-century troubadours, a vision that survives today as a nostalgic programme of politicized culture.

In one respect the literary evocation of past splendour came closer to historical truth than the old foralist ones. By referring back (however vaguely) to the twelfth and thirteenth centuries, it recalled the great age of growth and prosperity that made possible the conquests of Valencia, Majorca, and Sicily: the age before the mountains gave way to the sea and to a spectacular but precarious destiny. Then and perhaps only then in the whole history of the Crown of Aragon were productive forces well balanced to support growing populations without social conflict. The cities overtook the old manses, hamlets, and farms in the later Middle Ages, draining them of men who were soon caught up in a new urban-maritime world, and who seldom looked back. Out of an inherently urban prosperity that peaked toward 1345 blossomed the institutional and cultural achievements of the medieval Crown of Aragon.

In the waning centuries the continuities were less vital, the blows less muffled. Demographic recovery in the sixteenth century was offset by expulsions of Jews (1492), Mudejars (1502), and finally of the Muslim converts (*moriscos*, 1609), causing economic dislocation and misery above all in Aragon and Valencia. When Catalonia refused to shoulder the burden of Castilian collapse, her revolt achieved little more than recognition of her liberties and escape from economic and social reforms. She was powerless to prevent the definitive loss of Roussillon (together with the Conflent and parts of Cerdanya) to France in the treaty of the Pyrenees (1659). Boundaries were hardening in ways that served distant rulers better than long settled peoples: the Aragonese (and Castilians) clung to their Catalan enclave of Ribagorza, the French imposed their language on Roussillon in 1700, and the Castilians theirs on the old Crown lands (1707–16). One last time the Crown of Aragon went on its own way, siding with the archduke Charles of Austria in the losing struggle for the Spanish succession; there could be no turning back. After the treaty of Utrecht in 1713 and the fall of Barcelona in 1714, the old lands, stripped of Minorca and the Italian domains, became a part of Spain. The Nueva Planta, imposed on Aragon and Valencia in 1707 and on Catalonia in 1716, swept away the old foralist regime and introduced a Castilian administration. As it happened the reforms were already in progress that would render Catalonia the most progressive state in a retrograde monarchy. The consequences of those events are live issues to this day.

The old stones are quiet now. They are none the less eloquent. They tell of fighting and protecting and exploiting; of rural toil and herding; of praying and endowing; of trading and talking, and of links and aspirations across sunny seas. So do the sculptures and paintings they sheltered, and the written artifacts of law, spirit, and imagination. In many a *masia* of Old Catalonian hills and vales the family's parchments survived intact until yesterday, reaching back like the rough-hewn stone of the house itself to the fourteenth century or before; in some few they are still there. Throughout the former Crown's lands the civil and ecclesiastical records are preserved in a relative abundance perhaps unmatched elsewhere in Europe—a national treasure that owes its existence partly to benign neglect, partly to the forbearance of modernizers, but chiefly to the pride of people for whom the medieval past retains vital immediacy. So rich a heritage is still far from having yielded all its secrets. No sketch such as this may pretend to comprehend it. But the sheet force of the Catalans' character and the amplitude of their vision may stand out clearly enough. They and their neighbours were the makers of a historic Mediterranean civilization.

Note on the Translation of Proper Names

How to render proper names in English is a problem of uncommon difficulty in a work dealing with peoples of different languages who had rulers in common. Some of these rulers and their princely offspring were Catalan by blood or preference, others Aragonese, still others Castilians; and the count-kings between 1162 and 1410, while speaking Catalan as a rule, bore the names and regnal numbers of an Aragonese dynasty. It therefore seemed awkward to refer to these rulers in the Catalan forms (and numbers) of their originally Aragonese names (Alfons I for Alfonso II, etc.), misleading to refer to them all as if Aragonese, and absurd to present some in one way and some in the other. Accordingly, I have adopted a compromise not uncommon in historical writing on other European lands but seldom preferred by Hispanists: namely, to Anglicize the given names of kings (or count-kings) in one or several of the realms making up the Crown of Aragon. More conventionally, I have rendered the names of popes, certain foreign rulers, and dynasties as well as of Hispanic countries—Catalonia, Majorca, Aragon, etc.—in familiar English forms.

With these exceptions, proper names, including toponyms, are normally given in the modern forms that prevail today in Catalan-speaking lands, Aragon, Castile, France, the Italian islands, etc. Castilian and Navarrese rulers, their relations and children, and those of Castilian or Aragonese descent not primarily concerned with Catalan-speaking lands are named in Castilian forms. Almost all others, including princes who subsequently became kings in the realms of the Crown of Aragon are named in Catalan forms: thus the son of James the Conqueror who became his main heir is called Pere in pages that deal with his brilliant pre-regnal career, and Peter III after his accession. On the other hand, his older half-brother of a Castilian mother who was squeezed out of a Catalonian destiny I call Alfonso.

Since no such system can pretend to solve the problem completely, I have tolerated a few exceptions. There is a stowaway Frederick or two to avoid the disconcerting usage Fadrique in reference to non-reigning princes. Because it is easy to confuse the count-king Martin with his like-named son, I speak of the latter as Martí even though he reigned in Sicily. I have preferred Lérida to Lleida not because I regard it an Aragonese city but because *Lerida* was a medieval Catalan name of the place. There are anomalies. Because even dynastic barons with chiefly Catalonian interests bore Aragonese names (Barcelona's dynastic names, practically limited to Ramon and Berenguer, soon died out), I refer to James I's great-uncle and his son as Sanç and Nunyo Sanç respectively; that is, in the Catalan forms of those non-Catalan names. When discussing a ruler as count-king (for example, John I, pp. 120 ff.), I retain the English form even when referring back to his earlier career. The Index provides cross-references to names in English and foreign-language forms, as well as regnal numbers for kings.

Glossary

In principle this list includes only terms that recur in the text or are not there explained or translated.

aljama: settlement or district of Jews or Moors.

almogàvers: mercenary warriors of the new frontier employed first to raid Moorish lands and later to support Catalan forces in Sicily and Greece.

Almohads (Arabic: Muwaḥḥid): a Berber dynasty of pious Muslims who invaded Spain in 1145.

Almoravids (Arabic: Murābiṭ): a Berber dynasty of pious Muslims who entered Spain in the later eleventh century.

Audiència: supreme royal court.

banal lordship: power to command peasants or to impose fiscal obligations on them.

Biga: coalition of patricians and landlords in Barcelona in the fifteenth century.

bovatge (Latin: *bovaticum*): tax to secure the peace in Catalonia.

braç: social 'arm' or estate in Catalonia or Valencia. The *braç reial* was the estate of towns. See also *estament*.

Busca: coalition of merchants, artisans, and labourers in Barcelona in the fifteenth century.

call: Catalan form of the Hebrew *qahal*, referring to the urban quarter of the Jews.

camp: open land dependent on a city.

carrer: street.

censal: annuity payable from municipal revenues.

ciutadans honrats: 'honoured citizens', or privileged townsmen eligible for public office.

comtors: barons of the old comital aristocracy.

condottiere: adventurer-leader, especially of mercenaries.

Consell de Cent: 'Council of one hundred' in Barcelona.

Constitucions: statutes or laws made by the count-kings in the Corts of Catalonia.

convivencia: literally, 'living together'. The traditional state of toleration in medieval Spain.

croat: silver coin established in 1285 originally valued at 12 pennies.

Diputació del general: committee of the *estaments* (*q.v.*) bearing the general power of the Catalonian Corts. Came to be known as the *Generalitat* in Catalonia. There were *diputacions* in the other realms.

diputats: commissioners of the Corts.

dirhem: Muslim silver coin.

doblench: 'double', referring to silver pennies of two-twelfths fine silver.

drassanes: shipyards of medieval Barcelona

écu: French gold coin, originally (1385) valued at one *livre tournois*.

estament: estate of society. See also *braç*.

Extremadura: Christian frontier against the Moors.

La fi del comte d'Urgell: 'The end of the count of Urgel', an anonymous Catalan chronicle written *c*.1466–79.

florin (fl.): gold coin of Florence, first struck in 1252 at a weight of about 3.5 grams.

foral: pertaining to *fueros* (or [Catalan]: *fors*; Latin: *forum*) and the regime thereof.

fuero(s): laws, customs, or privileges of Aragon or other non-Catalan regions; or charters containing them.

General estoria: 'General history' of Alfonso X of Castile, translated by order of Peter IV.

Generalitat: see *Diputació del general*.

honor(es): baronial tenure in Aragon.

Hospital de la Santa Creu: 'Hospital of the Holy Cross', the municipal hospital of Barcelona, built 1401–6.

Infant(e): first-born son of reigning count-king.

infanzones: Aragonese knights of less than baronial rank.

insaculació: system of balloting for public office by drawing names by lot.

Justicia: Aragonese official who came to defend privileges of the realm against the king.

Liber iudiciorum: 'Book of judgements', a compilation of Visigothic and Roman laws dating from 653 to 655.

llonja: see *llotja*.

llotja: public building of the merchants. Called *llonja* in Majorca and Valencia.

mals usos: 'Bad customs' or obligations imposed notably on the *remensa* peasants of Catalonia.

masia: manse or homestead of Catalonian peasants.

mazmudin: Almohad gold coin, originally worth one (gold) dinar.

merinado: district served by a *merinus* (q.v.).

merinus: king's bailiff or steward of domains in Aragon.

Mestre Racional: 'Accounting master', the king's supervisor of patrimonial revenues.

monedatge (Latin: *monetaticum*; Castilian: *monedaje*): tax to secure the stablity of coinage in Catalonia or (called *monedaje*) in Aragon.

morabetin: Almoravid gold dinar, long valued at 7 sous of Barcelona.

moriscos: baptized Moors or Mudejars.

mostassaf: see *muh-tasib*.

Mudejars: Moors under Christian domination, chiefly peasants and artisans.

muḥ-tasib: Moorish supervisor of markets and trade. The Catalan *mostassaf* was instituted by James I at Valencia and by Peter IV at Barcelona.

Murābiṭs: see Almoravids.

Occitania: an artificial designation for lands of southern France including Gascony and Guienne as well as the 'Languedoc' more narrowly defined by French administrators in the thirteenth century.

pactist(s): the disposition (or those so disposed) to set constitutional conditions on concessions to the count-king in the fifteenth century.

paers (Latin: *paciarii*): 'Peace-men', urban officers originally charged with surveillance of the Peace.

Placa del Rei: 'King's square'.

poble menut: 'Little people'.

Princeps namque: a title of the *Usatges of Barcelona* (*q.v.*) providing for a general summons to arms in case of the ruler's obligation to defend the land.

Procuració reial: 'Royal procuration', supervisory charge of the royal patrimony, exercised by the *procurador reial*.

procurador reial: see *Procuració reial*.

remença(es): peasants of Old Catalonia (or their status) subject to *mals usos* (*q.v.*). They could be freed only by heavy payments of 'ransom' (Latin: *redimencia*).

ricos hombres: 'Rich men', the greater barons of Aragon.

Siete Partidas: 'Seven parts', a law code promulgated by Alfonso X of Castile.

Tablas Alfonsíes: 'Alfonsine tables', astronomical tables of Alfonso X of Castile.

taifa: referring to the small 'party' states in Moorish Spain after the collapse of caliphal authority in the eleventh century.

Tarraconensis: a Roman imperial province corresponding in territorial extent to Aragon, Catalonia, and Navarre in their expanded forms.

Taula de Canvi: 'Table of Exchange', or municipal bank of deposit.

usatge: 'Usage' or custom, such as contained in the *Usatges of Barcelona* (*q.v.*).

Usatges of Barcelona: a collection of customs and laws for the principality of Barcelona compiled towards 1150.

vilanova de la mar: 'New village of the sea', a maritime suburb of medieval Barcelona.

wālī: Moorish governor.

Genealogical Tables

NB Given dates are normally those of reigns or deaths. Marriages are indicated by = ; or by $\doteq$ (etc.) to indicate plural marriages. Names of kings (and of count-kings) are in small capital lettering. Names of kings not of a Table's main series (as in Tables IV, and V) are in small capital italics. Broken lines indicate omissions in lines of descent, except as noted in Table VI. Not all marriages or offspring of all rulers are represented; in principle only persons mentioned in the text are included. Titles of the later count-kings cannot be fully represented. It should be borne in mind that Valencia, Majorca, and Sardinia came successively to be regarded as annexes of Aragon-Catalonia.

I. ARAGON (c.800 – 1137)

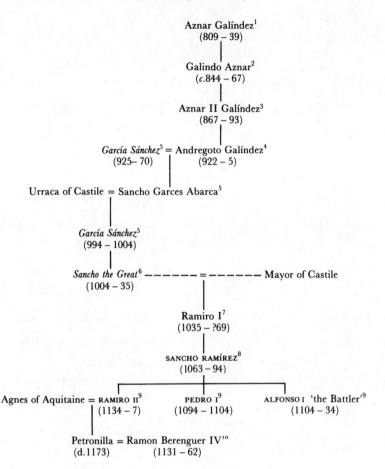

Aznar Galíndez[1]
(809 – 39)

Galindo Aznar[2]
(c.844 – 67)

Aznar II Galíndez[3]
(867 – 93)

García Sánchez[5] = Andregoto Galíndez[4]
(925– 70)   (922 – 5)

Urraca of Castile = Sancho Garces Abarca[5]

García Sánchez[5]
(994 – 1004)

Sancho the Great[6] — — — — — = — — — — — Mayor of Castile
(1004 – 35)

Ramiro I[7]
(1035 – ?69)

SANCHO RAMÍREZ[8]
(1063 – 94)

Agnes of Aquitaine = RAMIRO II[9]   PEDRO I[9]   ALFONSO I 'the Battler'[9]
(1134 - 7)   (1094 – 1104)   (1104 – 34)

Petronilla = Ramon Berenguer IV[10]
(d.1173)   (1131 – 62)

Notes to table I

1. Count of Aragon, Urgell, Cerdanya, Conflent.
2. Count of Aragon, Urgell, Cerdanya, Conflent, Pallars, Ribagorza.
3. Count of Aragon
4. Countess of Aragon.
5. King of Pamplona, Count of Aragon
6. King of Pamplona, Count of Aragon Ribagorza, Sobrarbe.
7. Quasi-king of Aragon, Count of Ribagorza and Sobrarbe.
8. King of Aragon and Pamplona.
9. King of Aragon, count of Ribagorza and Sobrarbe
10. See Tables II, III, IV.

II. EAST PYRENEAN COUNTIES (c.800 – 1162)

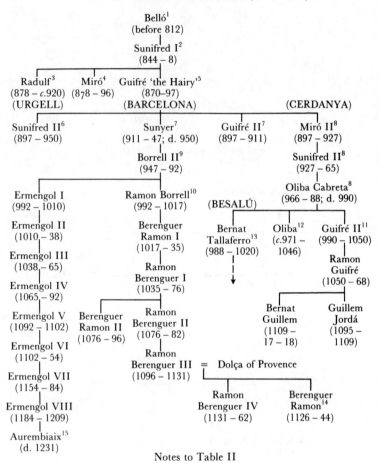

Belló[1]
(before 812)

Sunifred I[2]
(844 – 8)

Radulf[3] Miró[4] Guifré 'the Hairy'[5]
(878 – c.920) (878 – 96) (870–97)
(URGELL) (BARCELONA) (CERDANYA)

Sunifred II[6] Sunyer[7] Guifré II[7] Miró II[8]
(897 – 950) (911 – 47; d. 950) (897 – 911) (897 – 927)

Borrell II[9] Sunifred II[8]
(947 – 92) (927 – 65)

Oliba Cabreta[8]
(966 – 88; d. 990)

Ermengol I Ramon Borrell[10]
(992 – 1010) (992 – 1017) (BESALÚ)

Ermengol II Berenguer Bernat Oliba[12] Guifré II[11]
(1010 – 38) Ramon I Tallaferro[13] (c.971 – (990 – 1050)
  (1017 – 35) (988 – 1020) 1046)

Ermengol III Ramon Ramon
(1038 – 65) Berenguer I Guifré
  (1035 – 76) (1050 – 68)

Ermengol IV
(1065 – 92) Bernat Guillem
  Guillem Jordá

Ermengol V Berenguer Ramon (1109 – (1095 –
(1092 – 1102) Ramon II Berenguer II 17 – 18) 1109)
  (1076 – 96) (1076 – 82)

Ermengol VI Ramon
(1102 – 54) Berenguer III = Dolça of Provence
  (1096 – 1131)

Ermengol VII
(1154 – 84) Ramon Berenguer
  Berenguer IV Ramon[14]

Ermengol VIII (1131 – 62) (1126 – 44)
(1184 – 1209)

Aurembiaix[15]
(d. 1231)

Notes to Table II

1. Count of Carcassonne.
2. Count of Urgell-Cerdanya, Barcelona-Girona, Narbonne.
3. Count of Besalú.   4. Count of Conflent, Roussillon.
5. Count of Urgell-Cerdanya, Barcelona-Girona-Osona.
6. Count of Urgell, as were the Ermengols below in this column.
7. Count of Barcelona.   8. Count of Cerdanya, Besalú.
9. Count of Barcelona, Urgell.
10. Count of Barcelona, as were his descendants in this column.
11. Count of Cerdanya, followed by descendants in this column.
12. Abbot of Ripoll and Cuixà; bishop of Vic.
13. Count of Besalú. His successors were: Guillem I (1020–52); Guillem II (1052 – 66); Bernat II (1066 – 1100); Bernat III (c.1100 – 11).
14. Count of Provence.   15. Titular viscountess of Urgell (1220 – 31).

III. PROVENCE (1112 – 1285)

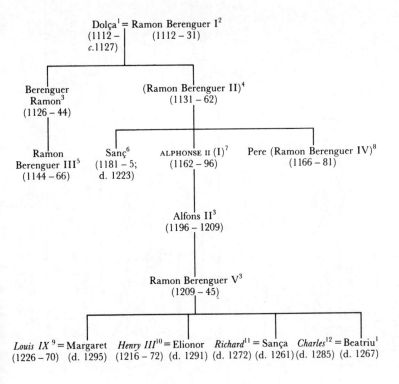

Dolça[1] = Ramon Berenguer I[2]
(1112 – | (1112 – 31)
c.1127)

Berenguer Ramon[3]
(1126 – 44)

(Ramon Berenguer II)[4]
(1131 – 62)

Ramon Berenguer III[5]
(1144 – 66)

Sanç[6]
(1181 – 5; d. 1223)

ALPHONSE II (I)[7]
(1162 – 96)

Pere (Ramon Berenguer IV)[8]
(1166 – 81)

Alfons II[3]
(1196 – 1209)

Ramon Berenguer V[3]
(1209 – 45)

Louis IX[9] = Margaret   Henry III[10] = Elionor   Richard[11] = Sança   Charles[12] = Beatriu[1]
(1226 – 70)   (d. 1295)   (1216 – 72)   (d. 1291)   (d. 1272)   (d. 1261)   (d. 1285)   (d. 1267)

Notes to Table III

1. Countess of Provence, viscountess of Millau, Gévaudan, Carladès.
2. Count of Provence by marriage; count of Barcelona (Ramon Berenguer IV, 1096 – 1131).
3. Count of Provence, viscount of Millau, Gévaudan, Carladès.
4. Ramon Berenguer IV, count of Barcelona; perhaps marquis of Provence from 1146.
5. Count of Provence and Melgueil; viscount of Millau, Gévaudan, Carladès.
6. Procurator or count of Provence; later count of Roussillon and Cerdanya.
7. King of Aragon, count of Barcelona; marquis of Provence, 1166–96.
8. Count of Provence and Carcassonne.
9. King of France.
10. King of England.
11. Earl of Cornwall; king of the Romans from 1257.
12. of Anjou. Count of Provence; king of Sicily, 1266–82.

IV. THE COUNT-KINGS (1150 – 1410)

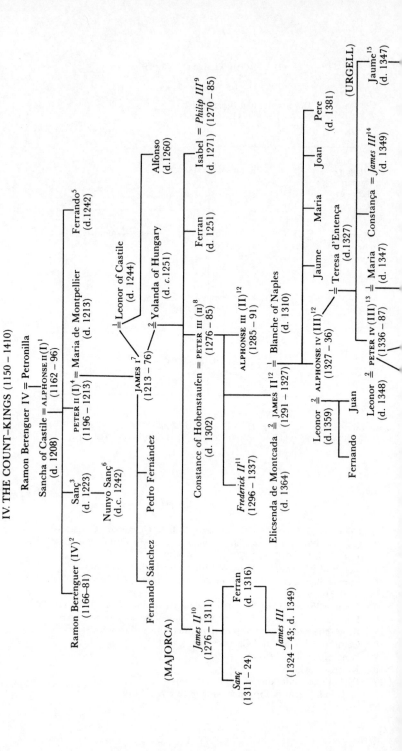

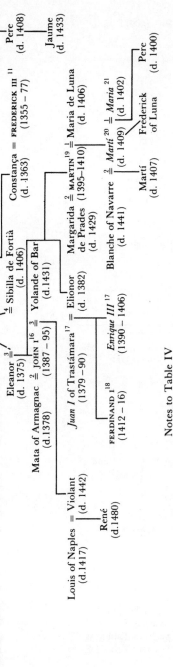

Notes to Table IV

1. King of Aragon, count of Barcelona, sometime marquis of Provence.
2. Count of Provence, etc. (see Table III).
3. Titular count of Cerdanya, procurator or count of Provence, 1181–5.
4. King of Aragon, count of Barcelona, lord of Montpellier from 1204.
5. Abbot of Montearagón.
6. Count of Roussillon, Cerdanya, and Conflent (1212–41).
7. King of Aragon, Majorca, and Valencia; count of Barcelona and Urgell; lord of Montpellier.
8. King of Aragon and Valencia, count of Barcelona, king of Sicily from 1282, etc.   9. King of France.
10. King of Majorca, as were his descendants in this column.
11. King of Sicily. See Table V.
12. King of Aragon and Valencia, count of Barcelona, and (after Alphonse III) lord of Sardinia and Corsica, etc.
13. King of Aragon, Valencia, and (from 1343) Majorca; count of Barcelona; lord of Sardinia, Corsica, Romania; etc.
14. King of Majorca; see this table at note 10.
15. Count of Urgell, as were his descendants in this column, until 1414, when Jaume, claimant at Caspe and subsequently rebel, was captured and imprisoned.
16. King of Aragon, Valencia, and Majorca; count of Barcelona; etc.
17. King of Castile.
18. of Antequera, elected count-king at Caspe in 1412. See Table VI.
19. King of Aragon, Valencia, Majorca, and (from 1409) Sicily; count of Barcelona; etc.
20. King of Sicily, 1390–1409.
21. Queen of Sicily, 1377–1402.

V. SICILY (1197 – 1409)

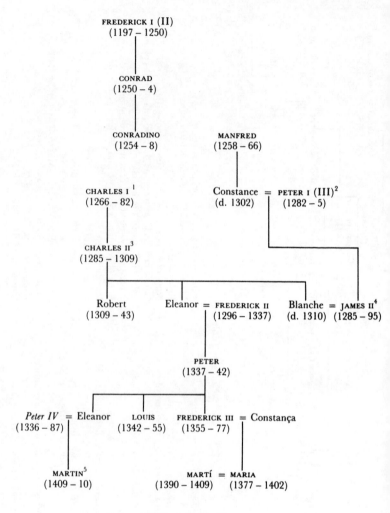

FREDERICK I (II)
(1197 – 1250)

CONRAD
(1250 – 4)

CONRADINO
(1254 – 8)

MANFRED
(1258 – 66)

CHARLES I [1]
(1266 – 82)

Constance = PETER I (III) [2]
(d. 1302)   (1282 – 5)

CHARLES II [3]
(1285 – 1309)

Robert   Eleanor = FREDERICK II   Blanche = JAMES II [4]
(1309 – 43)   (1296 – 1337)   (d. 1310) (1285 – 95)

PETER
(1337 – 42)

Peter IV = Eleanor   LOUIS   FREDERICK III = Constança
(1336 – 87)   (1342 – 55)   (1355 – 77)

MARTIN [5]   MARTÍ = MARIA
(1409 – 10)   (1390 – 1409) (1377 – 1402)

Notes to Table V.

1. of Anjou; count of Provence from 1246; king of Sicily.
   Also called Charles of Naples.
2. Count-king, 1276 – 85. See also Table IV.
3. King of Naples, count of Provence.
4. Count-king, 1291 – 1327. See also Table IV.
5. Count-king, 1395 – 1410. See also Table IV.

VI. THE TRASTÁMARAS (1369 – 1479)
AND THEIR CASTILIAN ASCENDANTS

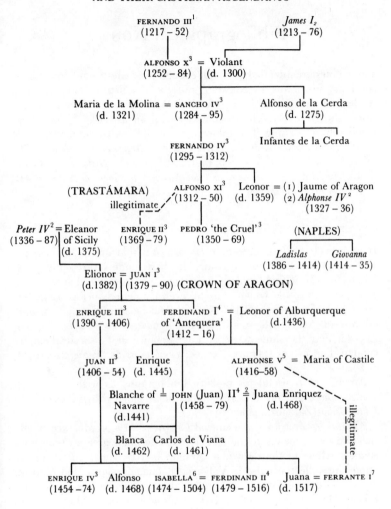

Notes to Table VI.

1. King of Castile and, from 1230, León.
2. Count-king. See Table IV.
3. King of Castile-León.
4. King of Aragon and Sicily, count of Barcelona.
5. King of Aragon, Sicily, and Naples; count of Barcelona.
6. Queen of Castile.
7. King of Naples.

Bibliographical Notes

THESE notes are intended to be full enough to orientate students or non-specialist historians to research, not too detailed to baffle general readers who merely wish to go further. With the latter in mind certain titles, chiefly in English, are marked with an asterisk (*) as recommended basic reading. The following abbreviations are employed: *AEM = Anuario de estudios medievales*; *CDIACA = Colección de documentos inéditos del Archivo de la Corona de Aragón*; *CHCA = Congreso de Historia de la Corona de Aragón*; *EEMCA = Estudios de Edad Media de la Corona de Aragón*; *EHR = English historical review*.

GENERAL

It is difficult to find up-to-date *bibliographies* that are focused on the realms of the Crown of Aragon. The best guide is presently J. N. Hillgarth, *The Spanish kingdoms, 1250–1516*, 2 vols. (Oxford, 1976–8), i, 409–36); ii, 634–85, which is useful even for periods before 1250. See also Ch.-E. Dufourcq and Jean Gautier-Dalché, 'Histoire de l'Espagne au Moyen Age (1948–1969)', *Revue historique*, ccxlv (1971), 127–68, 443–82; and the same writers' 'La naissance et l'essor de l'empire catalan d'après des travaux récents', *Les Cahiers de Tunisie*, xx (1972), 101–24.

Among *serials* useful for modern bibliography as well as research studies, see especially the *AEM* (Barcelona, since 1964); *Aragón en la Edad Media* (Zaragoza, since 1977).

Archival resources for the medieval Crown of Aragon are exceedingly rich and by no means yet fully explored. The single greatest repository is the Archive of the Crown of Aragon in Barcelona, but there are important collections also in Valencia, Palma, Zaragoza, and Madrid, to say nothing of French and Italian depots. Two recent guides are: Frederic Udina i Martorell, *L'Arxiu de la Corona d'Aragó* (Madrid, 1980; also published in Castilian); and Josep Baucells i Reig, *Guia dels arxius eclesiàstics de Catalunya-València-Balears* (Barcelona, 1978), The major collection of printed documents is *CDIACA*, ed. Pròsper de Bofarull y Mascaró and others, now some 50 volumes (Barcelona, 1847 to date).

Secondary: H. J. Chaytor, *A history of Aragon and Catalonia* (London, 1933) is a readable synthesis but now very dated. R. B. Merriman, *The rise of the Spanish empire in the old world and the new*, 4 vols. (New York, 1918–34), i, Book II, although no longer fully adequate, remains useful for institutional history. There is a suggestive sketch by Joan Reglà, *Introducció a la història de la Corona d'Aragó* . . . (Palma, 1973), which devotes only 75 pages to the medieval period. J. F. O'Callaghan, *A history of medieval Spain* (Ithaca, 1975) is a reliable survey not quite at its best on Catalonia, Aragon, and Valencia. Angus MacKay, *Spain in the Middle Ages. From frontier to empire, 1000–1500* (London, 1977) has some thoughtful summations of east peninsular developments; while Gabriel Jackson, *The making of medieval Spain* (London, 1972) is a well illustrated but brief sketch, necessarily very thin on the Crown of Aragon. J. N. Hillgarth, *The Spanish kingdoms** (cited above) is an excellent non-narrative history of the later Middle Ages, but is not meant to be read as a history of the Crown of Aragon, whose great age of origins lies outside its scope.

For *Catalonia* the standard modern authority is Ferran Soldevila, *Història de Catalunya*, 2nd edn. (Barcelona, 1963), finely informed but sometimes tendentiously Catalanist. *Història de Catalunya*, 6 vols. (Barcelona: Salvat, 1978), and *Histoire de la Catalogne*, ed. Joaquim Nadal Farreras and Philippe Wolff (Toulouse, 1982; also published in Catalan) are recent collaborative works. For *Aragon* J. M. Lacarra, *Aragón en el pasado** (Madrid, 1972) is a masterly sketch. For *Valencia* see Joan Reglà, *Aproximació a la història del país Valencià* (Valencia, 1968); and the articles in *Gran enciclopèdia catalana*, xv (Barcelona, 1980), 164–81, 192–4. A new stress on social and economic history may be found in Jaime Vicens Vives, *Approaches to the history of Spain**, tr. Joan Connelly Ullman (Berkeley-Los Angeles, 1967); in this vein Pierre Vilar, *La Catalogne dans l'Espagne moderne. Recherches sur les fondements économiques des structures nationales*, 3 vols. (Paris, 1962), i, is a powerful study. For the geographical setting, see J. M. Houston, *The western Mediterranean world: an introduction to its regional landscapes* (London, 1964).

I. Before the Union

Orientation to current discussion of *prehistory and romanization* may be found in chapters by Lluis Solé Sabaris and Pere de Palol in Nadal and Wolff, *Histoire de la Catalogne*; see also Miquel Tarradell, *Les arrels de Catalunya* (Barcelona, 1962). On the *Visigoths* E. A. Thompson, *The Goths in Spain* (Oxford, 1969); P. D. King, *Law and society in the Visigothic kingdom* (Cambridge, 1972); Ramon d'Abadal i de Vinyals, *Dels visigots als catalans*, ed. Jaume Sobrequés i Callicó, 2 vols. (Barcelona, 1969–70), i, part 1. On the *Muslim conquests and settlements* see W. M. Watt, *A history of Islamic Spain* (Edinburgh, 1965); J. Mª. Millàs Vallicrosa, 'La conquista musulmana de la región pirenaica', *Pirineos*, ii (1946), 53–67; and the important work of Pierre Guichard, *Structures sociales 'orientales' et 'occidentales' dans l'Espagne musulmane* (Paris-La Haye, 1977), with a fine bibliography of Arabic sources and secondary studies. See also T. F. Glick, *Islamic and Christian Spain in the early Middle Ages. Comparative perspectives on social and cultural formation* (Princeton, 1979); and on language A. M. Badia i Margarit, *La formació de la llengua catalana . . .* (Barcelona, 1981).

Primary Sources: For the early history of Aragon and Catalonia the sources are chiefly charters preserved in ecclesiastical collections, of which the monastic series are mostly to be found in the Archivo Histórico Nacional (Madrid) and the Arxiu de la Corona d'Aragó (Barcelona). For *Aragon* many original series and cartularies have been edited, such as the *Colección diplomática de la catedral de Huesca*, ed. Antonio Durán Gudiol, 2 vols. (Zaragoza, 1965–9); the useful editions in *Textos medievales*, ed. Antonio Ubieto Arteta and others (Valencia, 1960 to date) are of uneven quality. A fundamental collection is 'Documentos para el estudio de la reconquista y repoblación del valle del Ebro', ed. J. Mª. Lacarra, *EEMCA*, ii (1946), iii (1949), and v (1952), indexed.

For *Catalonia* the major printed collections are *Catalunya carolíngia*, ed. Ramon d'Abadal i de Vinyals, 2 vols. in 4 parts (Barcelona, 1926–55); Federico Udina Martorell, *El Archivo condal de Barcelona en los siglos IX–X. Estudio crítico de sus fondos* (Barcelona, 1951); and *Liber feudorum maior. Cartulario real que se conserva en el Archivo de la Corona de Aragón*, reconstituted and ed. Francisco Miquel Rosell, 2 vols. (Barcelona, 1945–7). The diplomatic collections of cathedral churches are only beginning to be put into print; those for Vic and Urgell are in progress. A major monastic record is *Cartulario de 'Sant Cugat' del Vallés*, ed. José Rius, 3 vols. (Barcelona, 1945–7); indexes were published in 1981.

Secondary. For *Aragon* the pioneering work is Geronimo Zurita y Castro, *Anales de la Corona de Aragón*, 6 vols. (Zaragoza, 1562–80), book I; now best used in the edition by Angel Canellas López, 8 vols. (Zaragoza, 1967–77), or in the modernized Catilian and annotated version by Antonio Ubieto Arteta and María Desamparados Pérez Soler, 4 vols. (Zaragoza, 1967–72). See also Lacarra, *Aragón en el pasado**, pp. 11–73; Antonio Ubieto Arteta, *Historia de Aragón. La formación territorial* (Zaragoza, 1981), ch(apters) 1–6. Bernard Reilly, *The kingdom of León-Castilla under Queen Urraca, 1109–1126* (Princeton, 1982) has some useful matter on Aragon. See also Elena Lourie, 'The will of Alfonso I, "El Batallador", king of Aragon and Navarre: a reassessment', *Speculum*, l (1975), 635–51, together with A. J. Forey in *Durham University Journal* lxxiii (1980), 59–65; L. H. Nelson, 'The foundation of Jaca (1076): urban growth in early Aragon', *Speculum* liii (1978), 688–708, with useful maps; and J. Mª. Ramos y Loscertales, *El reino de Aragón bajo la dinastía pamplonesa* (Salamanca, 1961).

For the *early Catalan counties* see above all Ramon d'Abadal i de

Vinyals, *Els primers comtes catalans* (Barcelona, 1961; 2nd edn., 1965); *idem, L'abat Oliba, bisbe de Vic i la seva època*, 3rd edn. (Barcelona, 1962); also Santiago Sobrequés i Vidal, *Els grans comtes de Bracelona* (Barcelona, 1961); *idem, Els barons de Catalunya* (Barcelona, 1957). J. M. Salrach has re-examined the earliest evidence in *El procés de formació nacional de Catalunya (segles VIII–IX)*, 2 vols. (Barcelona, 1978), but the title of his book is misleading. The authoritative treatment of social and economic growth is Pierre Bonnassie, *La Catalogne du milieu de X^e à la fin du XIe siècle. Croissance et mutations d'une société**, 2 vols. (Toulouse, 1975–6). See also A. M. Mundó, 'Monastic movements in the east Pyrenees',* *Cluniac monasticism in the central Middle Ages*, ed. Noreen Hunt (London, 1971), pp. 98–122; and Michel Zimmermann, 'La prise de Barcelone par Al-Mansûr et la naissance de l'historiographie catalane', *L'Historiographie en Occident du Ve au XVe siècle . . . Annales de Bretagne et des pays de l'Ouest*, lxxxvii (1980), 191–218. On the church see Odilo Engels, *Schutzgedanke und Landesherrschaft im östlichen Pyrenäenraum (9.–13. Jahrhundert)* (Münster i.W., 1970).

II. The Age of the Early Count-Kings (1137–1213)

Primary Sources: Major records of the period of dynastic union are printed in *CDIACA*, iv and viii; even more important are the charters, oaths, and conventions collected toward 1194 in the *Liber feudorum maior*. See also *La documentación pontificia hasta Inocencio III (965–1216)*, ed. Demetrio Mansilla (Rome, 1955). For *Catalonia* the printed cartularies of Poblet (Barcelona, 1938) and Santes Creus (ed. Federico Udina Martorell, Barcelona, 1947) are of great importance for this period; and the *Cartas de población y franquicia de Cataluña*, ed. J. Mª. Font Rius, 3 vols. in 2 parts (Madrid-Barcelona, 1969–83) is a splendid edition. Early administrative records are gathered in *Fiscal accounts of Catalonia under the early count-kings (1151–1213)*, ed. T. N. Bisson, 2 vols. (Berkeley-Los Angeles, 1984). The *Usatges de Barcelona*, ed. Ramón d'Abadal and Ferràn Valls Taberner (Barcelona, 1913) are now known to have been compiled about 1150; while the *Gesta comitum Barcinonensium . . .*, ed. Louis Barrau Dihigo and J. J. Massó Torrents (Barcelona, 1925) begins with a primitive genealogy composed toward 1150–62, a work more useful for the study of the twelfth than of earlier centuries. For *Aragon* the collections mentioned for Chapter I remain important, while narrative sources (as in Catalonia) are meagre.

Secondary: There is no thorough investigation of the incipient Crown of Aragon. P. E. Schramm, J.-F. Cabestany, and Enric Bagué, *Els primers comtes-reis. Ramon Berenguer IV, Alfons el Cast, Pere el Catòlic* (Barcelona, 1963) is well informed but thin. A. J. Forey, *The Templars in the Corona de Aragón* (London, 1973) is useful on its theme, as are articles by J.

Mª. Lacarra, Yves Renouard, Johannes Vincke, and J. Mª. Font Rius in *VII CHCA*, 3 vols. (Barcelona, 1962), i. On *Catalonia* see chiefly Soldevila, *Història de Catalunya*, 2nd edn., chs. 7–10. The problem of political and ideological formation is examined by Michel Zimmermann, 'Aux origines de la Catalogne. Géographie politique et affirmation nationale', *Le Moyen Age*, lxxxix (1983), 5–40; and T. N. Bisson, 'L'Essor de la Catalogne: identité, pouvoir, et idéologie dans une société du XIIᵉ siècle', *Annales: Economies, sociétés, civilisations*, xxxix (1984), 454–79; and the institution of government in Catalonia is the larger theme of my *Fiscal accounts of Catalonia* (cited above), Introduction.* See also Charles Higounet, 'Un grand chapitre de l'histoire du XIIᵉ siècle: la rivalité des maisons de Toulouse et de Barcelone pour la prépondérance méridionale', *Mélanges d'histoire du moyen âge dédiés à la mémoire de Louis Halphen* (Paris, 1951), pp. 313–22; and Ramon d'Abadal i de Vinyals, 'A propos de la "domination" de la maison comtale de Barcelone sur le Midi français', *Annales du Midi*, lxxvi (1964), 315–45 (reprinted in Catalan in *Dels visigots als catalans*, ii, 281–309). P. H. Freedman, *The diocese of Vic. Tradition and regeneration in medieval Catalonia* (New Brunswick, 1983), and J. C. Shideler, *A medieval Catalan noble family: the Montcadas, 1000–1230* (Berkeley-Los Angeles, 1983) are pioneering studies. Lawrence McCrank's dissertation (University of Virginia, 1974) 'Restoration and re-conquest in medieval Catalonia: the church and principality of Tarragona, 971–1177' remains, unfortunately, unpublished.

Aragon after the dynastic union has been relatively neglected. See generally Zurita, *Anales*, book II. On 'territorial formation' see Ubieto Arteta, *Historia de Aragón*, chs. 7–9, who cites specialized studies of *fueros* and settlement. Also Jesús Lalinde Abadía, *Los fueros de Aragón* (Zaragoza, 1976), ch. 1. J. Mª. Lacarra, '"Honores" et "tenencias" en Aragon (XIᵉ siècle)', *Les structures sociales de l'Aquitaine, du Languedoc et de l'Espagne au premier âge féodal* (Paris, 1969), pp. 143–86, despite its title,is useful for this period. More specialized are Agustín Ubieto Arteta, 'Aproximación al estudio del nacimiento de la nobleza aragonesa (siglos XI y XII): aspectos genealógicos', *Homenaje a don José María Lacarra de Miguel . . . Estudios medievales*, ii (Zaragoza, 1977), 7–54; Antonio Ubieto Arteta, 'Sobre demografía aragonesa del siglo XII', *EEMCA*, vii (1962), 578–98; and Miguel Gual Camarena, 'Precendentes de la reconquista valenciana', *Estudios medievales* (Valencia), i (1952), 167–246.

III. James the Conqueror (1213–1276)

Primary Sources: The *Colección diplomática de Jaime I, el Conquistador*, ed.

Ambrosio Huici Miranda, 3 vols. (Valencia, 1916–20) is being re-edited
and expanded by María Desamparados Cabanes Pecourt, *Documentos de
Jaime I de Aragón*, 3 vols. to date (Valencia, 1976; Zaragoza, 1978). Also
in progress is a new edition of the *Libre del repartiment del regne de Valencia*,
i, ed. María Desamparados Cabanes Pecourt and Ramon Ferrer
Navarro, i (Zaragoza, 1979); the *Repartimiento de Mallorca*, ed. Próspero
de Bofarull y Mascaró, is in *CDIACA*, xiii. Major legal collections are
Los fueros de Aragón . . ., ed. Gunnar Tilander (Lund, 1937); and *Furs de
València*, ed. Germà Colon and Arcadi Garcia, 3 vols. (Barcelona,
1970–8). Records of thirteenth-century Corts are printed in *Córtes de los
antiguos reinos de Aragón y de Valencia y principado de Cataluña*, 26 vols.
(Madrid, 1896–1920), i[1]. Narrative sources assume much greater
importance. The *Gesta comitum Barcinonensium* was continued through the
reign of James I (cited for Chapter II). The *Libre dels feyts* may be found
in *Els quatre grans cròniques*, ed. Ferran Soldevila (Barcelona, 1971); and
in a mediocre English translation by John Forster, *The chronicle of James
I, king of Aragon*, 2 vols. (London, 1883).

    Secondary: See generally Ferran Soldevila, *Els grans reis del segle XIII.
Jaume I, Pere el Gran*, 2nd edn. (Barcelona, 1965); idem, *Història de
Catalunya*, 2nd edn., chs. 11–13; Zurita, *Anales*, Book III; Lacarra,
Aragon en el pasado*, pp. 73–125; Hillgarth, *Spanish kingdoms**, i, 233–51;
and *ponencias* collected in *Jaime I y su época* (Zaragoza; X CHCA, 1979).
F. D. Swift, *The life and times of James the First, the Conqueror** (Oxford,
1894) remains readable and useful. Ferran Soldevila, *Els primers temps de
Jaume I* (Barcelona, 1968) is the most thorough study of any period of
the reign; see also for the preconquest years Luis González Antón, 'La
revuelta de la nobleza aragonesa contra Jaime I en 1224–1227',
Homenaje a don José María Lacarra de Miguel . . . Estudios medievales, ii
(Zaragoza, 1977),143–63; T. N. Bisson, 'Las finanzas del joven Jaime I
(1213–1228), *Jaime I y su época*, 1 y 2 (Zaragoza: X CHCA, 1980),
161–208; and idem, 'A General Court of Aragon (Daroca, February
1228)', *EHR*, xcii (1977), 107–24. For the conquests of Majorca and
Valencia see J. Mª. Quadrado, *Historia de la conquista de Mallorca* (Palma,
1850); and R. I. Burns, SJ, *Islam under the crusaders. Colonial survival in the
thirteenth-century kingdom of Valencia** (Princeton, 1973). See also T. F.
Glick, *Irrigation and society in medieval Valencia** (Cambridge, Mass.,
1970). Father Burns has essayed a portrait of King James in *Jaime I y su
época*, 1 y 2 (cited above), pp. 323–57. On towns and trade J. Mª. Font
Rius, *Orígenes del régimen municipal de Cataluña* (Madrid, 1946), which is
important also for the eleventh and twelfth centuries; and A.-E. Sayous,
Els mètodes comercials a la Barcelona medieval (Barcelona, 1975), ch. 1. On
the church see Peter Linehan, *The Spanish church and the papacy in the
thirteenth century** (Cambridge, 1971), chs. 1–5, 11, 12; and R. I. Burns,

The crusader kingdom of Valencia: reconstruction on a thirteenth-century frontier, 2 vols. (Cambridge, Mass., 1967).

IV. Mediterranean Expansion (1276–1336)

Primary Sources: The great Catalan chronicles of Bernat Desclot and Ramon Muntaner can be found in *Els quatre grans cròniques*, ed. Soldevila; they are respectively translated by F. L. Critchlow, *Chronicle of the reign of King Pedro III of Aragon*, 2 vols. (Princeton, 1928–34); and Lady Goodenough, *The chronicle of Muntaner*, 2 vols. (London, 1920–1). A basic gathering of archival records is *Acta aragonensia*, ed. Heinrich Finke, 3 vols. (Berlin-Leipzig, 1908–22). Ecclesiastical order is well shown by the *Rationes decimarum Hispaniae (1279–1280)*, ed. José Rius, 2 vols. (Barcelona, 1946–7). Records of Corts are in *Cortes de Cataluña*, i[1].

Secondary: See generally Soldevila, *Els grans reis*; idem, *Història de Catalunya*, 2nd edn., chs. 14, 15; Zurita, *Anales*, books IV–VI; Hillgarth, *Spanish kingdoms*, i, 251–86; and on the nature of expansion J. N. Hillgarth, *The problem of a Catalan Mediterranean empire, 1229–1327** (London: *EHR* Supplement 8, 1975). Ferran Soldevila, *Pere el Gran* (Barcelona, 1950–62) is a massive work left incomplete at the author's death. For later reigns J. E. Martínez Ferrando, Santiago Sobrequés, and Enric Bagué, *Els descendents de Pere el Gran. Alfons el Franc, Jaume II, Alfons el Benigne* (Barcelona, 1954) is excellent; see also Roger Sablonier, 'The Aragonese royal family around 1300', *Interest and emotion. Essays on the study of family and kinship*, ed. H. Medick and D. W. Sabean (Cambridge, 1984), pp. 210–39. A major monograph on the theme of expansion is Ch.-E. Dufourcq, *L'Espagne catalane et le Maghrib aux XIIIᵉ et XIVᵉ siècles* (Paris, 1966); while Luis González Antón, *Las Uniones aragonesas y las cortes del reino (1283–1301)*, 2 vols. (Zaragoza, 1975) deals in fine detail with the great constitutional crisis of medieval Aragon. Two other major works are Juan Reglá Campistol, *Francia, la Corona de Aragón y la frontera pirenaica* . . ., 2 vols. (Madrid, 1951); and Vicente Salavert y Roca, *Cerdeña y la expansión mediterránea de la Corona de Aragón, 1297–1314*, 2 vols. (Madrid, 1956). An old classic on the longer history of expansion is Lluís Nicolau d'Olwer, *L'expansió de Catalunya en la Mediterrània oriental* (Barcelona, 1926; 3rd edn., 1974). On the Catalan companies see K. M. Setton, *The Catalan domination of Athens, 1311–1388*, revised edn. (London, 1975); A. E. Laiou, *Constantinople and the Latins, the foreign policy of Andronicus II, 1282–1328* (Cambridge, Mass., 1972), pp. 131–242.

V. Peter the Ceremonious and his successors (1336–1410)

Primary Sources: The principal narratives are *Crónica de Pere el Cerimoniós*, ed. Soldevila, *Els quatre grans cròniques*; tr. Mary and J. N. Hillgarth, *Pere*

III, Chronicle, 2 vols. (Toronto, 1980); and *Crònica dels reys d'Aragò e comtes de Barcelona*, ed. A. J. Soberanas Lleó (Barcelona, 1961), of which the Latin version is edited by Antonio Ubieto Arteta, *Crónica de San Juan de la Peña* (Valencia, 1961). The speeches of Peter IV and his sons will be found in *Parlaments a les Corts catalanes*, ed. Ricard Albert and Joan Gassiot (Barcelona, 1928). Records of Corts are in *Córtes de Cataluña*, i²–vi, to which may be added *Actas de las Cortes Generales de la Corona de Aragón de 1362–63*, ed. J. Mª. Pons Guri *CDIACA*, l (1982). For other non-narrative records, see Hillgarth, *Spanish kingdoms*, i, 430–1.

Secondary: See generally Rafael Tasis, *El segle XIV. Pere el Ceremoniós i els seus fills* (Barcelona, 1957); Soldevila, *Història de Catalunya*, 2nd edn., chs. 16–21; Zurita, *Anales*, books VI–X; Hillgarth, *Spanish kingdoms*, i, 347–71; and the remarkable essay by Ramon d'Abadal i de Vinyals, 'Pedro el Ceremonioso y los comienzos de la decadencia política de Cataluña',* in *Historia de España*, ed. Ramon Menéndez Pidal, xiv (Madrid, 1966; republished in Catalan in 1972). There are valuable studies in *La Corona de Aragón en el siglo XIV*, 3 vols. (Valencia: *VIII CHCA*, 1969–73), and in *AEM*, vii (1970–1); to which may be added J. A. Robson, 'The Catalan fleet and Moorish sea-power', *EHR*, lxxiv (1959), 386–408. On the last kings of Majorca, J. E. Martínez Ferrando, *La tràgica història dels reis de Mallorca* (Barcelona, 1960). On the dilapidation of the royal patrimony Mª. Teresa Ferrer i Mallol, 'El patrimoni reial i la recuperació dels senyorius jurisdiccionals en els estats catalano-aragonesos a la fi del segle XIV', *AEM*, vii (1970–1), is a remarkable study.

VI. The Trastámaras (1412–1479)

Primary Sources: Pere Tomich, *Històries e conquestes dels Reys d'Aragó e comptes de Barcelona* (Barcelona, 1886), completed in 1438, is useful for baronial history and Mediterranean affairs after 1390. The *Dietari de la Diputació del General de Cathalunya* is newly edited for the years 1411–58 in *CDIACA*, xlvi (1974). For the Compromise of Caspe see *Córtes de Cataluña*, vii–x (1903–6); and for the case against Jaume of Urgell, *CDIACA*, xxxv–xxxvi. For Aragon see *Cortes del reino de Aragón, 1357–1451*, ed. Angel Sesma Muñoz and Esteban Sarasa Sánchez (Valencia, 1976). Records of the Catalonian civil war are in *CDIACA*, xiv–xxv (1858–63). For the Corts see *Córtes de Cataluña*, xi–xxvi.

Secondary: See generally Jaime Vicens Vives, *Els Trastàmares (segle XV)* (Barcelona, 1956); and in more depth his *Juan II de Aragón* (Barcelona, 1953); also Hillgarth, *Spanish kingdoms**, ii, 215–99. See also Soldevila, *Història de Catalunya*, 2nd edn., chs. 22–6; and for Aragon Zurita, *Anales*, books XI–XX; Angel Canellas López, 'El reino de Aragón en el siglo XV', in *Historia de España*, ed. Ramon Menéndez Pidal, xv (Madrid,

1964), 323–594; Lacarra, *Aragón en el pasado**, chs. 6, 7; and articles in *IV Congreso de Historia de la Corona de Aragón, Mallorca . . . 1955*, 3 vols. (Palma, 1959; Barcelona, 1970, 1976). On government see J. Mª. Font Rius, 'The institutions of the Crown of Aragon in the first half of the fifteenth century',* in *Spain in the fifteenth century, 1369–1516*, ed. J. R. L. Highfield (London, 1972), pp. 171–92; and Alan Ryder, *The kingdom of Naples under Alfonso the Magnanimous** (Oxford, 1976). On the Corts see Peter Rycroft, 'The role of the Catalan "Corts" in the late Middle Ages', *EHR*, lxxxix (1974), 241–69; and especially Santiago Sobrequés Vidal, 'Los orígenes de la revolución catalana del siglo XV: Cortes de Barcelona de 1454–1458', *Estudios de historia moderna*, ii (1952), 1–96. For the Cortes of Aragon, Luis González Antón, *Las Cortes de Aragón* (Zaragoza, 1978). On the Catalonian civil war, see Santiago Sobrequés i Vidal and Jaume Sobrequés i Callicó, *La guerra civil catalana del segle XV. Estudis sobre la crisi social i econòmica de la baixa Edat Mitjana*, 2 vols. (Barcelona, 1973). There is something of interest on fifteenth-century Aragon in R. E. Giesey, *If not, not. The oath of the Aragonese and the legendary laws of Sobrarbe* (Princeton, 1968).

VII. Prosperity and Crisis in the Later Middle Ages

Primary Sources: Editions of the hearth-registers are listed by Josep Iglésies, 'El poblament de Catalunya durant els segles XIV i XV', *VI CHCA* (Madrid, 1959), to which should be added his edition of the record of 1365–70, *Memorias de la Real Academia de Ciencias y Artes de Barcelona*, xxxiv (1962), 247–356. On trade the classic gathering of texts is Antoni de Capmany de Montpalau i Suris, *Memorias históricas sobre la marina, comercio y artes de la antigua ciudad de Barcelona* (1779–92); new edn. E. Giralt y Raventós and Carme Batlle, 3 vols. (Barcelona, 1961–3). For plague see 'Documentos acerca de la peste negra en los dominios de la Corona de Aragón', ed. Amada López de Meneses, *EEMCA*, vi (1956), 291–447. On culture *Documents per l'història de la cultura catalana mig-eval*, ed. Antoni Rubió i Lluch, 2 vols. (Barcelona, 1908–21); 'Documentos culturales de Pedro el Ceremonioso', ed. Amada López de Meneses, *EEMCA*, v (1952), 669–771. There are convenient editions of Francesc Eiximenis, *Regiment de la cosa publica*, ed. Daniel de Molins de Rei (Barcelona, 1927); and Bernat Metge, *Lo somni*, 2nd edn., ed. J. Mª. de Casacuberta (Barcelona, 1925).

Secondary: On society and economy see generally Jaime Vicens Vives, *An economic history of Spain,** tr. F. M. López-Morillas (Princeton, 1969), chs. 14–19; Vilar, *La Catalogne*, i, 131–520; Hillgarth, *Spanish kingdoms,** i, parts 1 and 2 (ch. 1); ii, part 1. On nobility see Sobrequés i Vidal, *Els barons de Catalunya*. On the *remença* peasants the standard works are Eduardo de Hinojosa, *El régimen señorial y la cuestión agraria en Cataluña* *durante la Edad Media* (Madrid, 1905), and Jaime Vicens Vives, *Historia de los remensas en el siglo XV* (Barcelona, 1945); current work by Paul Freedman is likely to throw new light on the problem of origins. On slavery see Charles Verlinden, *L'esclavage dans l'Europe médiévale*, i (Bruges, 1955). On urban trade, money, and banking see Sayous, *Els mètodes comercials*, chs. 2–4; E. J. Hamilton, *Money, prices, and wages in Valencia, Aragon, and Navarre, 1351–1500* (Cambridge, Mass., 1936); A. P. Usher, *The early history of deposit banking in Mediterranean Europe* (Cambridge, Mass., 1943); on urban labour Pierre Bonnassie, *La organización del trabajo en Barcelona a fines del siglo XV* (Barcelona, 1975). On Valencia city Francisco Sevillano Colom, *Valencia urbana y medieval a través del oficio del mustaçaf* (Valencia, 1957). On culture and religion see generally Miquel Batllori, SJ, 'La cultura catalano-aragonesa durant la dinàstia de Barcelona, 1162–1410 . . .', *VII CHCA*, i (Barcelona, 1962), 327–407. On particular topics see J. N. Hillgarth, *Ramon Lull and Lullism in fourteenth-century France* (Oxford, 1971); Jill Webster, *Francesc Eiximenis. La societat catalana al segle XIV* (Barcelona, 1967); Sigismund Brettle, *San Vicente Ferrer und sein literarischer Nachlass* (Fribourg, 1924); Julio Rey Pastor and Ernesto García Camarero, *La cartografía mallorquina* (Madrid, 1960). On the church Johannes Vincke, *Staat und Kirche in Katalonien und Aragon während des Mittelalters* (Münster i. W., 1931); Manuel Riu, 'El monaquismo en Cataluña en el siglo XIV', *AEM*, vii (1970–1), 593–613; Agustí Altisent, *Història de Poblet* (Poblet, 1974); and other works listed by Hillgarth, *Spanish kingdoms*, i, 415–17; ii, 645–8. On Mudejars see John Boswell, *The royal treasure: Muslim communities under the Crown of Aragon in the fourteenth century* (New Haven, 1977); and on Jews, Yitzhak Baer, *A history of the Jews in Christian Spain*, 2 vols. (Philadelphia, 1971), especially ii; A. A. Neuman, *The Jews in Spain*, 2 vols. (Philadelphia, 1942); and Philippe Wolff, 'The 1391 pogrom in Spain: social crisis or not?',* *Past and Present*, no. 50 (1971), 4–18. On piracy, J. Mª. Ramos y Loscertales, *El cautiverio en la Corona de Aragón durante los siglos XIII, XIV y XV* (Zaragoza, 1915).

On the nature and chronology of socio-economic change and the place of Catalonia (and Barcelona) in the later medieval Crown of Aragon, see further Carmen Batlle y Gallart, *La crisis social y económica de Barcelona a mediados del siglo XV*, 2 vols. (Barcelona, 1973); Claude Carrère, *Barcelone, centre économique à l'époque des difficultés, 1380–1462*, 2 vols. (Paris-La Haye, 1967); and Mario del Treppo, *I mercanti catalani e l'espansione della Corona d'Aragona nel secolo XV* (Naples, 1972).

Index

PERSONS of less than royal estate are indexed by given name when they lived before about 1300 and by family name thereafter, with appropriate exceptions. Cross-references are supplied in numerous cases. The abbreviations are: abp. = archbishop; abt. = abbot; bp. = bishop; ct. = count; ctess. = countess; cty. = county; k. = king; q. = queen; vct. = viscount; vctess. = viscountess; vcty. = viscounty.